Enhancing Thinking
Through
Cooperative Learning

Enhancing Thinking Through Cooperative Learning

Edited by
NEIL DAVIDSON
and
TONI WORSHAM

Teachers College, Columbia University
New York and London

Published by Teachers College Press, 1234 Amsterdam Avenue
New York, NY 10027

Library of Congress Cataloging-in-Publication Data

Enhancing thinking through cooperative learning / edited by Neil
    Davidson and Toni Worsham.
        p. cm.
    Collection of essays sponsored by the Maryland Center for Thinking
Studies and the International Association for the Study of
Cooperation in Education.
    Includes bibliographical references and index.
    ISBN 0-8077-3158-7. — ISBN 0-8077-3157-9 (pbk.)
    1. Group work in education. 2. Thought and thinking—Study and
teaching—United States.   I. Davidson, Neil. II. Worsham, Toni.
III. Maryland Center for Thinking Studies. IV. International
Association for the Study of Cooperation in Education.
LB1032.E54   1992
371.3'95—dc20   91-37660

ISBN 0-8077-3158-7
ISBN 0-8077-3157-9 (pbk.)

Printed on acid-free paper
Manufactured in the United States of America

99 98 97 96 95 94 93   8 7 6 5 4 3 2

To my dearest parents, Clinton and Anna Worsham—
". . . you are my heroes, the wind beneath my wings."

—Toni

To a wonderful man, my father Morris Davidson,
engineer and philosopher.

—Neil

Contents

Acknowledgments

This text is sponsored by the Maryland Center for Thinking Studies (MCTS) and the International Association for the Study of Cooperation in Education (IASCE).

The Maryland Center for Thinking Studies is a unique, multifaceted resource for students and parents across the educational spectrum in Maryland. The Center has a Saturday Program for children in grades 4 through 9, a classroom research incentive program, a graduate program for teachers, and a "Teaching Thinking at Home" program for parents. It also provides curriculum and staff development programs for schools and colleges across Maryland. Its primary purpose is to improve instructional approaches for thinking improvement at all levels (K through graduate) across the curriculum.

Maryland Center for Thinking Studies
Coppin State College
2500 W. North Avenue
Baltimore, Maryland   21216
(410) 383-5575

The International Association for the Study of Cooperation in Education, which sponsors the publication *Cooperative Learning*, is a nonprofit educational association dedicated to the study and practice of cooperation in education. This field includes the increasingly popular cooperative classroom methods in which students work together in learning teams to master academic content and social skills. But cooperation in education also includes teachers working together to support and coach each other, to develop and share curriculum materials, and to join with students, parents, and business and community leaders to improve the physical, social, and intellectual quality of their schools.

International Association for the Study of Cooperation in Education
Box 1582
Santa Cruz, California   95061-1582
(408) 426-7926

Introduction
HOTSICLE—Higher Order Thinking Skills in Cooperative Learning Environments

Neil Davidson and Toni Worsham

Competition has characterized educational practice from its beginnings in American history through the better part of this century. There are few among us who cannot recall the classroom scenario in which the return of graded test papers prompted students to compare their scores, each hoping to have done better than the others. "What'd you get? I got a 92!" "Ha! Beat you! I got a 94!" Dialogues such as these have occurred over and over again in American classrooms. This spirit of competition seems to go with our system of free enterprise and the American preoccupation with being number one. However, educationally speaking, we seem to be a long way from the top, with the students of many other countries scoring higher than American students on international achievement tests.

The chapters in this volume highlight the development of a new paradigm in education that has evolved through the linkage of two powerful educational movements. Already, as separate entities, the thinking improvement movement and the cooperative learning movement have provided education with new strategies for improved learning for well over a decade. As the chapters will illustrate, the body of educational research that supports the effectiveness of many of the approaches in both movements is growing constantly. The natural symbiosis that each of the two provides to the other further amplifies the value of their union by fostering the development of higher order thinking skills in cooperative learning environments.

WHAT IS COOPERATIVE LEARNING?

Cooperative learning procedures are designed to engage students actively in the learning process through inquiry and discussion with their peers in small groups. The groupwork is carefully organized and structured so as to promote the participation and learning of all group members in a cooperatively shared undertaking. Cooperative learning is more than just tossing students into a group and telling them to talk together.

A class period might begin with a meeting of the entire class to provide an overall perspective. This may include a teacher presentation of new material, class discussion, posing problems or questions for group discussions, and clarifying directions for the group activities.

The class is then divided into small groups, usually with four members apiece. Each group has its own working space, which might include a flipchart or section of the chalkboard. Students work together cooperatively in each group to discuss ideas, clarify their understanding, think and reason together, solve problems, make and test conjectures, and so forth. Students actively exchange ideas with one another, and help each other learn the material. The teacher takes an active role, circulating from group to group, providing assistance and encouragement, and asking thought-provoking questions as needed.

In each type of small group learning, there are a number of leadership and management functions that must be performed. These are generally handled by the teacher, although some of them may be explicitly delegated to the students. A basic list of functions includes:

- Initiating group work
- Presenting guidelines for small-group operation
- Fostering group norms of interdependence and mutual helpfulness
- Forming groups
- Preparing and introducing new material in some form (orally to entire class, orally to separate groups, via written materials)
- Interacting with small groups in various possible ways (observing groups, checking solutions, giving hints, clarifying notation, asking and sometimes answering questions, giving specific feedback, pointing out errors, providing encouragement, reinforcing social or group skills, helping groups function, furnishing overall classroom management)
- Tying ideas together
- Making assignments of homework or in-class work
- Evaluating student performance

Each of these functions can be performed in various ways and to varying degrees, depending upon the model of cooperative small-group instruction in effect. Additional functions such as teaching social skills, team-building, fostering perspective-taking, and applying status treatments are employed in some cooperative learning models.

There is no single universal method of cooperative learning and no single guru who can speak for the entire field. The diversity of approaches includes the following: the principles approach of the Johnsons (1989), the structural approach of Kagan (1990), the student team learning methods of Slavin (1990), the group investigation approach of Sharan (1980, 1990), the complex instruction approach of Cohen (1986), and the collaborative approach described by Brubacher, Payne, and Rickett (1990). These diverse methodologies have certain key points in common and various areas of difference.

The following critical attributes are common to all methods of cooperative learning:

- A task or learning activity suitable for group work
- Student-to-student interaction in small groups
- Interdependence structured to foster cooperation within groups
- Individual responsibility and accountability

The following attributes are found in some, but not all, approaches to cooperative learning:

- Heterogeneous or random grouping (or some other grouping procedure)
- Explicit teaching of social skills
- Processing social skills: reflecting on the way social skills were employed and on how their use could be improved in a future lesson
- Means of structuring positive interdependence (goals, tasks, resources, role assignments, rewards)
- Team building and class building to foster a sense of inclusion, cohesiveness, and common identity in the team or class
- Perspective taking: learning to understand the perspectives of others, even when these differ from one's own
- Status treatments designed to recognize the competence of low status students and to enhance their status in the classroom
- Shared leadership within groups
- Use of structures: for example, interview, round-robin, think-pair-share, jigsaw

Cooperative learning is not necessarily conceived of as a total instructional system. Cooperative learning can be used as part of a cycle of classroom activities including a variety of other instructional methods such as lecture, large group discussion, individual work, and so on.

In the 1960s and 1970s terms were commonly employed such as "small group learning," "small group teaching," and "group work." The term "cooperative learning," used to designate a variety of organized and structured small-group procedures, has become more prevalent in the 1980s.

Research on the effects of cooperative learning has been quite extensive. Hundreds of studies have compared the effects of cooperative learning with other instructional methods such as the lecture or individualized instruction. See for example the extensive reviews by the Johnsons (1989), Slavin (1990), and Sharan (1980, 1990). Research has shown positive effects of cooperative learning in the following areas: academic achievement, development of higher order thinking, self-esteem and self-confidence as a learner, intergroup relations including cross-race friendships, social acceptance of mainstreamed students, development of social skills, and ability to take the perspective of another person. According to Slavin, the most powerful achievement effects of cooperative learning occur when there is a combination of group goals and individual accountability.

WHY TEACH THINKING?

Traditionally, the "curriculum" that should be taught has been viewed as a body of knowledge (Hobbs, 1980). Educators, for many years, have aligned themselves with either this content/knowledge camp or instead with the process/thinking improvement camp. The content supporters see the delivery of important facts and concepts to students as the primary task of educators (Cheney, 1987; Finn & Ravitch, 1987; Hirsch, 1987). The process supporters, on the other hand, contend that the mere accumulation of facts by students is ineffective if they are not taught how to construct their own schema for organizing and internalizing the information they acquire so that it becomes truly their own (Costa, 1991; Day, 1981; Worsham, 1988). These educators see the primary mission of schooling as the development of thinking abilities for both acquiring and processing information.

During this century, the tremendous increases in knowledge have outstripped our abilities to learn or even gather it all in a lifetime. The need, then, for effective information-processing skills has received greater attention than ever, with even the "knowledge" camp concurring that better delivery systems for the meaningful acquisition of knowledge are necessary for effective learning. So the artificial and inappropriate dichotomy between a "content" or "process" focus has been greatly diminished.

With the realization that teachers do most of the thinking and talking in our classrooms, and that students must process information in order to learn it, a greater emphasis has been placed on shifting the teacher's role to facilitator rather than information-giver. Additionally, with studies such as Goodlad's (1983) showing that less than 1% of teacher talk requires that students think beyond the recall level, the need for instructional approaches that actively engage the student in thinking has become critical.

Many programs and instructional methods have emerged to help students think more effectively to process knowledge, to construct their own learning schemas, to question artfully, to solve problems, to make decisions, to seek alternatives, and to create new ideas. While some of these have been more successful than others, all have contributed to giving increased attention to finding ways of teaching thinking more effectively.

OVERVIEW OF THE TEXT

Enhancing Thinking Through Cooperative Learning is about cooperative thought between students, between and among students and teachers, and between and among students and the thoughtful constructs that they generate when they are allowed to actively process and create the contexts in which they learn best. It is about theory and practice, content and process, product and performance, and autonomy and cooperation. It is about learning to think better by thinking in an educational community. Beyond the recognition of the value of "two (or more) heads" the cooperative thinking movement, as presented in this text, offers frameworks for the effective development of cooperation, mutual respect, and the willingness to share ideas.

Chapter 1 examines the conceptual base of cooperative learning as an instructional approach and the goals of teaching thinking in the classroom. Barbara Presseisen presents a brief historical review of research literature on both topics from early in the 20th century through recent socioinstructional interventions in current classroom practice. One of the main emphases of the chapter is a consideration of how young children learn. The importance of speech development, interactions between perception and action, and the different ways that information can be treated and related to human learning are explored. Another emphasis of this chapter is the role of metacognition in cooperative classroom endeavors. The significance of self-awareness, self-talk, and self-regulation are highlighted as common concerns of both cooperative learning and cognitive instruction.

In Chapter 2, Robert Marzano notes that little work has been done on describing the cognitive roles of cooperative learning across the various aspects of the learning process. In this chapter, a model of learning is described along with the functions of cooperative learning within each phase of the model. Specifically, five "dimensions" of learning (i.e., five different types of thinking) involved in the learning process are articulated. These include the thinking needed to

1. Develop attitudes and perceptions that create a positive classroom climate
2. Acquire and integrate knowledge
3. Extend and refine knowledge
4. Make meaningful use of knowledge
5. Develop favorable habits of mind

Within each of these dimensions, the cognitive role of cooperative learning changes. These changes have implications for the use and further development of cooperative learning.

Robert Samples, in Chapter 3, presents cooperation as a natural expression of human beings and describes tasks in which "true inquiry" is experienced when participants do not know in advance the answers that may arise from their explorations. The relationships among autonomy, cooperation, and authenticity are discussed. The author shows that cooperation and autonomy are not mutually exclusive in either education or life in general, but in fact can coexist and nurture each other. The chapter provides indicators of authenticity in cooperation and of authenticity in autonomy. The author argues that cooperative inquiry as classroom methodology can be linked with a larger vision of cooperation throughout the world and should, therefore, be seen as a life skill.

Chapters 4 through 11 are highly practice oriented, although each relies on scaffolds of theory in cognitive and cooperative research. These scaffolds provide the support for practical translations and applications to classroom settings. Examples connect the "why to" and "how to" in each chapter.

In Chapter 4, Arthur Costa and Pat O'Leary state that human intellect is enhanced through reciprocity. While research in cooperative learning has yielded much supportive data about its positive effects on creativity, critical thinking, and achievement, this chapter contends that the development of intellectual abilities should be viewed as a goal, not merely as a positive by-product of cooperative learning. Eight indicators of intelligent behavior are described. Suggestions for teaching, observing, and evaluating growth are presented for each indicator.

Chapter 5 provides an eight-step procedural model for incorporating thinking skills across the curriculum. Toni Worsham outlines a cooperative, metacognitive framework for making the selected skills as integral to the instructional program as the "other" informational content to be learned. Finally, it provides metacognitive strategies and performance assessment formats for gauging student progress in the application of the selected thinking skills.

Twelve instructional models which vary in degree of student involvement are presented by Robin Fogarty and James Bellanca in Chapter 6. Each model is introduced with a source name, a brief description of the interaction, and a prescription for recommended use. A classroom vignette illustrates the student-to-student or student-to-teacher interactions that define the model.

In Chapter 7, Richard Solomon, Neil Davidson, and Elaine Solomon demonstrate a synergistic relationship between thinking skills, social skills, and cooperative learning. Certain thinking skills and social skills facilitate cooperative learning activities, while many cooperative activities provide opportunities to apply these same thinking skills and social skills. The chapter provides a taxonomy of social skills on four levels, and offers a seven-step model for teaching both social skills and thinking skills along with cooperative learning.

Chapters 8 and 9 focus on constructive group discussions as vehicles for improving critical thinking and metacognitive thought. In Chapter 8, David Johnson and Roger Johnson stress the importance of structuring a "cooperative context" for academic controversy. Without these cooperative frameworks, students tend to see winning the argument rather than resolving the issue as their main objective. The chapter shows how a cooperative controversy can be structured by a sequence of steps including preparation and presentation of opposing viewpoints, active discussion, reversal of position, and group decision-making regarding the most appropriate solution. Attitudes toward controversies and the skills necessary to resolve them become valuable assets both in and out of school.

Chapter 9 deals with large group cooperative discussions. Howard Zeiderman, Geoffrey Comber, and Nicholas Maistrellis emphasize that cooperative thinking is not synonymous with seeking universal concurrence. Rather, perspectives need to be shared on a common ground. The Touchstones Project provides a discussion model designed to develop the following skills of cooperative thought:

- To realize that radically different approaches can illuminate a problem

- To cooperate with others whose backgrounds, perspectives, and skills are different from one's own
- To explore a problem whose solution doesn't follow a preexisting model
- To think in conditions where there are no experts or authorities

The integration of concept teaching and specific cooperative learning strategies are described by Linda Mauro and Lenore Cohen in Chapter 10. Suggested procedures for applying several cooperative structures with models of concept attainment and concept formation are outlined in both general terms and with specific examples of lesson plans at the elementary, middle, and high school levels. The chapter demonstrates the potential effectiveness of cooperation in the development of conceptual thinking.

In Chapter 11, Frank Lyman presents an explication of several specific cognitively oriented cooperative learning procedures, leading to the creation of a thoughtful classroom. Specifically, think-pair-share, think-trix, thinklinks, and weird facts are described to illustrate how their interactions play crucial roles in creating an ecosystem for cooperative thinking.

Jay McTighe, in Chapter 12, shows that graphic organizers may be used productively at any stage in the instructional process (before, during, and after). Graphic organizers are especially effective when applied in conjunction with cooperative classroom groups. By working with a graphic organizer as part of a collaborative group, students are encouraged to expand their own thinking by considering different points of view. This chapter includes descriptions of eight specific graphic organizers, provides a detailed instructional procedure, and illustrates practical applications in cooperative classrooms at the elementary, middle, and high school levels.

In Chapter 13, Charles Wiederhold and Spencer Kagan address teaching and learning using student-generated questions. The methodology presented is an extension of Kagan's structural approach to cooperative learning. A question matrix is employed to help students generate more than 36 different types of questions. Structures are designed either to help students generate their own questions or to help students process questions with other students. The chapter discusses a curriculum delivery system involving four elements: teacher attitude, cooperative learning, critical thinking, and student question generation.

Chapter 14 is based on a review of the literature, on Carla Beachy's classroom research, and on her experiences in teaching writing and thinking skills in the middle school classroom. Using examples of actual

writing assignments and classroom situations, the chapter contains procedures for teaching the peer editing phase of writing, including information on cooperative learning structures, the writing prompt, the grading
checklist, and the direct instruction of thinking skills. In addition, this
chapter offers strategies for fostering group cooperation, information on
the various roles of the students, teacher, and parents, and instruction on
assessing the students' work.

In Chapter 15, Anita Stockton notes that science has traditionally
required that students work in pairs or groups in the laboratory. This
chapter presents some strategies that orchestrate these groupings to promote higher level thinking and total participation. Several cooperative
learning strategies are linked with specific examples from the science
classroom to illustrate the design of "cooperatively thoughtful" science
lessons. Finally, the importance of staff development for classroom transformation and a staff development model are discussed.

Tom Bassarear and Neil Davidson, in Chapter 16, provide a rationale
for the use of cooperative learning in mathematics, which has often been
taught by individualistic or competitive modes. The chapter is based
upon the recent *Standards* of the National Council of Teachers of Mathematics and upon research by Bruner. Several specific examples are given
of mathematics lessons that require and develop the use of thinking skills
in the cooperative solution of challenging problems.

The final chapter in the text parallels the "school world" cooperative
thinking experiences with the "real world" demands for cooperative
problem-solving. Author Paul Hilt contends that student experiences with
thoughtful innovation and teamwork, the cornerstones of workplace
achievement, will provide students with a solid foundation for career
success. Students who learn problem-solving skills by dealing with real
issues in their school environments, who are able to reflect on their own
thinking, and who work cooperatively with others are not only better
prepared to succeed in living a quality life, but also ensure a society of
informed and contributing citizens.

WHY THINK TOGETHER?

There are many perspectives on the beneficial relationship between
thinking and cooperative learning. In a recent review of thinking improvement programs, Resnick (1987) observed that the more effective
programs had cooperative problem-solving components and advocated
cooperative thinking for enhanced learning. In this text, several descriptions and models of cooperative thinking are presented by the chapter

authors. All would concur that thinking is the *personal* process individuals use to create their own understanding; why, then, is *cooperative* exchange so beneficial? One answer is that shared visions and understandings enlarge the processing spheres that individuals may explore, thus making the enhancement of individual thought as boundless as the visions shared. Each chapter in this text presents a unique perspective on how this enhancement is achieved.

REFERENCES

Brubacher, M., Payne, R., & Rickett, K. (1990). *Perspectives on small group learning: Theory and practice.* Oakville, Ontario: Rubicon.

Cheney, L. V. (1987). *American memory.* Washington, DC: National Endowment for the Humanities.

Cohen, E. G. (1986). *Designing groupwork: Strategies for the heterogeneous classroom.* New York: Teachers College Press.

Costa, A. L. (Ed.). (1991). *Developing minds: A resource book for teaching thinking* (rev. ed.). (Vol. 1). Alexandria, VA: Association of Supervision and Curriculum Development.

Day, M. C. (1981, October). Thinking at Piaget's stage of formal operations. *Educational Leadership,* 44-47.

Finn, C. E., Jr., & Ravitch, D. (1987, October 25). Opportunity can be made. *Los Angeles Times,* p. 24.

Goodlad, J. (1983). *A place called school.* New York: McGraw-Hill.

Hirsch, E. D., Jr. (1987, April). The essential elements of literacy. *Education Week, 6,* 27.

Hobbs, N. (1980, April). Feuerstein's instrumental enrichment: Teaching intelligence to adolescents. *Educational Leadership,* 566-568.

Johnson, D. W., & Johnson, R. (1989). *Cooperation and competition: Theory and research.* Edina, MN: Interaction Book Company.

Kagan, S. (1990). *Cooperative learning: Resources for teachers.* San Juan Capistrano, CA: Resources for Teachers.

Resnick, L. B. (1987). *Education and learning to think.* Washington, DC: National Academy Press.

Sharan, S. (1980). Cooperative learning in small groups: Recent methods and effects on achievement, attitudes, and ethnic relations. *Review of Educational Research, 50,* 241-271.

Sharan, S. (Ed.). (1990). *Cooperative learning: Theory and research.* New York: Praeger.

Slavin, R. (1990). *Cooperative learning: Theory, research, and practice.* Englewood Cliffs, NJ: Prentice-Hall.

Worsham, T. (1988, September). From cultural literacy to cultural thoughtfulness. *Educational Leadership,* 20-21.

Enhancing Thinking
Through
Cooperative Learning

A Perspective on the Evolution of Cooperative Thinking

Barbara Z. Presseisen

Cooperative learning is an instructional approach that integrates social skills objectives with academic content objectives in education. When allied with the purposes of teaching thinking in the classroom, cooperative learning becomes an extension of cognitive research and the pursuit of more intelligent learning outcomes from instruction. In the last decade of the 20th century, such an alliance seems natural and, in many ways, an expected outgrowth following years of cognitive-developmental psychological theory development.

It is Bruner (1985) who cites the work of Lev Semovich Vygotsky as a major milestone of early cognitive research. Vygotsky's (1962) *Thought and Language* appeared in Russia in 1934 and was such a departure from Marxist psychological studies, then dominated by Pavlov, that it was immediately suppressed. The volume was not published in English until the early 1960s, when Bruner's own studies of thinking and education were becoming influential in the United States. Essentially, both authors advocate that children solve practical problems with the help of their speech, as well as with their eyes and hands. Learning, suggested the cognitive researchers, is a holistic process in which perception, speech, and action serve as instruments of mental internalization. Social exchange in learning constitutes the central subject matter for analyzing the unique human behavior of thought development and provides a basis for studying how youngsters become conscious of and learn to act upon the world in which they exist. It is no accident that the current, renewed interest in Vygotsky's research—particularly with regard to the learner's *potential* for progress—parallels the focus on cooperative learning as a major approach to organizing the thinking classroom (Belmont, 1989; Fireman & Kose, 1990; Kozulin, 1990; Wertsch, 1985).

In Vygotsky's interpretation, socially meaningful activity serves as the generator of consciousness; he particularly emphasizes dialogue, such as between teacher and student, as the important instrument in building new-found conceptions. Later proponents of cooperative learning, such as Johnson (1986), Johnson and F. Johnson (1987), Johnson and R. T. Johnson (1989), and Slavin (1983, 1986, 1987, 1990), extend this social thesis into educational practice literature that is focused on particular problems of organizing effective instruction. These researchers deal with individual needs of students and their challenges in becoming cognitively engaged with basic contents, such as reading and mathematics, and more importantly, with transforming the culture of the classroom. These proponents of cooperative learning emphasize the linguistic exchange between and among students and the experience of team building in the construction or mastery of knowledge through systematic classroom interaction. Their socioinstructional approach is particularly effective for elementary age youngsters who need to be socialized into the educational environment, and for whom social exchange seems to be especially developmentally appropriate. As Belmont reports, "Older children's spontaneous activity tends to happen in the head, whereas younger children's tends to be done out loud, as speech" (1989, p. 143).

Cooperative learning as a peer-mediated intervention in the classroom emphasizes collaboration among learners. At the heart of this collaboration is a group processing of the information to be studied and an exchange of the thinking involved in the cognitive processing. Students must explain *how* they reach a conclusion or arrive at an answer. First and foremost, they find the need to examine their own thought processes. Students engaged in cooperative learning need to reflect on what they think about the particular tasks of instruction, but they must also consider how they arrived at such thoughts and what the significance of a particular act happens to be. Thus, initially, they are engaged in a *metacognitive* involvement, one of the first acts of constructive thinking (Costa, 1984). Bransford and Vye (1989) discuss various characteristics of knowledge mastery in thinking; many of their observations apply to understanding the reflective learner engaged in cooperative learning. Master thinkers develop skills for recognizing and constructing meaningful "chunks" of information; they are pattern-seekers. Successful thinkers develop their own self-talk; they try to figure out why a particular aspect of a solution is applicable to the problem at hand. Eventually, usually with multiple experiences, they develop a notion of generalization or rule incidence and they actively search for comparable situations or other cases upon which they might generalize types of particular solutions. Less successful thinkers, say Bransford and Vye (1989, p. 181), are more prone to using memorization strategies and show less concern for analytic confirmation.

Instruction in the cooperative learning classroom requires students to share how they think, thus to act as mediators of other students' thinking. Such discussion with their peers often calls for an elaboration of the meaning first ascribed to a situation, perhaps the need to express ideas in exemplary, parallel structures. Metaphor or analogical thought (Sternberg, 1977), or even related lateral thinking (de Bono, 1970), can be developed through such dialogue, perhaps more effectively between peers than from adult teacher to student. Through such dialogue, say Palincsar and Brown (1988), students—even remedial or "at-risk" learners—can come to understand the strategic aspects of metacognition, become more aware of their own thoughts as tools to apply tentatively to given problems, and, in the dynamic exchange between and among their classmates, teach themselves more powerful dimensions of thinking. Like debaters and trial lawyers, cooperative thinkers are benefited by a vital exchange with their colleagues, but they are usually spared the anxiety of competitive risk-taking and the embarrassment of ultimate failure. It seems that cooperative learning combined with cognitive instruction is capable of creating a user-friendly approach to conceptual development.

Cooperative learning also provides an environment for mastering two of the most essential skills in learning to be an effective thinker: posing good questions and formulating significant problems. With properly designed tasks, and with appropriate materials, cooperative learning can facilitate students' search for needed, new information. Bransford and Vye (1989) see this characteristic as related to the elaboration of meaning skills and, ultimately, to the "inert knowledge" problem (p. 189). Students need to enter into cooperative tasks, not to learn information by rote, to memorize and treat data as fixed, unchanging fact. They need to consider the significance or potential meaning of such information, to see where it might lead, to find new relationships. Critical understanding can be accompanied by creative insight if a question is posed by a member of a learning group or if a problem is cast in an innovative or different light. It is such characteristics of team learning that have caused Johnson and R. T. Johnson (1990) to propose that being effective in such social and small-group interaction is vitally important in meeting the employment and career requisites of the modern job market. Palincsar and Brown (1988) suggest that predicting, questioning, summarizing, and clarifying are group learning skills that ultimately help students integrate new information with the prior knowledge they have already mastered.

One of the most powerful aspects of combining cooperative learning and teaching thinking in the classroom is that they provide a context in which many students spend much more time at school actively engaged in learning, using knowledge to solve problems. As Tharp and Gallimore (1988) found in their research in Hawaii, cooperative engagement in learning for students made it necessary to remove the teacher from the center of the learning process. Recitation by the "sage on the stage" was not only an inappropriate approach for the children, it actually wasted the limited time they had in the instructional setting. The paradigm shift involved in the intervention these researchers introduced made it possible, for the first time, for select Hawaiian children to become engaged in their own cognitive learning.

Cooperative learning in the thinking classroom is only recently becoming an object of rigorous research. Several chapters in this volume include summaries of such research. Examinations like the Tharp and Gallimore project (1988) and research on reciprocal instruction, as reported by Palincsar and Brown (1988), represent a limited supply of reports whose findings tell what really happens when theoretical ideals become actual classroom interventions. We need more of these studies and we need to relate them to the research embedded in other aspects of educational literature based on similar assumptions and objectives (Link, 1985; Luria, 1976). There is also some debate about the notion that cooperative learning is a beneficial instructional approach for all students. Some gifted program educators fear that mixed-ability groups for cooperative learning experience may shortchange youngsters of high ability (Willis, 1990; Allan, 1991). Advocates of cooperative learning indicate that it can benefit gifted students and that it is very important to understand the rationales behind policy and research, and to understand implications of assessment (Slavin, 1991). Obviously, a full menu of research developed to study a variety of practices, such as cooperative learning, and to ask questions that parallel the complexity of the educational environment in the country today, is still very much down the road. A great deal needs to be examined in the findings of any educational innovation. Nevertheless, Vygotsky would be pleased that his socio-instructional approach is alive and well in current American education. He would be even more surprised to find that his long-suppressed research might even become an educational reality in his native Russia.

REFERENCES

Allan, S. D. (1991). Ability-grouping research reviews: What do they say about grouping and the gifted? *Educational Leadership, 48*(6), 60–65.

Belmont, J. M. (1989). Cognitive strategies and strategic learning. *American Psychologist, 44*(2), 142–148.

Bransford, J. D., & Vye, N. J. (1989). A perspective on cognitive research and its implications for instruction. In L. B. Resnick & L. E. Klopfer (Eds.), *Toward a thinking curriculum: Current cognitive research* (pp. 173-205). Alexandria, VA: Association for Supervision and Curriculum Development.

Bruner, J. S. (1985). Vygotsky: A historical and conceptual perspective. In J. V. Wertsch (Ed.), *Culture, communication and cognition: Vygotskian perspectives* (pp. 21-34). New York: Cambridge University Press.

Costa, A. L. (1984). Mediating the metacognitive. *Educational Leadership, 42*(3), 57-62.

de Bono, E. (1970). *Lateral thinking: Creativity step by step.* New York: Harper & Row.

Fireman, G., & Kose, G. (1990). Piaget, Vygotsky, and the development of consciousness. *Genetic Epistemologist, 18*(2), 17-23.

Johnson, D. W. (1986). *Reaching out: Interpersonal effectiveness and self-actualization.* Englewood Cliffs, NJ: Prentice Hall.

Johnson, D. W., & Johnson, F. (1987). *Joining together: Group theory and group skills.* Englewood Cliffs, NJ: Prentice Hall.

Johnson, D. W., & Johnson, R. T. (1989). *Cooperation and competition: Theory and research.* Edina, MN: Interaction Book Company.

Johnson, D. W., & Johnson, R. T. (1990). Social skills for successful group work. *Educational Leadership, 47*(4), 29-33.

Kozulin, A. (1990). *Vygotsky's psychology: A biography of ideas.* Cambridge, MA: Harvard University Press.

Link, F. R. (1985). Instrumental enrichment: A strategy for cognitive and academic improvement. In F. R. Link (Ed.), *Essays on the intellect* (pp. 89-106). Alexandria, VA: Association for Supervision and Curriculum Development.

Luria, A. R. (1976). *Cognitive development: Its cultural and social foundations.* Cambridge, MA: Harvard University Press.

Palincsar, A. S., & Brown, A. L. (1988). Teaching and practicing thinking skills to promote comprehension in the context of group problem solving. *Remedial and Special Education, 9*(1), 35-39.

Slavin, R. E. (1983). *Student team learning: An overview and practical guide.* Washington, DC: National Education Association.

Slavin, R. E. (1986). *Using student team learning* (3rd. ed.). Baltimore, MD: Johns Hopkins University Press.

Slavin, R. E. (1987). Cooperative learning and the cooperative school. *Educational Leadership, 45*(3), 7-13.

Slavin, R. E. (1990). *Cooperative learning: Theory, research, and practice.* Englewood Cliffs, NJ: Prentice Hall.

Slavin, R. E. (1991). Are cooperative learning and "untracking" harmful to the gifted? Response to Allan. *Educational Leadership, 48*(6), 68-71.

Sternberg, R. J. (1977). *Intelligence, information processing, and analogical reasoning: The componential analysis of human abilities.* Hillsdale, NJ: Erlbaum.

Tharp, R., & Gallimore, R. (1988). *Rousing minds to life: Teaching, learning, and schooling in social context*. New York: Cambridge University Press.

Vygotsky, L. S. (1962). *Thought and language* (E. Hanfmann & G. Vakar, Eds.). Cambridge, MA: MIT Press.

Wertsch, J. V. (Ed.). (1985). *Culture, communication and cognition: Vygotskian perspectives*. New York: Cambridge University Press.

Willis, S. (1990). Cooperative learning fallout? *ASCD Update, 32*(8), 6, 8.

2

The Many Faces of Cooperation Across the Dimensions of Learning

Robert J. Marzano

It is no exaggeration to say that cooperative learning is quickly becoming the most widely used instructional innovation in American education. However, it is also no exaggeration to say that cooperative learning is conceptualized in a variety of sometimes inconsistent ways, both in form and function. Fortunately, with regard to form, there have been some clear guidelines as to the distinctions of cooperative learning. For example, Johnson, Johnson, Roy, and Holubec (1984) have clearly defined those aspects of cooperative learning that distinguish it from simply having students work in groups. These include positive interdependence, heterogeneity, shared responsibilities, and social skills development.

Unfortunately, with regard to the functions of cooperative learning, not as many useful distinctions have been made. Although Slavin (1983) has identified some functions of cooperative learning, to date there has been no attempt to correlate the functions of cooperative learning with the phases of learning. That is, no research or theory has articulated how cooperative learning interacts differently within the various aspects of the learning process. This chapter offers such an articulation. Specifically, in this chapter the changes in the function or purpose of cooperative learning are discussed across five aspects of the learning process.

FIVE DIMENSIONS OF LEARNING

Although there is no agreement as to the exact process or sequence of events relative to the learning process, there is agreement as to some basic types of thinking that occur during effective learning. These "types of thinking" have been referred to as "dimensions of learning" (Marzano, in press; Marzano, Pickering, & Brandt, 1990) and are a translation of an effort sponsored by the Association for Supervision and Curriculum Development to create a framework that organizes the current research and theory on the teaching of thinking (Marzano et al., 1988). The five dimensions of learning that have been identified are

1. Thinking needed to develop attitudes and perceptions that create a positive classroom climate
2. Thinking needed to acquire and integrate knowledge
3. Thinking needed to extend and refine knowledge
4. Thinking needed to make meaningful use of knowledge
5. Thinking needed to develop favorable habits of mind

Although these dimensions are presented in a linear fashion, this in no way implies a linear process (i.e., a linear progression of the five types of thinking). Rather the interrelationship among the five dimensions is that depicted in Figure 2.1.

As Figure 2.1 illustrates, learners' attitudes and perceptions (Dimension 1) and their habits of mind (Dimension 5) form the backdrop of any learning experience. Briefly, every learner comes to every learning situation with attitudes and perceptions about such factors as their comfort, safety, and acceptance. Negative attitudes and perceptions relative to any of these factors will negatively affect the learning process. Hence, certain attitudes and perceptions constitute the context or backdrop within which learning occurs. Similarly, a learner must utilize certain positive mental habits, such as "being sensitive to feedback" and "seeking accuracy," during an effective learning experience. Like attitudes and

Figure 2.1. The Five Dimensions of Learning

Attitudes & Perceptions

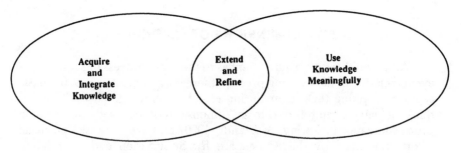

Habits of Mind

perceptions, these mental habits are part of the context or backdrop of learning because their use (or lack of use) by the learner drastically affects the learning process.

Given the existence of the types of thinking specified in Dimensions 1 and 5, learning is a matter of acquiring and integrating new knowledge (Dimension 2). In Piagetian terms, new information is assimilated into the existing knowledge base—integrated with what is already known. Over time, though, knowledge changes, sometimes in drastic and unpredictable ways. In effect, over time new knowledge structures are formed that are not simple additions to existing knowledge. They are new entities with unique distinctions. In Piagetian terms, accommodation occurs. The types of thinking that play a major role in accommodation are extending and refining knowledge (Dimension 3) and using knowledge meaningfully (Dimension 4). More precisely, the shift from assimilation to accommodation is an integrated one involving the types of thinking in Dimensions 2 through 4. This is indicated by the interlocking circles in Figure 2.1. As learners acquire and integrate knowledge, they also begin to extend and refine it. Extending and refining knowledge is also an aspect of using knowledge meaningfully. The shift from assimilating to accommodating knowledge, then, can be thought of as occurring on something of a continuum, with all the types of thinking alluded to in Dimensions 2 through 4 used throughout.

It is not the purpose of this chapter to defend the five dimensions of learning. For such a defense the reader is referred to Marzano et al. (1990). It is the purpose of this chapter to use the dimensions to identify the various roles cooperative learning can play within the learning process. Consequently, in the remainder of this chapter, each of the five dimensions is described along with the manner in which the type of thinking inherent in the dimension can be reinforced through cooperative learning and the function or role cooperative learning takes on in such an endeavor.

DIMENSION 1: DEVELOPING ATTITUDES AND PERCEPTIONS CONDUCIVE TO A POSITIVE MENTAL CLIMATE

The 1970s produced a great deal of research supporting the importance of classroom climate in the learning process (e.g., Brophy, 1982; Fisher & Berliner, 1985). Within that body of research and theory, climate was conceptualized in very general terms such as the extent to which effective classroom management procedures are used. Since then cognitive psychologists have considered climate from the perspective of the learner. Specifically, a positive climate is more a matter of attitudes and perceptions on the part of the learner than it is the presence or absence of factors external to the learner. The attitudes and perceptions that constitute a positive mental climate include

1. A sense of physical comfort
2. A positive affective tone
3. A sense of order
4. A sense of safety and acceptance

A sense of physical comfort is a by-product of the actual physical environment of the classroom including temperature, arrangement of furniture, and attention paid to physical activity. It is intuitively obvious and scientifically valid that a student cannot learn optimally if he or she is too hot or cold, cramped in a tiny space, not free to move about, and otherwise physically uncomfortable.

Affective tone refers to the overall level of affect within a classroom. Although affect does not necessarily have to be positive, it cannot be negative. Specifically, Mandler (1983) has shown that a negative affective tone will inhibit learning, and a positive affective tone will enhance it. A neutral affective tone will neither inhibit nor enhance learning.

A sense of order, the third type of attitude and perception, is affected by explicit and consistent rules and procedures. That is, research on classroom management (Anderson, Evertson, & Emmer, 1980; Emmer, Evertson, & Anderson, 1980) indicates that explicitly stated and reinforced rules and procedures create a climate conducive to learning. Presumably, students need to know the parameters of behavior within a learning situation. Without these parameters, the psychological environment can become chaotic.

The final type of attitude and perception necessary for a positive climate is a sense of safety and acceptance. Safety refers to both physical and psychological safety. Obviously, students must believe that they are physically safe within the classroom, school, and surrounding areas (Combs, 1982). Not so obviously, students must perceive the classroom as a place where risks can be taken as part of the learning process. Specifically, students must believe that their ideas will be honored and valued and their failures will not be met with ridicule (Covington, 1983). Closely related to a sense of psychological safety is a sense on the part of students that they are accepted by their teacher and their peers (Combs, 1982).

These four categories of attitudes and perceptions are central to effective learning. If one or more are not present, learning is inhibited.

Using Cooperative Learning to Establish
a Positive Mental Climate

Although the teacher will and should always have a role in establishing these attitudes and perceptions, all can be affected from a cooperative perspective. First, a class acting as a cooperative group can identify desired features of the physical environment in which they will learn. Specifically, research and theory on learning styles (Carbo, Dunn, & Dunn, 1986; McCarthy, 1990) indicates that students define physical comfort in different ways. Some desire an atmosphere with no noise, some desire an atmosphere with music, some like an environment free of extraneous materials, some like a certain amount of clutter, and so on. To accommodate such diversity, students operating cooperatively can make decisions as to the physical characteristics of the classroom. For example, group decisions can be made relative to the arrangement of desks and furniture, the number and types of breaks that will be taken, and the display of bulletin boards and other classroom accessories. Once these standards have been identified, students can be involved in their implementation. For example, students can schedule and orchestrate classroom breaks. They can also be in charge of planning and maintaining bulletin boards.

Second, students can plan and carry out activities that enhance the perception of a positive affective tone. For example, a class operating as a cooperative group can be responsible for identifying activities that will be used to change a negative affective tone that might exist at any given moment. These activities might include class discussions about the source of the negative affect, calling for "time-outs" to alleviate a negative affective tone, and regularly scheduled activities for enjoyment and relaxation.

Third, a class can be responsible for generating and implementing classroom rules and procedures. For example, students can identify the specific classroom rules that will govern their treatment of other people, their behavior in class, and responsibilities for assignments. With regard to classroom procedures, students can help identify the specific routines that will be used during seatwork, transition times, and group work.

Finally, students can help establish and implement the rules for physical and psychological safety as well as those for a sense of acceptance. For example, students can identify a classroom "code of conduct" that would cover such areas as how to listen attentively to each other, how to show respect for each other's opinions, how to be sensitive to the feelings and knowledge base of others, and how to disagree without attacking.

In short, all four categories of attitudes and perceptions that constitute a positive classroom climate can be created and maintained in a cooperative manner.

The Importance of Cooperative Learning in Establishing a Positive Mental Climate

When used to establish and maintain a positive mental climate, cooperative learning has two primary functions: (1) building group norms and (2) diffusing responsibility.

According to Deutsch's (1949) theory, group norms are a powerful dynamic within cooperative behavior. If the four types of attitudes and perceptions described above are central to learning, then the extent to which they are established by group norms should be critical to effective learning. Deutsch's theory, then, strongly suggests that having these norms generated and reinforced by a group rather than imposed by the teacher increases the probability of adherence to them. Just as student acceptance of academic norms is a strong predictor of academic success (Brookover, Beady, Flood, Schweitzer, & Wisenbaker, 1979), so is group acceptance of the norms that reinforce the types of attitudes and perceptions necessary for a positive mental climate.

Diffusion of responsibility is another role cooperative learning plays in establishing a positive mental climate. Where diffusion of responsibility can have negative effects on group task performance (Slavin, 1983), it can have a positive effect on students' sense of self-efficacy. On the negative side, performance in academic tasks will erode if it is unclear who is responsible for specific elements of a task. However, when responsibility is diffused relative to maintaining the climate for learning, students can have an enhanced sense of control because of the transfer from teacher to students of an important regulatory function. Specifically, recent research and theory in the self-system (Harter, 1980, 1982; McCombs, 1984, 1987) has shown that effective learning includes a perception by learners that they have control over their environment. Diffusing responsibility relative to establishing group norms directly places students in a position to regulate their environment. They, as much as the teacher, are the ones establishing and maintaining the physical environment, the affective tone in the classroom, and so on.

In summary, when used to establish a positive mental climate, cooperative learning serves the function of establishing group norms. Additionally, cooperative learning diffuses responsibility for maintaining the environment, which in turn provides students with a sense of self-efficacy.

DIMENSION 2: ACQUISITION AND INTEGRATION
OF KNOWLEDGE

The initial acquisition and integration of knowledge involves at least two types of content: declarative and procedural (Paris & Lindauer, 1982; Paris, Lipson, & Wixson, 1983). *Declarative knowledge* is concerned with who, what, where, and when; for example, information about who was involved in Watergate, what occurred, and where and when it occurred. Researchers commonly subdivide declarative knowledge into (in order of specificity) facts, time sequences, causal networks, problems/solutions, episodes, generalizations, and concepts. *Procedural knowledge* is knowledge of "how to," such as how to write a research paper. Sometimes the components of procedural knowledge are represented as steps that must be applied in a particular sequence, for example, the algorithm for doing long division. Others, like the procedure for reading a bar graph, are much more loosely ordered.

Content in any field can be subdivided into these two major types of knowledge. A course in geography might include concepts and principles (declarative knowledge) about the distribution of land, along with processes (procedural knowledge) such as how to read a contour map. According to recent research and theory (Wittrock, 1974), the first job of the learner when presented with new declarative or procedural knowledge is to use prior knowledge to comprehend the information and then assimilate it into the existing knowledge base. That is, the acquisition and integration of declarative and procedural knowledge requires the construction of internal representations of the information. This internal representation is a combination of the learner's previous knowledge base and the new information within the learning situation. For example, when learners view a film on Watergate (declarative knowledge), they construct an internal representation of the information in the film. That representation comprises what they already know about Watergate and the new information about Watergate contained in the film. Similarly, when learners are first presented with the process for performing three column addition (procedural knowledge), they must again create an internal representation of it based on their existing knowledge (e.g., what they know about two column addition). Kintsch & van Dijk (Kinsch, 1974; Kintsch & van Dijk, 1978; van Dijk, 1980) refer to this process as creating a "macrostructure."

There are two aspects of a given macrostructure that render it useful or not useful relative to learning: (1) the extent to which the macrostructure contains the "top level" information from the learning situation and (2) the extent to which the macrostructure does not contain misconceptions. To illustrate, reconsider the example of the film on Watergate. Any film (or textbook chapter or teacher lecture) will contain "levels" of information. The top level of information is that which organizes the most important information presented. The top level information in the film on Watergate might be a generalization about Watergate with a number of supporting details. However, the film might also contain lower level patterns of information such as a brief description of the security guard who discovered the break-in. When creating a macrostructure for the information in the film, a student might use accurate information but not that which represents the top level structure. For example, a student might focus on the description of the security guard and totally ignore the overall generalization about Watergate with its supporting details. Similarly, when learning a new process or skill, a student might miss the major pattern of steps or heuristics and instead focus on special details. This tendency to miss the top level structures within declarative knowledge has been documented in much of the research on notetaking (Peper & Mayer, 1978; Smith, 1984). This tendency with procedural knowledge is evidenced in the research on the development of "buggy" algorithms (Anderson, 1990).

A related problem in the initial acquisition and integration of knowledge is that of misconceptions. That is, when creating a macrostructure, a student might use inaccurate information. This is because a macrostructure is always a hybrid of *new* information from the learning experience and *old* information from the learner's long-term memory. If a learner has misconceptions in long-term memory, these will commonly be inserted into the macrostructure created for the learning experience. For example, if the learner has the misconception that Watergate was a general plot participated in by all high-ranking officials of the Republican party, this will be inserted into the learner's macrostructure about the film on Watergate unless that information is directly contradicted *and* the contradiction is noticed. Similarly, if a learner has misconceptions about two column addition, they will be inserted into her initial macrostructure representing three column addition. This phenomenon has been cited frequently in research on scientific learning (Osborne & Freyberg, 1985).

Characteristically, it has been the teacher's job to ensure that top level information is noticed. One common strategy teachers use to facilitate student recognition of top level structures within declarative knowledge is to present students with advanced organizers in the form of questions presented prior to a learning situation (e.g., questions presented to students before they read a chapter) and outlines of the important information presented prior to or during a learning experience. Both of these techniques have been shown to produce favorable results in students' learning (Weinstein & Mayer, 1986). Modeling is a technique used to help students recognize the top level information in procedural knowledge. With modeling the teacher presents the important steps or heuristics for the skill or process in their most useful order. This has been shown to be highly effective, especially in learning mathematical skills and processes (Good, Grouws, & Ebmeier, 1983).

Guarding against misconceptions within a macrostructure is a much more difficult proposition because a teacher does not have the time or resources to check every student's understanding in a detailed fashion. In fact, it has been noted that many misconceptions on the part of students commonly go unnoticed by the teacher (Pressley, Ghafala, Woloshyn, & Pirie, 1990).

Using Cooperative Learning to Acquire and Integrate Knowledge

The initial acquisition and integration of knowledge can be greatly enhanced by cooperative learning. In fact, it is probably true that knowledge acquisition and integration is best accomplished in a cooperative manner. When students cooperatively identify the top level information within a learning experience, there is less chance of an individual student settling on a subordinate structure.

Because top level structures are commonly not explicit in declarative or procedural information, learners frequently must try a variety of organizational structures to establish which has the "best fit." Usually, the more alternatives considered, the better the fit of the final macrostructure. To illustrate, consider expository declarative information (e.g., information presented in textbooks). A top level structure in an expository text might have few overt linguistic or visual markers, there might be few or no headings or formatting cues as to the nature and content of the top level information. For such a situation learners have the tendency to settle on structures with which they are familiar (e.g., narrative structures) rather than those that best capture the gist of the information presented in the text (Hill, 1991). However, when top level information is identified by a group, a wider variety of alternatives is generally considered, especially with poorly marked information. For example, when a group acting in cooperation identifies the main idea in a passage (i.e., the top level information), participating students will inevitably propose a variety of alternatives. One student might propose a generalization with supporting examples as the best way to organize the information. Another student might propose a causal network as the most appropriate organizational scheme. Still another might propose a time line. When a variety of organizational schemes are considered, the probability of capturing the gist of the information is maximized (McTighe & Lyman, 1988).

Cooperative learning also helps students avoid the infusion of erroneous information into a macrostructure. Because an individual learner is not aware of his misconceptions, when he or she generates a macrostructure there is little or no possibility of checking the accuracy of the information; the learner will not question the insertion of information from long-term memory. However, quite the opposite is true when a macrostructure is constructed by a group. Given that individuals have different knowledge bases from which to insert information into the new macrostructure, there is a higher probability of informational errors being detected when meaning is constructed in a cooperative manner. As various members of a cooperative group propose ways of organizing information, other members will more than likely point out fallacies or inconsistencies that might be embedded in the proposals.

The Importance of Cooperative Learning in Acquiring and Integrating Knowledge

As evidenced in the previous discussion, cooperative learning has two primary functions in the knowledge acquisition and integration dimension of learning: (1) generating rich and varied alternatives and (2) serving as a check for accuracy. Generating alternatives is a type of cognition fundamental to most mental tasks. For example, Torrance (1988) notes that the flexibility and fluency with which ideas are generated are key aspects of creativity. Additionally, without an ability to generate a variety of alternatives, an individual cannot adapt well to a changing environment (Sternberg, 1977). With few exceptions, effective performance on cognitive tasks is a function of the extent to which alternatives are generated and assessed relative to their utility.

Checking for accuracy is equally important to most tasks because it involves assessing the truth or validity of information used within tasks. Checking for accuracy is particularly important in guarding against errors due to automaticity, the ability and propensity to perform a mental process with little or no conscious thought (Anderson, 1983; Fitts, 1964; LaBerge & Samuels, 1974). Although automaticity is necessary for effective processing of information during complex tasks, it also creates blocks or "blind spots" to recognizing errors. In extreme cases the blind spots can be so pervasive that a task will fail because of uncorrected errors.

In summary, knowledge acquisition and integration can be greatly enhanced by cooperative learning because it supports the act of generating rich and varied alternatives and checking the accuracy of the information used to create macrostructures, neither of which are commonly done by learners operating independently.

DIMENSION 3: EXTENDING AND REFINING KNOWLEDGE

Knowledge, once acquired, is frequently developed in such ways as to create new, unique cognitive structures. But this does not occur automatically. In fact, unless the learner engages in specific types of tasks, knowledge will frequently remain static. The types of tasks that help knowledge develop can be divided into two broad categories: those that help "extend and refine" knowledge and those that "use knowledge in meaningful ways." One type of thinking or dimension of learning, then, is thinking needed to extend and refine knowledge (Dimension 3); another is thinking needed to make meaningful use of knowledge (Dimension 4). In this section are considered the types of tasks that facilitate thinking needed to extend and refine knowledge and the roles of cooperative learning in facilitating that type of thought.

As the name indicates, knowledge extension and refinement involves making new connections among information and making refinements in existing knowledge. Tasks that engage students in the type of thinking necessary for these changes have, at least, two defining characteristics. They are (1) partially specified and (2) multidimensional.

Fully specified tasks, by their very nature, have outcomes that are completely determined. For example, they have only one right answer that must be expressed in a specific format. To illustrate, consider the task of answering a true/false question. Only one answer is correct and the format in which the answer is to be communicated is fully determined. Other tasks that are fully specified include answering matching items, most fill-in-the-blank questions, and typical short answer items.

Fully specified tasks do not engender knowledge extension and refinement because they do not require or allow learners to explain the reasoning behind their conclusions, and it is the act of explaining the reasoning behind conclusions that facilitates knowledge extension and refinement. That is, the process of articulating their thinking helps learners make adjustments in their thinking (Cazden, 1986). In contrast, partially specified tasks invite explanation on the part of the learner since their outcomes are not predetermined. Consider, for example, the task of classifying elements into categories. Because there are a number of ways of categorizing any group of elements (Smith & Medin, 1981), such a task would require learners to explain or defend why they selected specific categories and the criteria used to sort elements into those categories.

Closely related to the characteristic of partial specification is multi-dimensionality. That is, tasks that extend and refine knowledge have a variety of steps that interact in complex ways. This means that they cannot be done automatically as one might perform an algorithm that has been extensively practiced. Rather, multidimensional tasks require learners to consider many, if not most, of the steps involved in their execution.

Although there are probably many tasks that have the characteristics of partial specification and multidimensionality, there is a small set of tasks that are particularly applicable to knowledge extension and refinement within content area classrooms.

- *Comparing*. Identifying and articulating similarities and differences between bodies of information relative to their specific attributes
- *Classifying*. Grouping items into definable categories on the basis of their attributes
- *Inducing*. Inferring unknown generalizations or principles from observation or analysis
- *Deducing*. Inferring unknown consequences and necessary conditions from given principles and generalizations
- *Analyzing errors*. Identifying and articulating errors in one's own thinking or in that of others
- *Constructing support*. Constructing a system of support or proof for an assertion
- *Abstracting*. Identifying and articulating the underlying theme or general pattern of information
- *Analyzing value*. Identifying and articulating personal value and general value of information

Within the classroom, each of these cognitive operations can be used to engage learners in such a way as to extend and refine their knowledge of the content. In a social studies class, for example, students might compare different forms of government (democracy and dictatorship) to discover new distinctions between them. Similarly, making deductions, such as anticipating future events or conditions based on implicit or explicit principles, can help students better understand the information about which the deductions are made. In a science class, students might make deductions about whales based on known principles about mammals to refine and extend their knowledge about mammals and whales.

The extending and refining tasks listed above may also be used when acquiring knowledge. For example, when first learning about types of governments, students may engage to some degree in comparison, induction, deduction, and so on. At this stage, however, most such activity will be automatic and relatively unconscious. To extend and refine knowledge, these operations are used consciously, rigorously, and with greater complexity. When students first learn about democracies and republics, they might think casually about similarities and differences between the two. To extend and refine these concepts, however, they would be asked to list these similarities and differences, perhaps using some type of graphic or matrix representation. The difference is a matter of degree, focus, and conscious use.

Characteristically, the teacher initiates knowledge extending and refining tasks via questioning techniques. It is difficult to structure knowledge and extension refinement questions (Christenbury & Kelly, 1983), and such questions commonly tend to regress toward full specification. That is, even when teachers try to construct questions involving comparison, classification, induction, deduction, and so on, they tend to specify the form and content of the answer and, consequently, cut short or totally negate student explanation.

Knowledge Extending and Refining
Through Cooperative Learning

Knowledge extending and refining tasks like those listed above can be done in a cooperative manner with relatively powerful effects. Cooperative learning ensures that these tasks will be partially specified and multidimensional. This is because a cooperative format ensures a great deal of diversity of response and, consequently, necessitates a fair amount of student explanation and justification. For example, if students compare forms of government in cooperative groups, they will surely produce highly diverse and complex comparisons simply because of the variance of input and opinion within groups. This diversity establishes a need for explanation and justification. As each group explains the process by which they reached the conclusion made within their comparisons and the information used, they quite naturally extend and refine their knowledge.

The Role of Cooperative Learning in Extending
and Refining Knowledge

One of the major roles cooperative learning can play within knowledge extending and refining activities is through group rewards. Slavin

(1983) states that "group reward" means that the reward for each member of a group is a function of the extent to which all members have learned and performed within the task. This greatly enhances motivation for the extending and refining capacity of the tasks listed above. Within a group induction task, then, members of a cooperative group would necessarily have to ensure that each member of the group understood and could explain the observations that were made and the reasoning behind the generalizations derived from these observations. This interdependency would underscore the need for group interaction and dialogue—the *sine qua non* of knowledge extension and refinement. Additionally, Slavin notes that specific group rewards based on group member learnings increase instructional effectiveness because such rewards are likely to motivate students to do whatever is necessary to make it possible for the group to succeed—because no individual can succeed unless the group succeeds. In summary, complex knowledge extending and refining tasks lend themselves to cooperative learning and their effectiveness can be enhanced via the use of group rewards.

DIMENSION 4: MAKING MEANINGFUL USE OF KNOWLEDGE

Tasks that involve the meaningful use of knowledge have the characteristics discussed in the previous section. That is, they are partially specified and multidimensional. Additionally, they possess two other defining characteristics; they are (1) long-term and (2) student directed.

Long-term refers to the amount of time necessary to complete a task. Jacques (1985) and others assert that true knowledge development tasks, by definition, must span an extended period of time. In other words, meaningful use of knowledge probably cannot occur in a single class period. In the classroom this means that students should engage in tasks that span one, two, three weeks, and even more. Of course, this would rule out such activities as doing workbook exercises, answering specific questions at the end of a chapter and the like as tasks that enhance meaningful use of knowledge.

The second (and most important) characteristic of meaningful use tasks is that they are student directed. This means that students have a maximum amount of control over the knowledge development activities in which they engage. For example, students should be allowed to select what they will do to use the knowledge they have learned and the manner in which the product of their efforts will be reported. Where some students might decide to use their knowledge to solve a problem, others might use their knowledge to test out a hypothesis. Additionally, where some students might choose to report their findings orally, others might choose to construct a written report. Still others might make a videotape or an audiotape.

Meaningful use of knowledge, then, necessitates a measure of time and student control. Although the tasks listed under Dimension 3 could be adapted to include these characteristics (that is, they could be constructed to span extended periods of time and be controlled by students), there is another set of tasks that more readily involve extended periods of time and allow for maximum student control. These tasks are

- *Decision making.* Selecting among equally appealing alternatives
- *Investigation.* Developing an explanation for some past event or a scenario for some future event and then supporting the explanation or scenario
- *Problem solving.* Developing, testing, and evaluating a method or product for overcoming an obstacle or a constraint
- *Scientific inquiry.* Generating, testing and evaluating the effectiveness of hypotheses generated to explain a physical or psychological phenomenon and then using those hypotheses to predict future events
- *Invention.* Developing a unique product or process that fulfills some articulated need

Almost by definition, these tasks require extended periods of time to complete and maximize the amount of student control involved. This becomes evident when one considers the cognitive operations they involve. To illustrate, consider scientific inquiry tasks; the process involves

1. Explaining a phenomenon initially observed
2. Identifying the facts or principles behind the explanation
3. Making a prediction based on the facts and principles underlying the explanation
4. Setting up and carrying out an activity or experiment to test the prediction
5. Evaluating the results of the activity/experiment in terms of facts and principles that have been articulated
6. Making another prediction of future events based on the combined information from the original explanation and results of the activity

Given the number and complexity of steps involved in scientific inquiry, it is highly unlikely that students could complete such a task in a single class period. Additionally, regardless of the amount of structure imposed by the teacher relative to the task, it requires that students direct the flow of execution. For example, students must decide what predictions they will make based on their explanations. Additionally, they must determine how to test their predictions. Although the tasks listed encourage students to direct the flow, their effectiveness can be limited if the teacher specifies too many of their component parts. Consequently, students should be allowed to specify most, if not all, of the parts. To illustrate, consider decision making. A decision-making task will allow for maximum student direction if students are free to specify all components. That is, students should be allowed to determine the alternatives to be considered, the criteria, their weights and so on. However, if the teacher identifies these components (e.g., the teacher identifies the alternatives, the criteria and so on), then the task will provide less opportunity for students to manipulate the information and consequently develop their knowledge.

In summary, for knowledge to be developed, students must be engaged in tasks that are long-term and student directed. Unfortunately, such tasks are not very common within the current classroom setting. On the contrary, current research indicates that the majority of classroom tasks are teacher directed and short-term in nature (Fisher & Hiebert, 1988).

Using Knowledge Meaningfully Through Cooperative Learning

As is the case with knowledge extending and refining tasks, tasks involving the meaningful use of knowledge are well suited to cooperative learning. Each of the tasks listed above for Dimension 4 is probably done more efficiently by a cooperative group than by an individual, simply because each task is so taxing, both in terms of the knowledge and ability required for its effective completion. All necessitate large amounts of information for their execution, and a cooperative group can always provide more information than an individual. Additionally, because of the long-term nature of these tasks, they can easily overburden the energy and resources of a single individual, whereas the energy and resources available to a cooperative group are most probably sufficient to these tasks. In short, the very nature of meaningful use tasks calls for the knowledge, ability, resources, and energy available within cooperative groups.

The Role of Cooperative Learning In
Using Knowledge Meaningfully

As with tasks that extend and refine knowledge, one of cooperative learning's roles within tasks that use knowledge meaningfully is group rewards. That is, as cooperative groups engage in their decision making, investigation, problem solving, scientific inquiry, and invention tasks, the reward of each individual member should be a function of the extent to which every member has learned and performed well within the task. Cooperative learning within such tasks can also have the role of task specialization, which enhances performance because it maximizes the knowledge, ability, resources, and energy available for each component of the task. Where one student might not have the knowledge necessary to complete a component of a scientific inquiry task, another would; where one student might not have the ability to set up an experiment within such a task, another would. Slavin (1983) notes that for task specialization to be effective, each member of the group must be given a specific part of the task to do, and the members must depend on each other and not be able to substitute easily for each other in completing the task. Slavin also notes that when these components are in place, task specialization solves the problem of diffusion of responsibility by creating a high degree of individual accountability for each group member.

DIMENSION 5: DEVELOPING FAVORABLE HABITS OF MIND

The final dimension of learning is thinking needed to develop favorable habits of mind. This dimension springs from the current research finding that learning is maximized when directed by certain mental dispositions. Specifically, in recent years there has been great interest in identifying the components of higher level learning. Work by Resnick (1987), Paul (1984), Ennis (1987), Costa (1984), and others indicates that higher level learning occurs when the learner's actions are governed by mental dispositions or habits such as:

- Being sensitive to feedback
- Seeking accuracy
- Evaluating the effectiveness of your actions
- Being precise
- Engaging intensely in tasks even when answers or solutions are not available

- Pushing the limits of your knowledge and performance
- Generating and following your own standards
- Generating new ways of viewing situations

To illustrate, learners can engage in virtually all of the tasks listed under Dimensions 3 and 4 in a haphazard and uninspired manner. However, when learners engage in such tasks while utilizing the dispositions listed above, their learning is invariably enhanced. For example, evaluating the effectiveness of their actions always enhances learners' performance; being precise usually renders a task more effective, and so on. In short, the mental habits of higher level learning cut across all academic tasks, making their execution more effective and enhancing the knowledge base of the individuals engaging in them.

Characteristically, these dispositions or mental habits are reinforced by the teacher. For example, the teacher might notice students evaluating the effectiveness of their own actions. The teacher would reinforce this disposition by commenting positively on its use. Similarly, if the teacher noticed a student engaging intensely in a task even when solutions or answers were not available, the teacher might compliment the student on the use of this mental habit. Teachers also encourage the use of these dispositions by commenting on their absence. For example, if a teacher noticed that students were not pushing the limits of their abilities, the teacher might point this out, exhorting them to work harder. Specifically, if students were giving up on a task because they considered it too difficult, the teacher would remind them that they sometimes must perform at levels beyond what they are accustomed to.

Fostering Favorable Habits of Mind Through Cooperative Learning

The dispositions of higher level learning can be (but are not always) fostered by cooperative learning in that students can observe and comment on positive uses of the mental habits by their classmates. To formalize positive student comments about the mental habits, "process observers" can be used. For example, one student within each cooperative group working on the tasks described under Dimensions 3 and 4 could be asked to look for instances of use of a specific disposition. Specifically, a student in each group might be appointed the task of looking for instances of their peers generating new ways of viewing a situation. In addition to doing their own work, these observers would look for instances of that specific mental habit. At the end of the period, the process observer in each group would then report on the use of the targeted disposition by their classmates, pointing out specific examples of how peers attempted to view the task in new ways.

The Importance of Cooperative Learning in Fostering Favorable Habits of Mind

The primary function of cooperative learning in reinforcing favorable habits of mind is to provide feedback. Current research on the change process (Sawada & Caley, 1985) indicates that for habitual actions to change, individuals must have feedback about their behavior. Unfortunately, the dispositions, by their very nature, are difficult to self-observe. That is, individuals are usually not aware of the extent to which they are evaluating the effectiveness of their own actions, are being precise, and so on. It is because these mental habits are so difficult to self-observe that changing one's behavior relative to them is problematic. Cooperative groups, then, can create a "feedback loop" for learners relative to the mental habits. This could provide a rare opportunity for learners to receive objective data about their use of the mental habits of higher learning and the effects of these dispositions on their performance.

SUMMARY

In summary, there are five dimensions of learning that stem from some commonly accepted principles of learning. Cooperative learning can play a significant role in each of these aspects of learning. However, its role is different from dimension to dimension. Specifically, within the first dimension (thinking needed to develop attitudes and perceptions that create a positive mental climate), cooperative learning performs the functions of establishing group norms and diffusing responsibility. Within the second dimension (thinking needed to acquire and integrate knowledge), cooperative learning performs the functions of generating rich and varied options and promoting accuracy. Cooperative learning can perform the function of establishing group rewards within the third dimension of learning (thinking needed to extend and refine knowledge) and the function of task specialization within the fourth dimension (thinking needed to make meaningful use of knowledge). Finally, within the fifth dimension of learning (thinking needed to develop favorable habits of mind), cooperative learning can perform the function of feedback.

As this chapter illustrates, cooperative learning has many faces within the learning process. It will be through the specification of the distinctions between these faces that cooperative learning will develop into an even more powerful instructional tool.

REFERENCES

Anderson, J. (1983). *The architecture of cognition.* Cambridge, MA: Harvard University Press.

Anderson, J. (1990). *Cognitive psychology and its implications.* New York: Freeman.

Anderson, L., Evertson, C., & Emmer, E. (1980). Dimensions in classroom management derived from recent research. *Journal of Curriculum Studies, 12,* 343–356.

Brookover, W., Beady, C., Flood, P., Schweitzer, J., & Wisenbaker, J. (1979). *School social systems and student achievement.* New York: Praeger.

Brophy, J. (1982). *Classroom organization and management.* Washington, DC: National Institute of Education.

Carbo, M., Dunn, R., & Dunn, K. (1986). *Teaching students to read through their individual learning styles.* Englewood Cliffs, NJ: Prentice-Hall.

Cazden, C. B. (1986). Classroom discourse. In M. C. Wittrock (Ed.), *Handbook of research on teaching* (3rd ed.) (pp. 432–463). New York: Macmillan.

Christenbury, L., & Kelly, P. P. (1983). *Questioning: A path to critical thinking.* Urbana, IL: National Council of Teachers of English.

Combs, A. W. (1982). *A personal approach to teaching.* Boston: Allyn & Bacon.

Costa, A. (1984). Mediating the metacognitive. *Educational Leadership, 42,* 57–62.

Covington, M. V. (1983). Motivated cognitions. In S. G. Paris, G. M. Olson, & H. W. Stevenson (Eds.), *Learning & motivation in the classroom* (pp. 139–164). Hillsdale, NJ: Erlbaum.

Deutsch, M. (1949). A theory of cooperation and competition. *Human Relations, 2,* 129–152.

Emmer, E. T., Evertson, C. M., & Anderson, L. (1980). Effective management at the beginning of the school year. *Elementary School Journal, 80,* 219–231.

Ennis, R. H. (1987). A taxonomy of critical thinking dispositions and abilities. In J. Baron & R. Sternberg (Eds.), *Teaching thinking skills: Theory and practice* (pp. 9–26). New York: Freeman.

Fisher, C. W., & Berliner, D. (Eds.). (1985). *Perspectives on instructional time.* New York: Longman.

Fisher, C. W., & Hiebert, E. F. (1988). *Characteristics of literacy learning activities in elementary schools.* Paper presented at the annual meeting of the National Reading Conference, Tucson.

Fitts, P. M. (1964). Perceptual-motor skill learning. In A. W. Melton (Ed.), *Categories of human learning.* New York: Wiley.

Good, T. L., Grouws, D. A., & Ebmeier, H. (1983). *Active mathematics teaching.* New York: Longman.

Harter, S. (1980). The perceived competence scale for children, *Child Development*, *51*, 218–235.

Harter, S. (1982). A developmental perspective on some parameters of self-regulation in children. In P. Karoly & F. H. Kanfer (Eds.), *Self-management and behavior change: From theory to practice* (pp. 165–204). New York: Pergamon.

Hill, M. (1991). Writing summaries promotes thinking and learning across the curriculum—but why are they so difficult to write? *Journal of Reading*, *34*(7), 536–539.

Jacques, E. (1985). Development of intellectual capability. In F. R. Link (Ed.), *Essays on the intellect* (pp. 107–142). Alexandria, VA: Association for Supervision and Curriculum Development.

Johnson, D. W., Johnson, R. T., Roy, P., & Holubec, E. J. (1984). *Circles of learning: Cooperation in the classroom*. Alexandria, VA: Association for Supervision and Curriculum Development.

Kintsch, W. (1974). *The representation of meaning in memory*. Hillsdale, NJ: Erlbaum.

Kintsch, W., & van Dijk, T. A. (1978). Toward a model of text comprehension and production. *Psychological Review*, *85*, 363–394.

LaBerge, P., & Samuels, S. J. (1974). Toward a theory of automatic information processing in reading comprehension. *Cognitive Psychology*, *6*, 293–323.

Mandler, G. (1983). The nature of emotions. In J. Miller (Ed.), *States of mind* (pp. 136–153). New York: Pantheon.

Marzano, R. J. (in press). *Dimensions of learning and instruction*. Alexandria, VA: Association for Supervision and Curriculum Development.

Marzano, R. J., Brandt, R. S., Hughes, C. S., Jones, B. F., Presseisen, B. Z., Rankin, S. C., & Suhor, C. (1988). *Dimensions of thinking: A framework for curriculum and instruction*. Alexandria, VA: Association for Supervision and Curriculum Development.

Marzano, R. J., Pickering, D. J., & Brandt, R. S. (1990). Integrating instructional programs through dimensions of learning. *Educational Leadership*, *47*(5), 17–24.

McCarthy, B. (1990). Using the 4MAT system to bring learning styles to schools. *Educational Leadership*, *48*(2), 31–37.

McCombs, B. (1984). Processes and skills underlying intrinsic motivation to learn: Toward a definition of motivational skills training intervention. *Educational Psychologist*, *19*, 197–218.

McCombs, B. (1987, April). *Issues in the measurement by standardized tests of primary motivation variables related to self-regulated learning*. Paper presented at the annual meeting of the American Educational Research Association, Washington, DC.

McTighe, J., & Lyman, F. T., Jr. (1988). Cueing thinking in the classroom: The promise of theory embedded tools. *Educational Leadership*, *45*(7), 18–25.

Osborne, R., & Freyberg, P. (1985). *Learning in science: The implications of children's science*. Portsmouth, NH: Heinemann.

Paris, S. G., & Lindauer, B. K. (1982). The development of cognitive skills during childhood. In B. W. Wolman (Ed.), *Handbook of developmental psychology* (pp. 333–349). Englewood Cliffs, NJ: Prentice Hall.

Paris, S. G., & Lipson, M. Y., & Wixson, K. K. (1983). Becoming a strategic reader. *Contemporary Educational Psychology, 8,* 293–316.

Paul, R. W. (1984). Critical thinking: Fundamental to education for a free society. *Educational Leadership, 42*(1), 4–14.

Peper, R. J., & Mayer, R. E. (1978). Note-taking as generative activity. *Journal of Educational Psychology, 70,* 514–522.

Pressley, M., Ghafala, E. S., Woloshyn, V., & Pirie, J. (1990). Sometimes adults miss the main ideas in text and do not realize it: Confidence in responses to short-answer and multiple-choice comprehension questions. *Reading Research Quarterly, 25*(3), 232–249.

Resnick, L. B. (1987). *Education and learning to think.* Washington, DC: National Academy Press.

Sawada, D., & Caley, M. T. (1985). Dissipative structures: New metaphors for becoming in education. *Educational Researcher, 14,* 3–19.

Slavin, R. E. (1983). *Cooperative learning.* New York: Longman.

Smith, E. E., & Medin, D. L. (1981). *Categories and concepts.* Cambridge, MA: Harvard University Press.

Smith, L. R. (1984). Effects of teacher vagueness and use of lecture modes on student performance. *Journal of Educational Research, 78*(2), 69–74.

Sternberg, R. J. (1977). *Intelligence, information processing and analogical reasoning: The componential analysis of human abilities.* Hillsdale, NJ: Erlbaum.

Torrance, E. P. (1988). Teaching creative and gifted learners. In M. C. Wittrock (Ed.) *Handbook of research on teaching* (3rd ed.) (pp. 630–647). New York: Macmillan.

van Dijk, T. A. (1980). *Macrostructures.* Hillsdale, NJ: Erlbaum.

Weinstein, C. E., & Mayer, R. E. (1986). The teaching of learning strategies. In M. C. Wittrock (Ed.), *Handbook of research on teaching* (3rd ed.) (pp. 315–327). New York: Macmillan.

Wittrock, M. C. (1974). Learning as a generative process. *Educational Psychologist, 11,* 87–95.

3

Cooperation
Worldview as Methodology

Robert Samples

One of the most important models for education developed in the past 2 centuries is coming of age—again! It is education based on cooperation. In a social institution such as schooling, support for cooperation has been surprisingly absent, although it is clear that ancient tribal societies prized it highly (Turnbull, 1983). The majority of contemporary educational practitioners have been overly influenced by competition and the test scores it purports to produce. This emphasis on testing created a climate of competitiveness, forcing cooperative education to stand in the wings waiting for its own time. In the past decade, a significant number of researchers quietly gathered data suggesting that competitive practices were not accomplishing what had been hoped for. Robert Slavin (1983), Alfie Kohn (1986), David and Roger Johnson (1989), Shlomo Sharan (1980), and many others began to accrue a body of research that provided a rational argument for what many had come to know intuitively. Basically they found out that students like to cooperate and that when they do, they perform better not only cognitively but affectively as well. The students that are involved in cooperative approaches seem to experience both the cognitive and the affective in ways more consistent with the fulfillment patterns of real life.

BIOLOGICAL BASIS FOR COOPERATION

Just as the history of schooling has favored competition as a pervasive context for instructing and evaluating students, the history of biology has favored competition as a dominant explanation for the way nature manages itself. From the time of Darwin it was said that "all nature is at war" and "the world is a gladiator show and nature, red in tooth and claw." Cooperation was seen as something to be learned by creatures with large brains and could not be considered as contributing to the evolutionary continuity of the species.

Since the mid '70s a compelling literature has emerged that provides a new paradigm in scientific thinking. The revolution in physics was well addressed by Fritjof Capra (1977) when he challenged the dominance of the Newtonian worldview in scientific thought. His voice hit a resounding chord as a dozen or so books quickly appeared that addressed the same issues in other arenas of contemporary study. Among the authors were Erich Jantsch (1980), who introduced the biological world to the new paradigm in regard to systems thinking, and Norman Cook (1980) and his work in stability and flexibility in systems. I chose to explore a biological view of brain-mind function and apply it to education (Samples, 1975, 1981). Humberto R. Maturana and Francisco Varela (1988), Robert Augros and George Stanciu (1987), all biologists, wrote cogent perspectives of the new views of biology. More recent additions have been offered by James Lovelock (1988), who formulated the Gaia hypothesis, and Rupert Sheldrake (1991), the originator of the concept of morphogenetic fields. All of these authors present various facets of the argument for considering cooperation as a far better premise in organic evolution than is competition.

Competition is, by definition, the striving for a prize or reward that not all can attain. This is more of a cultural than a natural definition. In education our willingness to adopt the more culturally framed practices of competition creates a powerful dilemma. If leading scientists are rethinking their basic assumption about the role of competition in the natural world, then do we not owe as much to students in our homes and schools? In a sense we are talking here about a design characteristic of our species. *It is nature that built cooperation into us and we must realign our cultural practices so as to restore this basic component of our design.* Homo sapiens, as a species, is fundamentally designed to cooperate rather than compete.

A PERSONAL PERSPECTIVE

During the late '60s and early '70s, my colleagues and I were working on the development of science and social studies materials funded by the National Science Foundation. I worked with the *Elementary Science Study* and *Man a Course of Study*. Initially I was profoundly influenced by Jerome Bruner, Richard Jones, Margaret Donaldson, Eleanor Duckworth, and William Gordon, who were colleagues on these projects. Later I tried to apply these early learnings to the Earth Science Curriculum Project and Environmental Studies for Urban Youth project. For more than a decade we explored approaches that would create learning experiences that in our judgment were authentic for both our students and the disciplines explored. Toward the end of that time we began to realize that there were some underlying patterns in the context of learning that we could depend upon.

The most basic assumption that guided our work was the belief that true inquiry was experienced when those involved did not know the answer that lay at the end of their exploration. For too long inquiry learning had been seen as a journey in interrogative discourse and carefully contrived experiences toward already determined answers. For us, these were exercises in verifying what was already known and were not examples of inquiry at all. To be authentic to our vision we would initiate a process of inquiry where the "answers" would come honestly out of the exploration at hand. They would not be characterized by teacher-dominated intellectual coercion leading to a preordained conclusion. In effect we bought into the "reinvention of the wheel," since we were more interested in invention than wheels.

To accomplish this end we adopted a respect for the powerful invitation to learning that is initiated by ambiguity. When ambiguous assignments are given to students, they have no choice but to make decisions—the first of which is to decide what the assignment *means*. Consider some of the following assignments:

- Go outside and find a million of something and prove it.
- Go outside and find evidence for change.
- List ten things that cannot be photographed (part 1). Now photograph any three (part 2).
- Go outside in your community and find something that needs to be done—do it.

In the face of such ambiguity a remarkable phenomenon emerged. The groups of students returned with literally dozens of different responses. The search for "a million" produced solutions in terms of bricks in the school building, blades of grass in the lawn, and the number of leaves in the trees. Students became sensitive to problems of estimation and approximation. The search for "change" and "impossible photographs" brought an awareness of cause and effect and the nature of evidence. "Community action" produced a wide array of suggestions for improvement in areas such as the aesthetic ambience of the community, land use, and the safety of the citizens. It generated a richness in critical thinking around what was possible and an equal amount of creative thought about how to get it done.

Such assignments (with modification) have been successful from the primary grades through graduate seminars. Their primary advantage is that they honor true inquiry and they possess the possibility of authentic cognitive exploration and authentic affective experience. "Authentic" as I use it here means commitment without contrivance. It involves the initiation of experience from choice, interest, and dedication. When students embark on such explorations, a great deal of sorting out takes place at the outset. I can recall many examples of the collegial inquiry when we were forced to address issues such as measurement, skills of estimation, organizing responsibility, getting permissions, maintaining records, addressing the needs of children in wheelchairs, and the dozens of other demands of real world exploration. Cooperation is the basic medium of success in such explorations. In our experience, all parties recognize this in short order. Moreover, the students quickly shifted from the contrivance inherent in doing someone else's assignment into the posture of rephrasing the assignment so it had meaning to them. Because of the high diversity of the solutions proposed in each assignment, nearly all the students found a niche in the inquiry in which they could make a significant and meaningful contribution.

From these forays, the students return to the classroom with *real* work to do. The more ordinary lessons sparkle with the same sense of mutual responsibility that is common out of doors. Somehow much of the standard fare of skills work and drill and factual learning is played out in the context of authentic experience and seems less pedantic. Yet it is clear that individual students following the strand of inquiry that they personally choose are not isolated or ostracized. Cooperation and autonomy coexist and nurture each other.

THE INTERRELATEDNESS OF AUTHENTICITY, COOPERATION, AND AUTONOMY

Authenticity is a key issue in education. For countless students, schoolwork is some kind of game guided by the clock, calendar, and textbook rather than true intellectual and emotional immersion. Today's information-age students are far too sophisticated to accept contrivance as authentic. Thus, we as educators must address the way today's students fulfill their cognitive and affective yearnings to be whole, competent, and viable. It is clear that we must honor both the self and the group through school experiences that address real issues and real problems.

A few words about scale—it would certainly be inappropriate to suggest that learning the skill of punctuation is of the same scale as making a major life-style or career decision. Yet learning to punctuate is useful, adds richness to life, and for some child at some time it may be a highly focused, all important issue. It is the role of the teacher to greet the task with the passion it deserves and nurture grace in small scale experiences as well as larger ones. Both cooperation and autonomy are served when there is no distortion of the scale of the task. When students are rewarded for what they perceive as trivial tasks, they are likely to see the experience as potentially demeaning and coercive. They know that the quality of life that they are destined to experience is only superficially affected by accurate punctuation, and they affectively close down, losing the opportunity to experience the grace of expression that correct punctuation allows.

In much of parenting, schooling, and the other socializing institutions, young people are judged on how efficiently they adopt the skills and behaviors that adults favor. Most often these adult-favored skills and behaviors are clearly not things the children are interested in or value. As a result, many of the things children learn as they "grow up" are not accomplishments that come from their own choices, interests, and commitments. Though much of this extrinsically based learning is worthy and valid, it is still an accommodation on the part of the child to the extrinsic worldview of the adult. Many children grow up knowing how to sense, respond, and be defined by that which is outside themselves rather than by that which is inherently and intrinsically within them. Their behaviors are the result of someone else's motivation and the children grow up incomplete. Alfie Kohn (1986) elaborates on this condition in his explorations of the effects of competition on children.

Humans who have never responded to and never become confident in their own intrinsic motivation are hollow. A society made up of such humans is a natural resource for despotism. It does us no good to create students so dependent upon others outside of themselves that they are rendered helpless if the support of such a group disappears. Thus authenticity must guide the development of autonomy as surely as it must guide affiliation.

Cooperation by definition is a group activity. It is expressed and judged in the context of affiliation. By definition cooperation requires mutual and beneficial behavior that results in mutual action. Consider these working definitions:

1. Cooperation is the willful engaging of one's self with others through mutual action, ideas, and possibilities.
2. Autonomy is the willful engaging of one's self, dominantly with one's self, with little or no apparent involvement with others.

A common confusion exists in educational literature about how these two ideas, cooperation and autonomy, relate. For example, I see autonomy as the condition under which the skills of self-reliance mature. It is healthy, desirable, and most certainly *not* antisocial. Cooperation is the condition under which the skills of affiliation mature. It is also healthy, desirable, and is *not* an abdication of self. What I propose here is a way to track them conceptually—a way that is useful as we explore how to make educational experience honor both the skills of cooperation and the skills of autonomy, with both hopefully leading to authenticity.

Cooperation is dominantly an attribute of affiliation while autonomy is an attribute of self-reliance. Look at it this way:

COOPERATION is to AFFILIATION
as
AUTONOMY is to SELF-RELIANCE

Cooperative education enhances the skills, grace, and benefits of affiliation. An education that honors autonomy is one that enhances the skills, grace, and benefits of self-reliance. Both are vital to contemporary health. Authenticity in cooperation and affiliation is a measure of the student's sincerity, interest, and commitment to *the goals of the group*. Authenticity in autonomy and self-reliance is the measure of the student's intrinsic sincerity, interest, and commitment to goals aimed at the *fulfillment of one's self*.

R. Buckminster Fuller (1981), Margaret Mead (1980), Jonas Salk (1983), and many others claim that the future of the planet as a whole is dependent on the authenticity of how we affiliate and cooperate. Though I am as committed as my colleagues are to this view, I am compelled to suggest that the future will also require a matching integrity within individuals who devote themselves to the culture. For me, the results that emerge from global cooperation and affiliation will be dependent upon the authenticity and integrity of each person's autonomy and self-reliance as well.

Our fundamental obligation as educators, then, may be to ensure that the cooperation and autonomy that we nurture in classrooms is authentic. If cooperation is to be the medium through which authenticity is explored then the cooperation must be authentic as well. We, as teachers who choose to nurture cooperation in learning and living, must be courageous enough to make our goals sufficiently broad to allow students to experience the honoring of the persons they are and the contributions they make to the group. Figure 3.1 summarizes this.

Figure 3.1. Aspects of Authenticity

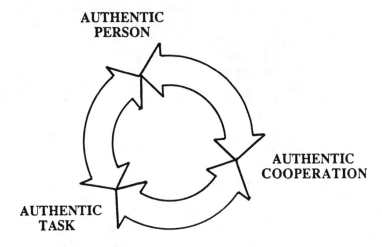

AUTHENTIC
PERSON

AUTHENTIC
COOPERATION

AUTHENTIC
TASK

Authenticity in Cooperation

Let us explore an example of authentic cooperation (Project WILD, 1986). In Lee County, Florida, a mixed group of gifted and at-risk students gathered to work individually and collectively on environmental topics of their choice. They were enrolled in grades 10 through 12 and were given each Monday to meet and attempt to accomplish their chosen inquiry. After several sessions the students decided to cooperate collectively in a single effort. They chose to try to save a pristine cypress swamp that was destined for destruction by developers and a projected highway. Once the decision was made, they enrolled the assistance of scientists, politicians, conservation groups, the park authority, garden clubs, school officials, the sheriff's department, and dozens of other groups. They created highly accurate maps, conducted a plant and wild-life census, and took their results to present at city council and county commissioners meetings. They led field trips by the dozens into the swamp and spoke before and lobbied developers ceaselessly. Finally their efforts got the proposal on a referendum ballot. They then can-vassed residents of the county and helped convince people to increase their own taxes by voting yes on the swamp. The results were totally unprecedented, as the vote passed by the largest margin in the history of Lee County. Today the Six-Mile Cyprus is a wildlife sanctuary in the midst of one of the fastest growing communities in the nation. The accomplishments of this group may at first seem to have been a casual choice. Yet it became clear that because the choice was real, they became highly committed to achieving results. It was true that profound changes took place in affective maturation, yet these affective accomplishments were accompanied by remarkable instances of cognitive growth. At the outset many of the students operated solely from emotion and feeling. Their presentations to city council and developers were, at first, near disasters. Under questioning the students discovered that they had not done their homework. The politicians and developers asked dozens of basic questions that the students were not prepared to answer. Wounded, they retreated to reorganize their plan of presentation and cut their losses. The need for rational understanding and accurate grounding became central to the efforts for several months. Rigorous planning, research, and the formulation of a new approach were central to the effort. The difference from conventional schooling was clear. These students were engaged in real world issues that required authenticity in the individuals and the group. Contrivance of the sort these students had experienced in the past was impossible.

The following are some of the characteristics that accompany cooperation-based experiences in which the tasks chosen for study are authentic.

- The students define the experience.
- There is a sense of scale. The inquiry is big enough so as not to be trivial and small enough to be manageable.
- True inquiry is involved since the outcomes are not known ahead of time.
- The primary reinforcement and reward comes from the experience itself rather than an external source such as the teacher.
- There are shifts in authority and responsibility within the group; leadership shifts with the nature of the task and the skills needed at the time.
- Wide ranges of resources are being used, both informational and human.
- The teacher's role is as a resource and guide rather than as a dominant authority.

Authenticity in Autonomy

Authenticity in autonomy comes from choosing and experiencing the consequences of that choosing. Autonomous choices are nearly always choices of some risk and they can only be experienced by addressing that risk. From these choices and that risk comes maturity. Autonomy is the apprenticing ground for individuals to become authentic members of a group. It requires that before individuals join a group and define themselves as a part of it, they first make an authentic, autonomous choice to join. In other words, self-reliance precedes the affiliation.

Some educators are, by the nature of circumstances and training, biased toward groups rather than individuals. Most certainly the popularity of cooperative learning nurtures a group perspective even though there may be individual assessment and evaluation. A possible negative effect of this may be that individuals are tacitly allowed to lose their identity to the group or to have their worth become a function of their conformity. It should be emphasized that the outcome of authentic cooperative education *may* be consensus but it is seldom conformity.

In one of the inner-city schools in which we tested the Environmental Studies for Urban Youth Project, I witnessed a poignant lesson in autonomy and self-reliance. A ninth grade student who was working on a cooperative group project related to pollution in the school environment had been discovered in the upper branches of a sycamore tree. The passerby who discovered the student promptly reported the situation to the principal. The student and his teacher were called to the principal's office. The student was asked what he was doing in the tree. He explained that he was determining, through smudge tests, the relative amount of solid particle deposition on the leaves at different levels in the tree. He said he had already discovered that the closer leaves were to the ground, the more particles were deposited on them. In spite of his earlier agitation, the principal was impressed. This student had visited the office many times before under more disciplinary conditions. After it was confirmed that the student was, in fact, carrying out a legitimate science assignment, the teacher and the student returned to the classroom, where the classmates were waiting. Neither the student, the teacher, nor the classmates made an issue of the event even though the whole project could have been in jeopardy. There was no blaming by others, no accusation by the teacher that the student lacked discretion, and no anguish about transgression by the student.

In an impassioned discussion the students asserted that they did not want to lose the right to outdoor study nor did they want to compromise their approach to the inquiry. Each of the working groups reviewed their methods and procedures in terms of discretion and school policies. Nearly all groups modified their tacit understanding about how to do what they had chosen while not creating undue concern on the part of others—particularly school officials.

In the era of cooperative education, we must be conscious of the true integrity of autonomy in the arena of cooperation. We must realize that "belonging to the group" and "fitting in" are not the only ways one can establish a positive self-image and self-esteem. We must honor the integrity of both the solitary self and the social self in the process of learning.

Some indicators of authenticity in autonomy:

- Students respect what they know and tacitly respect what they do not know.
- Students respect grades but do not hold their self-worth to be defined solely by them.
- Students recognize that what they know and believe applies to what they are learning and vice versa.
- Students are comfortable when they choose to be alone.
- Students occasionally choose "out" of a group for temporary exploration.
- Students grow comfortably in both affective and cognitive dimensions.

RETURNING TO OUR ORIGINS

Authenticity is a vital human goal. In schooling we often paint the concept of authenticity on a far too narrow canvas. With the profound responsibilities that will accompany our embracing of the methodologies of cooperative education, we must reexamine both cooperation and autonomy. Let us entertain the notion that we are really returning to a much more fundamental model—one popular during the Paleolithic era and with every tribal society since.

Cooperation is not a new idea born of our 20th-century technological consciousness. Rather it is an ancient legacy. It lives in residence in our biological make up—forming the basis for our earliest socialization and represents a powerful expression of human spirituality. Jonas Salk (1973) traces the evolution of human values from ancient times to the present and affirms the tendency toward inclusion and cooperation. I make much use of Salk's perception in my own explorations of evolutionary continuity (Samples, 1975, 1981, 1987). None of us is ignoring the profound evidence of competitiveness that characterize much of human literate history. Wars, aggression, and travail have been all too common to wash from our consciousness. We see these as representing the failure of a huge human experiment in behavior and motivation that are contrary to natural design. What we urge now is the restoration of natural tendencies of cooperation to ourselves and the institutions that have acquired the reflex to compete.

Learning has always been the medium through which these natural expressions of human grace are manifested. Jantsch (1980) extends the legitimacy of this biologically based vision when he claims that "creativity" and all learning "is simply evolution unfolding" (p. 296). And yet cooperation, as the heart of learning, is again a "new" star on our horizon. What are the reasons for this—is this a nature versus nurture issue?

Nature has taught us to *cooperate to learn*—society teaches us *how to learn to cooperate*. Both are vital but they are different. I see the contemporary interest in cooperative education in two ways. The first is sadly the possibility of a trivialization of the concept. For many, cooperative education seems to be a way of organizing experience so as to have students perform better in schoolwork. If it is successful in this form, supposedly test scores will rise, discipline will improve, and little of real consequence will change. I do not mean to diminish the successes that have been demonstrated in the literature about the schoolwork gains of many students (particularly those of low achievement). But I do stress that school and schooling, like all the institutions of our society, have the opportunity to make much larger scale contributions than were made in the past. Education is one of the few "industries" that often judges its total worth by the short-term report of a quality control officer waiting with standardized tests at the end of a 12 year long assembly line. Education and our society seem disinclined to see the whole of a graduate's life as the indicator of success. In the new role we have inherited as global citizens, the lives we live and the quality of life on the entire planet are destined to become the measures of our schooling.

Cooperation should become a life skill. I see it becoming the cohesive response for all those who learn in school that true human talent can flower through the cooperative experiences of students and teachers who honor authenticity and integrity. In this more provocative vision, I see schools and schooling adopting cooperation and cooperative education as a new worldview. That cooperative education may be cast in a perspective that sees it as more than solely another of education's technologies or methodologies is a major shift for our times. Largely, we have created limited though useful methodologies in the form of learning styles, learning modalities, multiple intelligences, cognitive coaching, and problem solving. These technologies should be seen not as ends in themselves but as means toward a larger vision. We must coordinate these various technologies into a commitment to diversification in instruction. If, in school, we experience free choice among authentic options and select approaches aimed at authentic problems, we may develop the skills that will embrace the global vision we aspire toward.

Cooperation is a much larger idea than any of the current educational technologies. We do have the privilege and responsibility to rein-troduce this primal evolutionary commitment to cooperate into our times. Never in history has the world demanded as much from its inhabit-ants. We are witnessing the first possibility of the entire planet being cloaked in peace—a peace that promises to invite us to recognize and honor our bonds with all life on earth—human and otherwise. These new times require new dreams and new commitments to cooperate. The grace of cooperation is becoming far more compelling a goal than the divisiveness of competition. As individuals we must seek to nourish our own personal integrity so that we offer worthy membership in the com-munities we help create. Through an authentic and high-integrity auton-omy a new cooperation can be born. Through a new cooperation a new worldview can be born.

REFERENCES

Augros, R., & Stanciu, G. (1987). *The new biology*. Boston: Shambhala.

Capra, F. (1977). *The Tao of physics*. New York: Bantam.

Cook, N. (1980). *Stability and flexibility*. New York: Pergamon.

Fuller, R. B. (1981). *The critical path*. New York: St. Martin's.

Jantsch, E. (1980). *The self organizing universe*. New York: Pergamon.

Johnson, D. W., & Johnson, R. T. (1989). *Cooperation and competition: Theory and research*. Edina, MN: Interaction.

Kohn, A. (1986). *No contest: The case against competition*. Boston: Houghton Mifflin.

Lovelock, J. (1988). *The ages of Gaia*. New York: Norton.

Maturana, H. R., & Varela, F. (1988). *The tree of knowledge*. Boston: Shambhala.

Mead, M., & Metraux, R. (1980). *Aspects of the present*. New York: William Morrow.

Project WILD secondary activity guide. (1986). Boulder, CO: WREEC.

Salk, J. (1973). *The survival of the wisest*. New York: Harper and Row.

Salk, J. (1983). *Anatomy of reality*. New York: Columbia University Press.

Samples, B. (1975). *The metaphoric mind*. Reading, MA: Addison-Wesley.

Samples, B. (1981). *Mind of our mother*. Reading, MA: Addison-Wesley.

Samples, B. (1987). *Openmind/wholemind*. Rolling Hills Estates, CA: Jalmar.

Sharan, S. (1980). Cooperative learning in small groups: Resent methods and effects on achievement, attitudes, and ethnic relations. *Review of Educational Research, 50*, 241-272.

Sheldrake, R. (1991). *The rebirth of nature*. New York: Bantam.

Slavin, R. (1983). *Cooperative learning*. New York: Longman.

Turnbull, C. (1983). *The human cycle*. New York: Simon & Schuster.

4

Co-Cognition
The Cooperative Development
of the Intellect

Arthur L. Costa and Pat Wilson O'Leary

> Every function in . . . cultural development appears twice: first, on the social level, and later on the individual level; first between people (interpsychological), and then inside (intrapsychological). This applies equally to voluntary attention, to logical memory, and to the formation of concepts. All the higher functions orginate as actual relationships between individuals. (Vygotsky, 1978)

Cooperative learning has been cited as a means for developing intellectual skills. Indeed, Johnson & Johnson (1989) and others have repeatedly supported this contention with much research, finding that there are strong positive effects upon achievement as well as the ability to think critically, perform higher order thinking, display more effective reasoning, and think more creatively when working in a group.

There are, however, other intellectual skills not necessarily measured on tests of critical thinking and reasoning: skills that facilitate efficient, effective problem solving; skills that enable people to behave intelligently. These skills should be more than mere by-products of cooperative learning; they should be the goals and the outcomes of collaborative efforts.

In teaching for thinking, we are interested not only in how many questions students answer correctly on a test; we are concerned also with students' knowing how to behave when they don't know an answer. Intelligent behavior is performed in response to questions and problems whose answers are not immediately known. We are interested in observing how students *produce* knowledge, rather than how they merely reproduce knowledge. The critical attribute of intelligent human beings is that they not only have information, they also know how to act upon it. We are interested in focusing on student performance under those challenging conditions that demand use of group strategic reasoning, insightfulness, perseverance, creativity, and craftsmanship to resolve complex problems.

41

What behaviors are indicative of the efficient, effective problem solver? What *do* human beings do when they behave intelligently? We are not describing performance on IQ tests. These have been shown by Sternberg (1984) to be little more than how a person performs on that test on that particular day, and have little relevance to intelligent life skills. Research in effective thinking and intelligent behavior by Feuerstein, Rand, Hoffman, and Miller (1980), Glatthorn and Baron (1991), Perkins (1991), Ennis (1991), and Gardner (1984) indicates that there are some identifiable characteristics of effective thinkers. Not only scientists, artists, and mathematicians demonstrate these behaviors. They have also been identified in successful auto mechanics, teachers, entrepreneurs, salespeople, and parents—people in all walks of life.

The eight indicators of intelligent behavior that we will discuss in this chapter are as follows:

1. Persistence
2. Restraining impulsiveness
3. Listening
4. Flexibility
5. Metacognition
6. Precision
7. Questioning
8. Creativity

This list is by no means complete. There are numerous indicators of intelligent behavior. The intent is to start you and your students thinking about characteristics of effective thinking behaviors and how working cooperatively can develop them. (For further references, see Costa, 1991.)

We believed that these intelligent behaviors can best be experienced, practiced, analyzed, and applied in collaborative settings. Co-cognition, moreover, is particularly fitting since a modern day problem is so complex that no one person can possibly have access to all the information necessary to solve it. The workplace increasingly necessitates group problem-solving skills.

For each indicator of intelligent behavior discussed in this chapter, an appropriate learner activity will be suggested to engage students in working cooperatively in groups. Suggestions will be offered as to the teacher behaviors needed to mediate students' learning from these experiences and applying or transferring experiences beyond the classroom setting. The teacher is critical as a mediator of this process. There are seven major roles of the teacher:

1. *Structuring* the group (including giving directions) to maximize positive interdependence; presenting the group with some dilemma, problem, or discrepancy to resolve; organizing/assigning tasks within the group; and communicating multiple and simultaneous goals.
2. *Mediating* the group's work by asking questions, building vocabulary, keeping clearly in mind the multiple nested objectives of the activity, responding nonjudgmentally, inviting the group's metacognition. (A dictionary and/or thesaurus will prove helpful here.)
3. *Processing* the cooperative efforts by debriefing after group work; reflecting on and labeling of actions and inviting transfer or bridging beyond this setting to other life situations.
4. *Teaching* students specific cooperative skills as needed including generating criteria, listening, empathizing, communicating, helping by not giving answers, observing, role playing, consensus seeking, and evaluating. (See Dishon & O'Leary, 1984, p. 57.)
5. *Monitoring* by observing students getting better at the intelligent behaviors, assisting students to become aware of their own and other's growth in these behaviors, providing specific feedback, finding other examples of the use of the behaviors beyond the context in which they were learned.
6. *Modeling* all the intelligent behaviors in their own conduct.
7. *Collaborating* as a member of a school-based team. Co-cognition is not just for classrooms. To work well, schools, too, must become collaborative. Teachers can reinforce these skills throughout the grade levels and across the subject areas. Parents can become involved in reinforcing these behaviors at home. Teachers should coach each other, plan together, construct collaborative visions, trust each other, and problem-solve together. Finally, they should assess themselves throughout the cooperative thinking process.

For more elaboration of the teacher's roles, see Dishon and O'Leary (1984).

Students and teachers may cooperatively assess their growth in the performance of intelligent behaviors in group and individual settings by using a "How are we doing?" checklist (see Figure 4.1). Checklists can be used with all the intelligent behaviors described in this chapter. For each, fill in the appropriate attribute and observable indicators, as discussed in the following sections. The columns for rating performance are labeled "Often," "Sometimes," and "Not Yet." The latter column is essential as a positive symbol of the potential for performance. (Our thanks to Bena Kallick of Westport, Connecticut, for this idea.)

The examples are meant to serve only as a model. The intent is to have students develop and keep a checklist of indicators of what they

Figure 4.1. "How Are We Doing?" Checklist

ATTRIBUTE:

Observable Indicators	Often	Sometimes	Not Yet

would see a person doing or hear a person saying if he or she were behaving intelligently. It is not intended for the teacher to use as a checklist to evaluate students. Rather, students should use the list to observe themselves and their performance in groups. In several of the activities, a group process observer should be invited to record indicators of performance on this checklist. After the activity, observers should share their observations with their group. It is desired that students become better able to develop, retain, and apply a set of internal criteria for monitoring and evaluating their own performance.

PERSISTENCE

Intelligent people persevere when the solution to a problem is not immediately apparent. They stick to a task and see it through to completion.

Some students, however, often give up in despair when the answer to a problem is not immediately known. They often crumple their papers and throw them away, saying, "I can't do this; it's too hard," or they write down any answer to get the task over with as quickly as possible. One teacher reported a student as saying, "I don't do thinking." They lack the ability to analyze a problem, to develop a system, structure, or strategy of attack. But though students are reluctant to go it alone they devote much energy and time to a difficult task when they do it with others. This is probably because of their feelings of responsibility to and camaraderie with others.

Suggestions for Teachers

Talk with your students about perseverance, and build their vocabulary related to it: persistence; stick-to-it; hang in there; if at first you don't succeed, try, try again; tenacity; focused. Discuss with them why it is necessary to persevere. Read them the story of *The Little Engine That Could* or something similar. Perhaps some of them have seen the movie *Stand and Deliver*, the story of Jaime Escalante, a teacher who coached Hispanic inner-city students to become math experts. Discuss how persistence by both the teacher and the students paid off. Another example is Nelson Mandela, who spent 27 years in prison but never gave up his beliefs.

Have them recall times when they persevered or persisted. In groups have them describe what they would see a person doing or hear a person saying that would indicate that he or she was persisting. Enter the following indicators on the "How are we doing?" checklist: seeks alternative sources of data; may take a break, but returns to the task; says, "Wait, I want to finish." A student can serve as a group process observer by tallying observations of a group's performance during and after the following activity.

Activity: Spatial Reasoning

Place your students in groups of three (or four if necessary). The task is easy enough for a small group, which helps keep more people involved more of the time. Give each group one piece of paper on which is a "maze" of geometric shapes, for example, many triangles or squares within a large triangle or square. Ask them to agree upon a system to use to count the shapes. Every person is responsible for knowing the final number, how to find all of the shapes recognized by the group, and to be able to explain the system. While working, one person serves as recorder, and every groupmate is to remember to "encourage."

After 15 minutes, time is called. Students sign the group paper, which means, "I understand and I helped." Several or all of the groups are checked. The teacher picks one person from each checked group to show all of the shapes without help from groupmates. Groups are above criteria if they come within two of the correct answer. Students are asked to recall specific behaviors they used to encourage each other.

Follow-up Discussion

During the processing ask students: "How long would you have worked on this task had I assigned it as homework for you to do at home alone?" Most, but not all, students will say they would have given up after only a brief period. Furthermore, they would have found one immediate solution that satisfied them and their job would have been finished.

Ask them to compare that response with what they actually did. They will often say they worked longer, found it more interesting, explored a variety of solutions, and checked more for accuracy.

Ask students to discuss and explain why people often persist longer in groups than when alone. Ask them when else it is necessary to persist and persevere. Have them interview their parents or grandparents to determine if persistence is required for their jobs. Have them describe what goes on inside their heads when they need to continue to work to solve a problem but don't know what else to do. Ask if there were ever a time when they wish they had persevered but didn't—what were the consequences?

Evidence of Growth/Improvement

Students may demonstrate growth in their capacity to persist by increasing their use of alternative strategies of problem solving. They collect evidence to indicate their problem-solving strategy is working, and if one strategy doesn't work, they know how to back up and try another. They realize that their theory or idea must be rejected and another employed. They have systematic methods of analyzing a problem, knowing ways to begin, knowing what steps must be performed and what data needs to be generated or collected.

RESTRAINING IMPULSIVENESS

Intelligent people have a plan of action before they begin a task. They have a clear goal and act with intentionality.

Often students blurt our the first answer that comes to mind, start to work without fully understanding the directions, and lack an organized plan or strategy for approaching a problem. They may make immediate value judgments about an idea, criticizing or praising it—without fully understanding it or gathering sufficient information to make an informed judgment. They may take the first suggestion given or operate on the first idea that comes to mind, rather than considering alternatives and consequences of several possible directions. They are often gullible, easily persuaded by others, and fail to explore the consequences of their actions. Working in cooperative groups provides an optimal opportunity for students to learn to restrain impulsiveness.

Suggestions for Teachers

Build the vocabulary of restraint of impulsiveness: patience, calm, keep your wits about you, look before you leap, and so forth. Read stories or fables, such as "The Hare and the Tortoise," whose moral is patience and the restraint of impulsiveness. Ask students why and when it is important to restrain impulsiveness. Ask them to interview their parents to determine when in their jobs they have to restrain their impulsiveness. Ask them to recall times when they wish they had restrained their impulsiveness but didn't. What were the consequences?

In groups, invite them to make a list of what people do when they restrain impulsiveness. What would you hear people saying or observe them doing if they were restraining impulsiveness? Enter the following indicators on the "How are we doing?" checklist to be used by the group process observer during an activity: listens to directions before starting; asks questions to clarify the task; thinks and talks with group before writing.

Activity: Below the Surface

After reading a story, poem, newspaper article, or a chapter, give your students five or six questions to answer. The questions need to be open ended, beginning, for example, "What if . . ." "How did the character/politician/scientist feel when . . ." "What would you have done if . . ." "Why do you suppose . . ."

Place your students in groups of four or five. This activity is fun and challenging with a larger group for added resources. Each group gets one worksheet with the questions and spaces for three possible answers. The writer writes the three answers to which the group agrees and then circles the one that the group agrees is their "best" choice. An appropriate social skill for this is "respond positively to ideas." This conversation (and group size) needs 20 to 30 minutes. When time is called, group members are asked to sign the worksheet, which means, "I participated and I agree." The group reader then reads the group answers to the class while the teacher facilitates perspective taking and continued thinking by noting similarities and differences in the answers from all groups. Students are asked to recall the ways in which they "responded positively" and how those behaviors kept them going in their conversation. Example: each groupmate tells his or her group, "I felt _____ when some paraphrased my idea because _____."

Follow-up Discussion

Invite the group process observer to share observations from the "How are we doing?" checklist. The teacher can also facilitate thinking by asking such questions as, "What happened in your group when you had to come up with the third alternative?" or "Did you find your group coming up with four or more alternatives to each question?" "Why?" "What did that do to your group's thinking?"

Ask when were times during this activity in which you restrained your impulsiveness. What went on in your head when you did so? What effect did the restraint of impulsiveness have on your group's functioning? When else in life or in other subjects is it important to restrain your impulsiveness?

Evidence of Growth/Improvement

As students decrease their impulsiveness, we might observe them clarifying their goals, planning a strategy for solving a problem, exploring alternative problem-solving strategies, and considering consequences of their actions before they begin. They will decrease trial and error, gather much information before they begin a task, take time to reflect on an answer before giving it, make sure they understand directions before beginning a task, and listen to alternative points of view without making premature value judgments.

LISTENING WITH UNDERSTANDING AND EMPATHY

The ability to listen may well be one of the highest forms of intelligent behavior. Intelligent people spend a lot of time trying to understand another person's point of view. People who lack intelligence spend most of their energy trying to persuade others to accept their point of view.

One of the most complex forms of listening is empathic listening. Carl Rogers said, "The way of being with another person which is termed empathic . . . means temporarily living in their life, moving about in it delicately, without making judgments . . . to be with another in this way means that for the time being you lay aside the views and values you hold for yourself in order to enter the other's world without prejudice . . . a complex, demanding, strong yet subtle and gentle way of being."

Suggestions for Teachers

Discuss the need for listening. Why is it important? Ask students to ask their parents if they need to listen in their jobs. What does it mean for them? Build the vocabulary of listening: attending, not interrupting, paraphrasing, discussing, discourse, dialectical, empathy, rapport, eye contact, and so on.

Have students describe the feelings they experienced while being listened to. Ask what went on inside their heads when they served as listeners. Invite them to share experiences in which they wish they had been listened to; and further, experiences in which they wish they had been better listeners.

Activity: Tape Recorder Dyads

Partners sit facing each other without desk or table. Partner A starts by responding to a question or topic presented by the teacher. After one minute the teacher stops the action and asks partner B, who has been listening quietly as the "tape recorder," to "play back" what partner A has just said. Partner A listens carefully and corrects or adds to what partner B has heard. Then the partners reverse roles. This method can be developed in stages: start with learning to summarize and paraphrase and then move on to reflecting feelings, and more active listening techniques (Graves & Graves, 1989).

As students practice their listening skills they will notice themselves and others practicing such skills as maintaining eye contact, paraphrasing other's responses, asking questions related to the subject, using body language like an appropriate nod, etc.

Follow-up Discussion

Discuss with students what people do when they listen to one another. Ask if they have ever been listened to. How do they know they have been listened to? What goes on in their heads when they listen? What would you see people doing or hear them saying if they were really listening? Enter their statements into the "How are we doing?" checklist. Use the checklists with their cooperative groups.

FLEXIBILITY IN THINKING

Have you ever known someone who says, "Don't confuse me with facts, my mind is made up." This person does not exhibit flexibility in thinking.

Intelligent people think flexibly when confronted with a problem. They can consider other points of view, they can generate alternative, creative solutions to problems, they can approach problems from differing vantage points. Flexible thinkers are able to celebrate uncertainty; they enjoy a state of tentativeness and are often uneasy with answers or solutions arrived at prematurely. Flexible people can think in several dimensions, time frames, and category systems simultaneously, having the capacity to deal with multiple data sources at the same time.

Some students have difficulty in considering alternative points of view or dealing with several sources of information simultaneously. Their way to solve a problem seems to be the only way. They may decide that their answer is the only correct answer. They are compelled to know whether their answer is correct, rather than being challenged by the process of finding the answer. They are unable to sustain a process of problem solving over time and, therefore, they avoid ambiguous situations. They have a need for certainty rather than an inclination to doubt or to pursue alternatives. Their minds are made up and they resist being influenced by data or reasoning that contradicts their set beliefs.

Solving problems in a cooperative setting will provide students many opportunities to develop, test, reflect upon, and apply alternative and creative solutions.

Suggestions for Teachers

Have students read stories or passages written from differing perspectives (Chris van Allsberg's *Two Bad Ants* (1988) is an example). Discuss with students the need for flexibility. Build the vocabulary of flexibility: alternatives, "shades of gray," tentative, vantage point, reorientation, paradigm shift, transformation, ambiguous. Share with them stories or incidences in which flexibility of thinking produced solutions to problems. Invite them to share examples of instances in which they have had to develop alternative, creative ways of solving problems.

The purpose of the following activity is to have students realize the possibility of considering alternative points of view. Students will find that there is more than one way to view a problem. They will need to exhibit and practice flexibility in considering others' solutions. Develop your "How are we doing?" checklist. Possible indicators are "All group-mates' points of view were heard," "Group reached consensus," and so forth.

Activity: Current Events

Every content area or grade level can address current events. Have groups of 3 or 5 pick a topic of current interest within the subject objective, grade level, or community—for instance, recycling of house-hold wastes, school policies regarding parties or field trips, issues of community government. Starting with less controversial issues will help build the use of social skills before emotion is strong around any inflammatory topics. Appropriate social skills to assign (one at a time) would be "respond positively to ideas," "paraphrase," "disagree in an agreeable way." Each group must reach consensus and write lists of reasons plus a rationale for at least two sides of that issue, and sign the group paper to indicate participation and agreement. The reporter from each group must present their decisions to the rest of the class.

Variation: Half of the class is divided into small groups working on rationale for one side of an issue while the other half is working on the opposite side of the same issue, then group members are asked to switch their position before reporting to the whole class. The analysis might result in the creation of a class continuum representing the many points of view regarding the issue and then lead into a problem-solving situation (see the Johnsons' chapter in this volume).

Follow-up Discussion

Invite the group process observer to share indicators. Discuss with students what went on inside their heads when they thought flexibly. How did they approach the problem from a different vantage point? What were the effects of their reorientation? Discuss with students when else in life do they need to remain flexible. Ask them what they will take from this learning to other subject areas, to home situations or other life situations.

When students are learning to be flexible in their thinking they will exhibit such behaviors as willingness to change his or her mind, ability to accept another point of view ("I understand . . .", "I see and . . ."), accepting or offering more than one alternative to the problem, being able to compromise, and so forth.

METACOGNITION: AWARENESS OF OUR OWN THINKING

Intelligent people seem to monitor their own problem-solving strategies. When they are confronted with a problem, they formulate a plan of action in their minds; then they monitor that plan while they are implementing it. After it is completed, they reflect on that plan to determine if it worked as they hoped it would to produce a reasonable conclusion.

Teaching is a prime example of this process. As a teacher, do you ever talk to yourself? For example, as you develop your lesson plan, do you envision that lesson inside your head? Do you see the action as it unfolds? Can you hear yourself asking questions and responding? Can you see the students performing the desired behaviors? Can you envision the arrangement of the room? If you can, you are metacogitating. While you are teaching, do you monitor that plan to determine if it is working and if the plan is producing the desired results? (Teachers report that they talk to themselves inside their head: "I need to speed up"; "Go back and review"; "Remember to teach that point in tomorrow's lesson"; "This isn't working!") Then, after the lesson, do you ever reflect to determine what worked and what didn't, where you should go next, or what you should do differently in future situations? If so, you are experiencing metacognition.

Some students are unaware of their own thinking processes while they are thinking. They lack a plan of action to solve a problem before they begin; they are unable to determine if that plan is working or if it should be discarded and another plan employed. They seldom evaluate their strategy to determine its efficacy or if there could have been a more efficient approach. When asked, "How did you solve that problem?" they may reply, "I don't know, I just did it." They are unable to describe the steps and sequences they used before, during, and after the act of problem solving. They cannot transform into words the visual images held in their mind. They seldom plan for, reflect on, or evaluate the quality of their own thinking skills and decision-making strategies.

Students can better learn metacognitive skills in cooperative groups (Webb, 1985; Weinstein et al., 1989; Yager et al., 1985, 1986). As students develop group criteria for their own performance of intelligent behaviors, they will develop operational indicators of what they would be doing or saying if they were persisting, listening, restraining impulsiveness, and so forth. These indicators serve as criteria with which to evaluate their own and others' performance. Thus, through collaboration students develop a common set of criteria, internalize those criteria, hold them in their heads as they work together, and then evaluate their own and the group's performance. Thus, *co-cognition* is the cooperative development of the intellect: collaboratively developing concepts, visions, and operational definitions of intelligent behavior, which, in turn, are used to guide, reflect upon, and evaluate one's own performance while in groups (co-cognition) or when alone (metacognition).

Suggestions for Teachers

Help students to understand metacognition with several of these activities: Read to students or have them read passages from such books as Tim Gallway's *The Inner Game of Tennis* (1974), Jack Nicklaus's *Golf My Way* (1974), and Charles Garfield's *Peak Performers* (1986). Interview athletic coaches, inviting them to describe how athletes positively envision their own performance inside their heads. Invite musicians to describe how they "audiate" or play tunes inside their heads. Ask students if they ever talk to themselves. Have them describe that process. Build the vocabulary of metacognition: inner speech, inner dialogue, talking to yourself, audiation, mental rehearsal, envisioning.

Activity: Thinking Aloud Allowed

Have students get into trios and assign the following tasks: One student will first be the problem solver. The problem solver's task is to solve the problem and to verbalize what is going on inside their head while doing this—what strategy is being attempted, what steps they are using to reach the solution.

The second student will be the listener. The teacher will need to teach listening skills, as it requires special abilities to listen effectively to another person's thought processes.

The third student should assume the role of the coach for the listener. The coach's task is to listen to, record evidence of, and give feedback regarding the listener's performance of the "effective listener" skills. The rules of listening that the teacher will need to demonstrate, give reasons for using, have the students practice, and help the coach give feedback about are as follows:

- *Check for accuracy.* Listeners are encouraged to enable the problem solver to check for accuracy by asking such questions as: "How do you know you are right?" or "Is there another way you could solve this problem to prove that you are correct?"
- *Clarify.* Listeners are encouraged to invite the problem solver to elaborate or explain more fully the strategy of solving the problem. Such

clarifications as "I still don't understand; help me," or "Run that by one more time." Listeners are cautioned not to interrupt the problem solver's thinking, but rather to wait until the problem solver comes to the end of a sentence or pauses, then ask for clarification.

- *Point out errors.* The listener may identify any errors the problem solver may have made such as in addition, in reading, or in listening adequately. Such statements as, "I don't think you added correctly" or "You misread the information" or "You didn't hear all the directions" would be some examples of pointing out errors.
- *Do not correct the error.* It is very tempting for the listeners to tell the problem solvers how to solve the problem or to tell them when they have arrived at the right answer. This must be avoided. Explain that the purpose of metacognitive discussions is to keep the problem solver thinking rather than arriving at the conclusion. Telling the partner that the answer is "correct" may discourage further thinking.
- *Keep talking.* Listeners will often have to remind the problem solvers to verbalize what is going on inside their heads as they are solving the problem. Particularly if the problem solvers write something on paper, they will be tempted to interact with the pencil and paper rather than verbalizing the strategy.
- *Encourage persistence.* There will be times when problem solvers might say, "I hate these kinds of problems" or "I'm not good at solving these problems." The listener may need to encourage the problem solver to persist with phrases like, "Keep it up," "You're making headway," "You're doing fine," "What would you do/say if you could solve these problems?"

Check to ensure that all members of the trio understand their roles. Present the trios with the following or similar problems suitable for their age/grade level:

1. A new student has just been transferred into your room. The teacher has asked if you will be study buddy/friend/mentor to the new kid. You agreed. When the new kid arrives you see that she has obvious learning and social disabilities. Your friends say, "You aren't going to help that girl, are you?" What do you do?
2. It is second semester final exam time. Someone has gotten a copy of the test for chemistry from last year. Do you take a look? Tell the teacher? Something else? Why?
3. You have taken an interest in computers. After an introduction during a 6-week enrichment class, you decide to do and learn more. Where do

you go for help? What goals do you set for yourself? How do you fit this extra study into your already full schedule of school and soccer.

After the problem solver has solved the problem and the listener has facilitated the metacognition, have the coach give feedback as to which of the behaviors the listener used. Invite the problem solvers to describe what the listeners did to help or hinder the problem-solving process. Ask what they might do differently next time to be even more helpful. Change roles and repeat the process with other similar problems.

The purpose of these activities is to cause students to become more aware of their own thought processes. Thinking and then talking about their thinking begets more thinking. Have students encounter many problems. Have them say what's going on inside their heads when they can't figure out the meaning of an unfamiliar word, or describe their decision-making process as they choose to purchase something or select a dish in the cafeteria.

Follow-up Discussion

Change the "How are we doing?" checklist to a "How am I doing?" checklist. Have students describe indicators of what people do when they metacogitate—when they are aware of their own thinking. Have them record their own experiences as they get better at their awareness of their own thinking. Some indicators are: "Can list the steps used to solve a problem," "Learns from mistakes," and so on.

Evidence of Growth/Improvement

Students are becoming more aware of their own thinking if they are able to describe what goes on in their heads when they think. When asked, they can describe what they know and what they need to know. They can describe what data are lacking and their plans for producing those data. They can describe their plan of action before they begin to solve a problem. They can list the steps and tell where they are in the sequence of a problem-solving strategy; they can trace the pathways and blind alleys they took on the road to a problem solution.

They can apply cognitive vocabulary correctly as they describe their thinking skills and strategies. We will hear students using such terms and phrases as: "I have a hypothesis . . . ," "My theory is . . . ," "When I compare these points of view . . . ," "By way of summary . . . ," "What I need to know is . . . ," or "The assumptions on which I am working are . . . ."

STRIVING FOR PRECISION AND ACCURACY

Another trait of intelligent people is their passion for accuracy and precision in their work. They want to communicate accurately in both oral and written language; they check their answers again and again; they ensure their task is complete. Critical thinkers use specific terminology, refrain from overgeneralization, and support their assumptions with valid data.

Students are often careless when turning in their completed work. When asked if they have checked their papers, they might say, "No, I'm done." They seem to feel little inclination to reflect upon the accuracy of their work, to contemplate their precision, or to take pride in their accomplishments. Speed in getting the assignment over with surpasses their desire for craftsmanship.

Some students' language is confused, vague, and imprecise. They describe attributes of objects or events with such nonspecific words as "weird," "nice," or "O.K." Objects are referred to as "stuff," "junk," and "things." Their sentences are punctuated with "ya' know," "er," and "uh." We might hear them use vague nouns and pronouns: "*They* told me to." "*Everybody* has one." "*Teachers* don't understand me." Verbs are often nonspecific: "Let's *do* it." Comparatives go unqualified: "This soda is better." "I like it *more*."

Suggestions for Teachers

Talk with students about the need for accuracy and precision. Ask them to think of situations in life, in school, in other subject areas in which checking for error, clarifying precise meanings, and striving for accuracy are essential. Describe other times when checking for accuracy and precision are not important; and how do you know when it is and when it is not important to be accurate and precise. Invite them to think of times when they have had to be extremely accurate because precision was essential to completing a task. Ask them if they have ever experienced a time when they wish they had been more accurate and precise but weren't. List such experiences on the board or a chart. Add your own situations to their list. Tell them stories in which lack of clear oral or written communication caused difficulty.

For example, Art was invited recently to participate in a national telephone network talk show beamed by satellite to participating school districts throughout the country. He agreed to participate and was given directions to call in at 12:50 P.M. to be prepared to be linked up by 1:00 P.M. sharp. Prior to the telephone conference he had a meeting of his department that was to last from 9:00 A.M. to noon; good timing, he thought. At 11:15 A.M. the secretary interrupted the meeting and told him he had an emergency telephone call. He left the meeting, rushed to the phone, and heard, much to his dismay, the program's producer frantically asking why he hadn't called at the assigned time as agreed. Much to his horror, he was supposed to have called at 12:50 *central standard time*. But he was on *pacific standard time*—2 hours earlier. Because he had not been precise about the time and did not check to ensure he was correct, he missed his conference call. (Most embarrassing for one who advocates intelligent behavior!)

Classify the list into various settings, types of errors, or situations. For example, students often need to check for accuracy in math—measurement, working problems, needing to go back and check multiplication or addition problems. And sometimes they need to check for accuracy and precision because of imprecise terminology or explanations or directions.

Build the vocabulary of precision and accuracy: Checking, accuracy, correct, error, mistake, proof, reliable, clarifying, clarity, vague, perfect, conscientious, exact, craftsmanship, pride, and so on.

Oral language is rife with omissions, vagueness, and generalizations. It is conceptual rather than operational, value laden, and sometimes deceptive. To encourage careful, precise, and accurate communication and thinking, teachers must teach students to define their terms, to become specific about their actions, to make precise comparisons, and to use accurate descriptors. They should also be alert to vague or unspecified terms in the speech of other group members.

Ask students to describe what they would see a person doing or hear a person saying if he or she were striving for precision and accuracy. Enter the behaviors in your "How are we doing?" checklist. Indicators could be, "demonstrates pride in quality of product," "uses correct names and labels," "uses precise analogies," and so forth. Have students keep track of their behaviors during the following activities.

Alert students to these vague terms. Practice with them by sharing some statements that need to become more specific. Have them respond by seeking clarity and specificity. In groups, have one student make a vague statement (examples in the left column below). Group members respond using such examples as those presented in the right hand column below.

"He *never* listens to me."	"Never? "Never ever?"
"*Everybody* has one."	"Everybody?" "Everybody in the whole world has one?"
"*Things* go better with . . ."	"Which things specifically?"

"Things *go* better with . . ."   "Go? Go? How, specifically?"
"Things *go better* with . . ."   "Better than what?"
"*They* made me take it."   "Who are they"?

Activity: Striving for Precision and Accuracy

Group editing of individual writing efforts can be perfect places for students to work on precision and accuracy. The goal is, of course, for students to transfer their editing efforts to their own work in future assignments. Begin students in groups of three on small tasks. Students read their sentence, paragraph, or paper to the group. Orally or in writing, each groupmate responds with one positive comment and one suggestion for change or revision. The student receiving the comments hears/takes all suggestions and says "thank you" or says nothing. It is not helpful for the receiver to defend or select options at present. Students then continue around the circle until everyone has received feedback from the group. Revisions are then done at home or during individual work time and brought back to the group at a later time. The complexity of the editing increases as students increase their writing skills and build trust within the group. Appropriate group skills for this activity include "using names," "eye contact," "responding positively to ideas." Ask students to make a quick verbal "whip" around their group after editing with one topic like "I felt _____ during the editing of my paper because _____" or "It is helpful to give and receive feedback in other situations like _____."

Follow-up Discussion

Ask students what they do when checking for accuracy. How do they remember to check and what do they do when they realize they've made an error?

Evidence of Growth/Improvement

You will be able to observe students growing in their desire for accuracy as they take time to check over their tests and papers, as they grow more conscientious about precision, clarity, and perfection. They go back over the rules by which they were to abide, the models and visions they were to follow, and the criteria they were to employ to confirm that their finished product matches exactly.

You will hear students seeking clarity from others. You should hear students asking, "Could you explain that one more time? I'm not sure I understand" or "How do you know you are correct—what evidence do you have?" You may even hear students question your directions or questions on assignments when they are vague. Value their alertness to imprecision!

As students' language becomes more precise, they will use more descriptive words to distinguish attributes. They will use more names correctly. They will spontaneously provide criteria for why they think one product is better than another. They will speak in complete sentences, voluntarily provide supportive evidence for their ideas, elaborate, clarify, and operationally define their terminology. Their oral and written expressions will become more concise, descriptive, and coherent. They will voluntarily seek corrective feedback and constructive criticism from their peers and their teacher.

QUESTIONING AND PROBLEM POSING

One of the distinguishing characteristics of humans is our inclination and ability to find problems to solve. Yet students depend on others to solve problems, find answers, and ask questions for them. They sometimes are reluctant to ask questions for fear of displaying ignorance.

Intelligent people know how to ask questions to produce the data they need. They know how to fill in the gaps between what they know and what they don't know.

Isadore Rabbi, a Nobel-prize winning physicist, tells a story of when he was growing up in the Jewish ghetto of New York. When the children came home from school, their mothers would ask them, "What did you learn in school today?" But Isadore's mother would ask him, "What good questions did you ask today?" Dr. Rabbi suggests that he became a physicist and won the Nobel Prize because he was valued more for the questions he was asking than the answers he was giving (Barell, 1988).

Suggestions for Teachers

Build the vocabulary of questioning and problem posing: dilemma, controversy, resolution, paradox, interrogation, examine, data collection, and so on.

Talk with students about the nature of questions, why they are important and what their various functions are. Some of the functions of questions might be: to gather data and verify information (what is your address?); to clarify meaning (could you explain what you mean by that?); to form experimental hypotheses (if we were to conduct this experiment in a darkened room, would the same results be reproduced?); to seek opinions (which painting do you think is most appealing?). The following activity will cause students to pose questions.

Activity: Posing Questions

One way to build ownership of asking questions is to ask students in medium-sized groups of 4 to determine what questions they want to answer in preparation for a test or assessment situation. First ask students to decide and write what questions they have. Then individuals join together to compare and contrast their questions and to come up with one list to pose to the rest of the class. Frequently they will have similar questions, which they find reassuring. Also, they will each have questions that others in the group don't understand. A discussion will clarify or delete the unclear questions. A master list is created by the teacher on easel paper as group readers report their list. Individuals can then use the list for home study, or further group investigation can offer possible answers as a review activity.

Follow-up Discussion

A useful debriefing can be to ask individuals to decide and explain what happened to their original questions as discussion within the group continued. Many of the questions asked in this assignment might be of the recall nature, mostly facts, dates, and basic information. However, it is a beginning for any age group of students who are not used to posing their own questions or being precise in their questioning. Then more complex questioning strategies can be added to the students' repertoire. (See Chapter 13 in this volume.)

Build your "How are we doing?" checklist. Possible indicators are, "asks thoughtful, focused questions," "seeks clarification and verification."

Evidence of Growth/Improvement

Use your checklists over time to observe a shift from the teacher asking questions and posing problems toward the students asking questions and finding problems for themselves. Furthermore, the types of questions students ask should change and become more specific and profound. For example: requests for data to support others' conclusions and assumptions—such questions as, "What evidence do you have . . . ?" or "How do you know that is true?"—will increasingly be heard. Students will pose more hypothetical problems characterized by "what-if" questions: "What do you think would happen if . . ." or "If that is true, then what might happen when . . . ?"

We want students to be alert to phenomena in their environment and to recognize discrepancies and inquire about their causes: "Why do cats purr?" "How high can birds fly?" "Why does the hair on my head grow so fast but the hair on my arms and legs grow so slowly?" "What would happen if we put a saltwater fish in a freshwater aquarium?" "What are some alternative solutions to international conflicts other than wars?" Keep a "How are we doing?" checklist for your class indicating increases in the frequency, complexity, and purposefulness of the questions.

INGENUITY, ORIGINALITY, INSIGHTFULNESS, AND CREATIVITY

Intelligent human beings are creative. They often try to conceive problem solutions differently, examining alternative possibilities from many angles. They tend to project themselves into different roles using analogies, starting with a vision and working backward, imagining they are the object being considered. Creative people take risks—they "live on the edge of their competence," testing their limits (Perkins, 1991). They are more intrinsically than extrinsically motivated, working on the task because of the aesthetic challenge more than the material rewards. Creative people are open to criticism. They hold up their products for others to judge and seek feedback in an ever-increasing effort to refine their technique. They are uneasy with the status quo. They constantly strive for greater fluency, elaboration, novelty, simplicity, flexibility, insightfulness, craftsmanship, perfection, beauty, harmony, and balance.

Intelligently functioning people know how to cause the "creative juices" to flow when the situation demands it. They know how to use such strategies as brainstorming, metaphor, or mind-mapping to generate new ways of perceiving problems and their solution.

Some students say, "I can't draw," "I was never very good at art," "I can't sing a note," "I can't think of anything." Some people think creative humans are just born that way, that it's in their genes. Increasingly we are coming to realize that all human beings have the capacity to generate novel, ingenious products, solutions, and techniques—if that capacity is developed.

Working in groups causes greater stimulation of ideas and thus provides a setting in which to generate creative thought. Students will want to pay attention to how their ideas flow more freely when they listen to and "bounce off" other's ideas in a freewheeling atmosphere.

Suggestions for Teachers

Build the vocabulary of creativity: insight, intuition, clever, creative, originality, fluency, inventive, divergent. Have them discuss the meaning of the old saying, "Necessity is the mother of invention." Invite them to think of times when they had to invent an original solution to a problem. What were the circumstances? Have them describe what went on in their heads when they had to think of an original idea.

Have the students interview their parents—when do they have to draw on their originality, ingenuity, and creativity? Have students read stories of Sir Isaac Newton, Albert Einstein, Michelangelo, Elizabeth Barrett Browning, Alexander Graham Bell, Emily and Charlotte Brontë, Thomas Edison, Madame Curie, Leonardo da Vinci, and other noteworthy artists, scientists, inventors, engineers, entrepreneurs, and philosophers who are noted for their inventions and creative insights.

Activity: Cheerios as a Metaphor

The following activities are intended to have students experience and describe the metacognition involved in three forms of creative thinking: fluency, metaphor, and personification.

Give each group of 4 to 6 students a handful of Cheerios. Place the pile of cereal in the center of the table on a piece of paper. (Some students will want to eat the cereal. Tell them they may after the activity.) Ask one student to be the recorder to capture as many of the group's ideas as possible.

Tell the students that the first activity will be one in which they experience *fluency*. Ask them to monitor what goes on in their heads when they are thinking fluently. Their task is to think of as many uses for a Cheerio as they can in one minute (e.g., life preserver for ants, wheels for a minicar, packing material, counters, keep babies quiet, etc.).

After one minute call time and have the recorders share the groups' lists of uses for the Cheerios. Then, ask them what went on in their heads when they were thinking fluently. They will often describe their thinking as building on ideas of others—they listened to each other and their ideas stimulated them to generate even more ideas. Others will say something like, "I let my mind run wild—to think of anything—sometimes different ideas" or "I opened my mind to anything it could think of."

Ask students to think of and tell about situations in which they might need to think fluently. Invite them to think of jobs or careers in which people get paid to think fluently (advertising agents, artists, composers, writers). These ideas are stated by volunteers, to the whole class.

The second activity in which they will engage is metaphorical thinking. Explain that similes are comparisons between two unlike objects or events, introduced by "like or as." Give some examples (e.g., "cheeks like roses"). Have students find examples of similes in short stories, advertising, speeches, and so on.

Now have the students complete the following: a Cheerio is like a _____ because _____. They will have one minute to think of as many similes as they can while the group recorder captures these.

After one minute, share the similes. (A Cheerio is like a doughnut, ring, circle because it's round. A Cheerio is like a sponge because it soaks up liquid. A Cheerio is like a dull book because it's dry, etc.)

Invite students to describe what went on in their heads when they were thinking metaphorically. They may say they searched their memory for comparisons. They may say they thought of the attributes of Cheerios: round, crunchy, spongy, tan color, puffy, and then thought of other similar objects. Again they will no doubt report that they built upon and "bounced" off others' ideas as they were stimulated to greater creativity when listening nonjudgmentally to others.

The third activity is personification—to become a Cheerio. Define personification as a person or the human form taking on the qualities of a thing or abstraction. Cupid, for example, is the personification of love. The Statue of Liberty is the personification of freedom. Have students generate other examples of personification.

Talk with students about personification as a way to solve problems creatively—by, for instance, imagining what it would be like to be an automobile tire or the tallest building in the world, or what it would feel like to be a zero. This causes a person to look at a situation from a different vantage point. Discuss with them times when that would be important.

Next, have them pretend to become a Cheerio. What would life be like? What is the greatest gift you could receive if you were a Cheerio? What would be the worst fate of being a Cheerio? Have students brainstorm life from a Cheerio's perspective.

Follow-up Discussion

Debrief by having students describe: what went on in their heads as they brainstormed? How did working in groups facilitate their creative thinking? When else in life do people succeed by working creatively in groups? Invite them to ask their parents how they must create, what are the circumstances, and how do they draw upon others to enhance their creativity.

Develop indicators of creativity/insightfulness. Have students monitor their own growth of originality, fluency, and cleverness by keeping their "How am I doing?" checklist. Indicators could be "Plays with ideas and things," "Thinks divergently," "When talking, extends ideas," "Uses prior skills and knowledge in new ways," and so forth.

SUMMARY

This chapter has discussed how cooperative learning can contribute to the development of the intellect. We believe that working in collaborative ways in classrooms, schools, school districts, and communities produces intellectual growth in all the parties involved. Co-cognition, interaction, dialogue, conflict resolution, problem solving, decision making, brainstorming, envisioning, and planning in groups not only enhance the quality of the solutions generated. They also contribute to the growth of the individual intellect of every member of the group, allowing individuals to become more precise, more creative, more persistent, more flexible, more curious, more thoughtful, more self-aware, and more empathic toward others. These are behaviors of intelligent human beings. These intelligent behaviors are traits we believe to be essential for human survival, productivity and enjoyment, now and in the future.

REFERENCES

Barell, J. (Ed.). (1988, April). *Cogitare: A Newsletter of the ASCD Network on Teaching Thinking,* 3(1).

Costa, A. (1991). The search for intelligent life. In A. Costa (Ed.), *Developing Minds: A resource book for teaching thinking* (pp. 100–106). Alexandria, VA: Association for Supervision and Curriculum Development.

Dishon, D., & O'Leary, P. (1984). *A guidebook for cooperative learning: A technique for creating more effective schools.* Holmes Beach, FL: Learning Publications.

Ennis, R. (1991). Goals for a critical thinking curriculum. In A. Costa (Ed.), *Developing minds: A resource book for teaching thinking* (pp. 68–71). Alexandria, VA: Association for Supervision and Curriculum Development.

Feuerstein, R., Rand, Y., Hoffman, M., & Miller, R. (1980). *Instrumental enrichment: An intervention program for cognitive modifiability.* Balitmore, MD: University Park Press.

Gallway, W. T. (1974). *The inner game of tennis.* New York: Random House.

Gardner, H. (1984). *Frames of mind: The theory of multiple intelligences.* Cambridge, MA: Harvard University Press.

Garfield, C. (1986). *Peak performers: The new heroes of American business.* New York: William Morrow.

Glatthorn, A., & Baron, J. (1991). The good thinker. In A. Costa (Ed.), *Developing minds: A resource book for teaching thinking* (pp. 63–67). Alexandria, VA: Association for Supervision and Curriculum Development.

Graves, N., & Graves, T. (1989). *What's cooperative learning? Tips for teachers 'n trainers.* Santa Cruz, CA: Cooperative College of California.

Johnson, D., & Johnson, R. (1989). *Cooperation and competition: Theory and research.* Edina, MN: Interaction Book Company.

Nicklaus, J. (1974). *Golf my way.* New York: Simon & Schuster.

Perkins, D. (1991). What creative thinking is. In A. Costa (Ed.), *Developing minds: A resource book for teaching thinking* (pp. 85–88). Alexandria, VA: Association for Supervision and Curriculum Development.

Sternberg, R. J. (1984). *Beyond I.Q.: A triarchic theory of human intelligence.* New York: Cambridge University Press.

van Allsberg, C. (1988). *Two bad ants.* Boston: Houghton-Mifflin.

Vygotsky, L. (1978). *Society of mind.* Cambridge, MA: Harvard University Press.

Webb, N. (1985). Interaction and learning in small groups. *Review of Educational Research, 52,* 421–445.

Weinstein, C., Ridley, D., Dahl, R., & Weber, S. (1989). Helping students develop strategies for effective learning. *Educational Leadership, 46*(4), 17–19.

Yager, S., Johnson, R., & Johnson, D. (1985). Oral discussion, group-to-individual transfer, and achievement in cooperative learning groups. *Journal of Educational Psychology, 77,* 60–66.

Yager, S., Johnson, R., Johnson, D., & Snider, B. (1986). The impact of group processing on achievement in cooperative learning groups. *The Journal of Social Psychology, 126*(30), 389–397.

5

The Inclusion Process
Cooperative Metacognition for Discovering, Describing, and Assessing Thinking Skills

Toni Worsham

Most educators recognize the truth of Charles Kettering's assertion that "there is a great deal of difference between knowing and understanding." One of the most memorable testimonies to this observation occurred for me about 5 years ago when I was working in a middle school in Maryland. I was officially the "English" supervisor, but because the teachers worked in interdisciplinary teams, it was not unusual for any teacher on a given day to invite any available supervisor into a classroom to observe or help with this or that.

On this particular morning, the sixth grade math teacher was especially pleased with the grades his gifted and talented class had received on a ratio and proportion test given the preceding day. He asked me to stop by and praise them because every student had scored either 90% or 100% on the 10-problem test. I was more than happy to carry out such a pleasant task and arrived promptly at the beginning of the class period to do so. I began by stating that the concept of ratio and proportion was a valuable one for students to have mastered by the sixth grade because it was needed for so many everyday calculations, from shopping in the supermarket to determining batting averages to figuring miles per gallon. This preamble to praise was met not with bright eyes and positive nods of understanding, but with an array of nonverbal responses ranging from eyes cast down to furrowed brows and "Is that so?" looks with an uneasy squirm popping up here and there around the room. I decided to see if this seeming "mastery" was a case of *true understanding* or *simply knowing* how to apply the right formula.

So I shifted from pontificating to questioning, asking who could explain exactly what was meant by miles per gallon and why this was important information to know about an automobile. Then I waited a moment or two to give the students some time to think. Still, only four

66

hands went up! But the student I selected gave a fine response. "It means," she said, "how far a car will go on a gallon of gasoline. My brother just bought another car. He wanted one that got at least 25 miles to the gallon because the old one he was driving was a real gas guzzler."

"Excellent!" I said. Now I was ready to pose the essential question. "How would we figure out how many miles a car will travel on a gallon of gas?"

I waited. I waited some more. Not one hand went up! Just as I suspected! Twenty-six bright students had demonstrated high computational skills on a ratio and proportion test, but not one of them was able to apply the concept in an authentic situation! The ratio and proportion formula was *known* but the ratio and proportion concept was *not understood*.

The task at hand was obviously to move these students to a level of understanding at which the proportional relationships of numbers could actually be conceptualized. The next 20 minutes involved paired "think aloud" discussions, with a process observer recording the procedures discussed by the two thinkers in response to a series of carefully framed questions. The intent was to get the students asking and answering the right questions to be able to explain exactly how miles per gallon can be calculated.

I wanted my probes to serve as a scaffold, providing structure, but not giving so much information as to require little or no high level thinking from the class. So I asked questions such as, "What are the questions you might ask in order to gather the information you need to solve this problem? How will you know you have worked out the most efficient way to solve the problem? How will you verify your findings? What level of accuracy will you expect?"

We were well past the midway point of the class period before most of the student pairs had come up with some procedure for calculating miles per gallon. While the procedures shared were not equally efficient, the concept seemed to be generally understood by most. It took time, cooperative thinking, and process observing to assist the metacognition. It took structured, broad-framed scaffold questions to move the students from merely knowing what numbers to put above and below the line to a true understanding of when and how to apply a ratio and proportion formula. Such is the stuff that true learning is made of! Yet few teachers design their instructional programs or their assessments to ensure that they are educating minds and not just memories. This problem of superficial fact or formula learning, rather than deeply internalized understandings of concepts and processes, continues to plague our classrooms despite the realization that such surface learning is short-term and of little real value for lifelong success in problem-solving skills.

NAEP results, SAT scores, the lamentations of employers and members of institutions of higher education all indicate that today's students seem less prepared to demonstrate higher order critical thinking and decision-making and problem-solving skills. They seem less able to be creative and autonomous. They are not able to function as mature, intelligent adults. They are not able to organize and synthesize information to solve authentic problems, draw conclusions, make predictions, and come up with new ideas. Lacking such intellectual skills, the vast majority of today's students will have great difficulty surviving in the increasingly complex information-processing world of the 21st century. Information currently doubles every 20 months (about the rate of 40% per year) in the areas of science and technology (Naisbett, 1984), and the projections are that by the year 2020, information may double every 35 days. These factors indicate that teaching needs to be dramatically restructured, yet many American educators continue to believe that moving faster is synonymous with doing better. They continue to teach as they were taught (i.e., lecturing and then testing primarily for recall of information) and attempting, somehow, to "cover" the ever-increasing amount of information exploding across every academic discipline!

Since our current teaching strategies do not seem to be succeeding in helping students to learn well, how can classrooms be restructured to do a better job? This chapter will describe both an instructional framework, the "Inclusion Process" (Worsham and Stockton, 1986), and several appropriate cooperative instructional strategies for increasing student understanding not only of subject matter, but also of the thinking process itself (metacognition). Specifically, the eight steps of the Inclusion Process will be described and discussed with the intent of providing simple operational guidelines for moving students from knowing to understanding, to a realization of how to understand more effectively and how to monitor their own progress in gaining understanding.

While the process of human thought is at once holistic and recursive, multifaceted and complex, critical and creative, it can be better comprehended by beginning to look at specific aspects of its functioning—i.e., thinking skills—in order to study how these various skills operate (description), what they mean (definition), and how each differs from the others while operating in concert with them. By generating a metacognitive conceptualization of some of the skills they use frequently, students learn to apply them more effectively and build up their own confidence in doing so. By working cooperatively with other students to analyze various thinking skills and discovering how they actually apply these skills, students learn that others can help them see, through objective lenses, exactly what they do as they think and give them new strategies for thinking better.

A REVIEW OF THE INCLUSION PROCESS

The Inclusion Process has two components: planning and implementation (Worsham, 1988). There are four steps in each phase (see Figure 5.1).

Phase One—Planning

The planning phase is primarily the responsibility of the teacher, although in some schools, older students have had some involvement in the decision regarding what skills need to be taught. This decision is made by looking at the curriculum objectives to determine what kinds of thinking are necessary to attain the objectives (Step 1). Based on past experience in teaching the program and an awareness of where students encountered difficulties (Step 2), a list of thinking skills is developed. Generally, it takes little time to produce a lengthy list of thinking skills that students have difficulty applying well. However, the objective here is not a long list but a rather *short* one that contains those key thinking skills that seem particularly related to the objectives of the subject and program being taught. Generally, from four to six thinking skills are selected for inclusion in the program during the school year (Step 3). A sample list is given later in the chapter.

Once the skills are selected, a long-range plan for including the skills throughout the school year needs to be developed (Step 4). This generally involves determining the sequence in which the skills will be introduced, the unit in which they will be taught, and the lessons in which they will be applied after they are taught. These decisions depend upon a number of factors including who is participating (total staff to single classroom) and the school's instructional organization (departmental, interdisciplinary, single grade, combined grades, etc.). Again, depending on the number of staff members and disciplines involved, this planning stage can take anywhere from 1 or 2 hours to several meetings. In instances where total school systems have adopted the model (i.e., Frederick County, Maryland) the planning has been done one grade level at a time (6, 7, 8) over a period of 3 years during the summer months by a committee of teachers from each grade level involved.

Figure 5.1. Inclusion Process

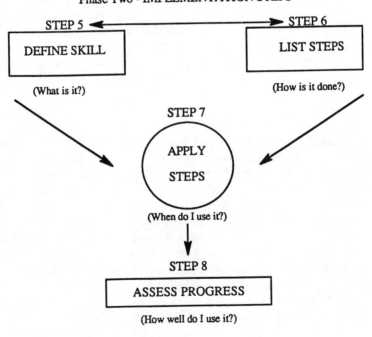

Phase One - PLANNING STEPS

STEP 1   STEP 2

CURRICULUM OBJECTIVES

(What must I teach?)

STUDENT NEEDS

(Whom must I teach?)

STEP 3

THINKING SKILLS

(What skills should I teach?)

STEP 4

LONG-RANGE PLAN

(When should I teach them?)

Phase Two - IMPLEMENTATION STEPS

STEP 5   STEP 6

DEFINE SKILL

(What is it?)

LIST STEPS

(How is it done?)

STEP 7

APPLY STEPS

(When do I use it?)

STEP 8

ASSESS PROGRESS

(How well do I use it?)

Phase Two—Implementation

The implementation component (Phase Two) requires that the teacher's role now shifts to "facilitator." The most critical piece of the entire process—the "focus" lesson—introduces the implementation phase. This lesson must be carefully designed to ensure that students are led to a discovery of how a selected skill operates when it is applied in a cognitive task. The objectives for this pivotal lesson (Steps 5 and 6) are always the same. *Students* will define the skills and describe the process (identify the steps) involved in applying the skill. This lesson usually takes at least two class periods, sometimes more, especially when it is first introduced.

Effective focus lessons provide a framework of cooperative, meta-cognitive structures to help the students help each other attain the lesson objectives. The activities are almost always inductive and can be either subject related, subject specific, or general. Students "discover" by engaging in the activities, the "how" and "what" of a specific thinking skill or process. The teacher's job is to ensure that the tasks are designed to lead students to this discovery. While the lessons following the focus lesson may have to be redesigned so that they are student centered, cooperatively structured, and include metacognition, the focus lesson is the only new addition to the regular program.

Following the focus lesson, several opportunities for affirmation of the skill's operation are provided in application lessons (Step 7). These lessons should be content specific and, ideally, fit naturally into the actual flow of the curriculum. Good planning in phase one places the focus lesson immediately prior to content lessons in which the selected skill is integral to the curriculum objective(s).

The application lessons provide students with the opportunity to refine and/or confirm their strategy for applying effectively the thinking skill in relation to the content to be learned. By working cooperatively in pairs and small groups, students help one another to apply and analyze the steps they've generated to determine their effectiveness. Metacognition is again most essential. Students must decide whether or not their "thinking plan" works in several different situations and, if not, how it needs to be adjusted. The thinking skills in both the focus and application lessons become part of the content to be learned and tested in relation to the curriculum to which they are so integral.

After several such practice activities, students rearrange their carefully honed "definitions" and "steps" to create a Performance Assessment Matrix (PAM) to determine their ability to apply the thinking skill just learned (Step 8). This final step in the Inclusion Process provides students with a nonthreatening "thinking in action" gauge of their own progress in applying specific thinking skills. The PAMS (to be discussed in detail later in this chapter) can be used for self, peer, or teacher assessment both independently or in combination with other assessment measures such as product assessments, exhibitions, portfolios, process folios, or written tests.

THE INCLUSION PROCESS IN PRACTICE

To provide a better "vision" of how the Inclusion Process takes shape, it might be useful to review the eight steps with examples of how they were actually incorporated into a school program. Beginning in 1985, a selected middle school in the state of Maryland began incorporating the Inclusion Process into all aspects of the middle school program (Worsham, 1988). Over the next 3 years the faculty proceeded, one grade level at a time (6, 7, 8), to follow the model by choosing four skills per year for inclusion in the instructional program. During the first year, in carrying out Phase One (the planning steps), the sixth grade academic interdisciplinary team, consisting of the math, science, social studies, and language arts teachers, selected the skills of predicting, reading charts and graphs, recognizing logical relationships, and understanding the main idea for direct instruction. They had little difficulty deciding, as a team, that the successful application of these four skills was essential to each of the four subjects and that, for the most part, their students did not perform them well.

The teachers then developed their long range plan for the year, based on the sequence of their respective units. They arranged their lessons to ensure that application lessons followed each focus lesson and fit naturally into each subject area. Each teacher was responsible for a focus lesson at the rate of one per quarter according to the following schedule:

Quarter	Skill Focus	Teacher Leader
1st	Predicting	Science
2d	Understanding the main idea	Language arts
3d	Reading charts, graphs, cartoons	Social studies
4th	Recognizing logical relationships	Mathematics

All four teachers then taught appropriate follow-up application lessons in their own subject area.

The seventh grade team, during the second year, reviewed the four sixth grade skills and added four new skills, according to the following monthly plan:

October	Defining	Social studies
November	Understanding the main idea	All teachers
December	Classifying	Science
January	Recognizing logical relationships	All teachers
February	Distinguishing facts from opinions	Language arts
March	Reading charts, graphs, cartoons	All teachers
April	Drawing conclusions	Mathematics
May	Predicting	All teachers

Finally, the eighth grade team reviewed the eighth, sixth, and seventh grade skills by pairing into math/science and social studies/language arts teams and dividing the skills to be reviewed between them. They also added four new skills according to the following schedule.

October	Identifying pertinent data	Language arts
November	Understanding the main idea	Social studies/ Language arts
	Predicting	Science/ Mathematics
December	Sequencing	Mathematics
January	Differentiating fact from opinion	Language arts/ Social studies
	Reading charts, graphs, and cartoons	Science/ Mathematics
February	Determining causes	Science
March	Defining	Language arts/ Social studies
	Drawing Conclusions	Science/ Mathematics
April	Comparing and contrasting	Social studies
May	Classifying	Language arts/ Social studies
	Recognizing logical relationships	Science/ Mathematics

As the teachers moved into Phase Two (the implementation phase), they worked independently on the focus and application lessons and then engaged in peer review as an interdisciplinary team. They found it was particularly important initially to go through the focus lesson activities themselves and generate their own definitions and steps for the selected skills. This enabled them to better assess the effectiveness of the activities and to directly experience the process that the students would follow as they moved through the focus lesson. Most of the teachers agreed that becoming metacognitive was more difficult than they had expected. With practice, however, both they and the students became better at getting in touch with and precisely describing their own thinking patterns.

This "walking in the thinking shoes" of their students also enabled teachers to become far more skillful in designing effective activities for leading the students to a truer understanding of the thinking skill being taught. They become experts in blending process and content with strategy and design in order to lead students skillfully to the discovery and conceptualization of the paths of their own thoughts and those of their classmates. The teacher's role became that of orchestrator and facilitator rather than information giver.

A PHASE TWO RE-CREATION

To illustrate how the implementation phase actually unfolds, it might be useful to select a thinking skill and re-create the focus, application, and assessment steps of the process to provide a better sense of what occurs in the classroom when the model is implemented. For this re-creation, let's assume that the skill is prediction. During the focus lesson the students, working in pairs, with a third student acting as a process observer, are directed to spend the first half hour of the period moving through the activity stations set up around the room. At each station the "thinking team" is to follow the listed directions and think aloud together while the process observer records the thinking steps the thinkers follow to complete the activity.

If this is the first time the students have engaged in cooperative, metacognitive thinking or if the group seems unsure of how to proceed, it is advisable for the teacher to model the procedure for the entire class, asking all the students to be process observers as the teacher thinks aloud. For example, using an incomplete comic strip (Figure 5.2) projected on the overhead, the teacher might say, "This comic strip has four frames but the fourth frame is missing. The directions tell me to describe what might belong in the missing frame, based on what I see in the first three. Well, in the first frame I see a small dog in the upper left corner of the

Figure 5.2. The Case of the Doggies and the Bone

frame looking intently at a big bone on the right. In the second frame, a much larger dog licking his chops can be seen in the lower left corner of the frame spying the same big bone. In the third frame both the big and the little dog are running toward the bone. They both seem to be moving at a full running stride" (refer to Figure 5.2). Then the teacher begins to think aloud: "What are the possibilities for the final frame of the cartoon? Will the big dog get the bone because the little dog will be frightened away? Will the little dog get the bone and quickly squeeze into some little hiding place where the big dog can't get him? Will the two dogs fight over the bone—the big one using his size and power to defeat the small one, or the small one using his quick agility to wear the big one out? Does physical strength have a definite edge? Not always! I recall the story of David and Goliath. Are there other possible outcomes based on what I see?"

And so the modeling continues with the teacher thinking aloud and reminding the students to record each thinking strategy observed. "Let me carefully study the three frames again." At this point some students may become eager to contribute to the teacher's brainstorming by offering their own visions of what could happen in the fourth frame. Rather than accepting alternative responses, the teacher can now turn the task of completing the comic strip over to the students by discontinuing the modeling, placing the students in thinking pairs, and asking a third student to continue serving as the process observer by adding to the list of steps already listed during the teacher's modeling.

There are many variations and graduated lead-ins to the focus lesson, which ultimately has the students doing *all* the thinking and metacognitive data-gathering. Knowing when to give the students the thinking task and how much autonomy to give is extremely important. The teacher must become very skillful at not doing so much that the students need not think or so little that the students experience frustration and failure. The teacher must decide whether to "walk through" the entire process of describing and defining a skill with the total class, or to model only a part of the process such as the thinking aloud or the process-observing tasks. Either the teacher or capable student volunteers working in pairs and trios can be used for the modeling segments.

Returning to our prediction lesson, let's assume that after the introductory "think aloud" by the teacher, the students have engaged in a "think-pair" discussion for several minutes, with the process observer recording thinking steps (see Chapter 11 in this volume). Again, the teacher must decide whether to move to a total class sharing of predictions and the observations of thinking steps gathered by the process observers, or to direct the students teams to complete the other activity station tasks before calling the total class together.

During the first two or three focus lessons it is generally best to check on the students' progress in a formative way immediately after the first activity. By re-forming the group as a total class, the teacher can first ask student volunteers to share their predictions regarding the fourth frame and, most importantly, explain how they can support their predictions by the evidence in the first three frames, their prior knowledge, and other appropriate supporting data.

The focus should now shift to the process observers' lists. They should be asked to share some of the thinking steps their team went through to arrive at their solution. To allow all or most process observers to contribute, it is advisable to ask for only one step from each group, at least until all who wish to respond have had a chance to do so.

A typical list might for this example include the following steps:

Study each frame carefully.
Gather as much information as possible.
Compare the positions of each dog in relation to the bone.
Contrast the advantages and disadvantages of each dog in this situation.
Consider the possible outcomes.
Select the most likely outcome (prediction).
Reconsider the other outcomes again.
Reaffirm or reject the original prediction.

Continue listing the steps shared by the process observers until no more are offered or those offered start becoming repetitive.

Direct the total class to look over the list generated (on the chalkboard, overhead projector, or chart paper) and direct the process observers to use the list for the following purposes as their team moves to each activity station:

1. To see if thinking pair actually uses the steps listed
2. To add any additional steps they may observe
3. To note any steps not used at a particular station
4. To see if there is any particular sequence to the steps when applied

Students should understand that this is a "working" list (a game plan, so to speak), not a rigidly cast set of steps to be followed in a particular sequence in all situations requiring the skill of prediction. It is also important to have students recall and restate, again and again, that thinking is a complex process requiring the simultaneous use of many skills in concert with each other and that no skill is ever really used in isolation. They should understand, however, that, metacognitive analysis of one skill is useful to help them understand how they currently apply that skill and in discovering how to use it more effectively. Finally, they need to recognize that it is equally important to learn how to be metacognitive in all intellectually challenging situations.

After the activities have been completed, the list of steps should be revised or affirmed according to the feedback given by the process observers and following any appropriate and/or necessary class discussion. This much of the process, without the modeling, will take at least a full class period. With teacher modeling and the midway formative checks of the steps developed, it can easily take two class periods. Whichever version is followed, the next class period should be spent developing and reaching class consensus on the definition of the skill.

Based on the steps developed, students are now ready to do a "think-pair-square-share" activity to generate and refine a class definition (see Chapter 11 in this text). The teacher should give a simple instruction such as: "Using the phrase, 'to predict means . . .', to start your sentence, come up with a clear, concise definition of the process you have gone through at each activity station. Your definition should be broad enough to relate to all the steps and specific enough to show how this skill is different from similar skills (such as drawing conclusions or identifying logical relationships)." Again, if the process of defining is new to the class, the teacher might select another thinking skill (such as sequencing or comparing) and think aloud to illustrate how a definition is generated.

After each pair has written its definition and "squared" (paired two pairs) with a second group to either select, combine, or revise the pair definitions to form a group-approved definition, all versions (from 5 to 8 depending on class size) are displayed on chart paper or the chalkboard for all to consider. By first finding commonalities among all the definitions and then selecting or revising those portions of the definitions in which differences exist, a class definition is developed through consensus.

The following definitions and steps for prediction were developed by middle and high school classes, respectively:

Middle School Definition:. To predict means to use what is already known to make an educated guess about what could happen in the future or when something is not known.

1. Gather information.
2. Sort our information to find what you need.
3. Discard unnecessary information.
4. Put information together to make a prediction statement.
5. Compare information with prediction for consistency.
6. Try other possibilities, if possible.
7. Revise and improve the prediction, if possible.
8. Select or state the best prediction statement.

High School Definition: To predict means to make a statement about an unknown based on knowledge, information, and experience.

1. Recall prior knowledge.
2. Gather information.
3. Examine all material carefully.
4. Identify important facts and details.
5. Look for relationships.
6. Analyze data.
7. Question.
8. Clarify.
9. List possibilities for the prediction.
10. Analyze and choose most likely prediction.
11. Test prediction (if possible).
12. Revise the prediction (if necessary).

The first took three class periods for a sixth grade. The second took a tenth grade honors class two periods.

Again, there are many variations for the focus lessons. For example, the definition may be attempted first *if* the group has sufficient experience in defining and knowledge of the skill being taught. The teacher may either tell the students what skill they will be analyzing or have the students discover what the skill is, based on the steps they are using.

While this second possibility offers a greater thinking challenge to the students, there is, of course, the possibility that the students won't come up with the "right" skill or will have no idea what the skill is called. In such instances, the teacher should make it clear that discovering and describing the process is far more important than coming up with the right name, which can be provided later.[1]

Once the definition and procedures (steps) have been developed and recorded (ideally, in a special "thinking skills" section) in the student notebooks, the focus lesson objectives (Inclusion Process Steps 5 and 6; refer to Figure 5.1) have been attained. The final steps of the model (Steps 7 and 8) should follow the focus lesson.

APPLICATION AND ASSESSMENT

During the application lesson(s) the students work to improve their abilities in performing the newly analyzed skill by using it in one or more of their subject areas where its application is essential to content comprehension. By recasting the definition and steps in a Performance Assessment Matrix (see Table 5.1), the students create a self and peer checklist to use as the skill is applied in the application lessons. In the PAM format the definition appears across the top of the matrix, and the steps are listed as "indicators" of thinking, vertically down the left side. Columns are provided for "key phrases" and the rating categories. The back of the form may be used for comments.

While the PAM may be used by a student independently for self-monitoring, it is somewhat disruptive to the thinking process to be checking oneself "along the way" and even more difficult to recall all the thinking that occurred after the activity is completed. Moreover, rating oneself objectively as having performed the steps "thoroughly," "to some extent," or "not at all" is very difficult. (For younger children just two rating columns, "yes" and "no" are enough.) Again, cooperative peer assessment seems to be far more effective.

Students need practice before actually monitoring their classmates' thinking progress. As a modeling introduction, let's imagine that the teacher displays a picture of several runners almost reaching the finish line in a race and explains that the task is to predict who will win the race. Two student volunteers are found who are willing to think aloud together, first reviewing their definitions and steps for prediction and then attempting to apply them as they study the picture. As they think aloud together, the rest of the students observe independently, record key phrases in the appropriate column on their PAM, and finally determine to

Table 5.1. PAM for the Thinking Skill of *Predicting*

Definition: Predicting means to make a statement about an unknown based on prior knowledge, information, and experience.

Indicators	Key Words	(3) Thoroughly	(2) To Some Extent	(1) Not At All
• Gathers or recalls prior knowledge/data or facts.	I know … I remember …	Recalls and gathers many facts.	Recalls a few.	Recalls no facts.
• Examines and organizes the data.	These are the pros or cons … This supports the ideas that … These facts indicate …	Describes and organizing scheme.	Does some organizing.	Confuses and jumbles facts.
• Identifies what is important.	This is important because …	Finds all important data.	Finds some important data.	Does not identify what is important.
• Seeks relationships among the data (cause-effect, sequencing, compare/contrast).	This happens(ed) because … This follows … These are alike/different.	Describes relationships.	Finds some relationships.	Finds no relationships.
• Questions/clarifies (optional, as needed).	What does this mean?	Questions until all un-certainties are clarified.	Questions somewhat.	Does not attempt to clarify or question.
• Makes a statement about the unknown or future (prediction).	This will happen … I predict …	States a prediction clearly.	Attempts to make a prediction.	Is unable to formulate a prediction.

Continuum: 10 — 0

Indicators	Key Words	Continuum		
		1 0 — — 0		
		(3) Thoroughly	(2) To Some Extent	(1) Not At All
• Uses the data to support the prediction.	This will happen because … This is supported by …	States reasons which support the prediction.	Give some supporting data.	Is unable to state reasons which support the prediction.
• Tests and evaluates the prediction.	This prediction is valid because … This will happen because … This may not happen because …	Provides data which supports the validity of the prediction or actually evaluates the prediction by trying it.	Seeks to test the the prediction to some degree.	Does not attempt to test the prediction.
• Revises (tests other possibilities) and then restates the prediction.	I'll change my prediction because … In view of these facts, I'll say …	Modifies predictions based on facts (data).	Attempts to revise the prediction if necessary.	Fails to revise prediction when data indicates a lack of validity.

Other Observations/Comments:

what extent they think the indicators (steps) were applied. Student observers should be encouraged to write supporting comments on the back of the form for the indicators they checked as "thoroughly" or "not at all." Other observations or additional steps should also be noted.

Students should then be directed to pair and compare their PAMs, discussing similarities and differences and, if so desired, make changes. As a total group, the PAMs should then be discussed in this same way. Such discussions help all to understand better what the expectations for each ranking should be. After one or two "practice" activities such as this one, students can become quite effective peer monitors.

The PAMs are currently being used in experimental fashion in the Saturday School Program by the faculty and students at the Maryland Center for Thinking Studies.[2] Additionally, students are keeping a "skill" folio (a folder) for selected thinking skills and other appropriate skill-related activities so they can collect their PAMs over the course of the year to see how they are making progress.

During this last stage of the Inclusion Process students learn not only how well they are doing in applying their skills, but also how to help one another improve in skill application. They come to recognize the value of working together and that two heads are, indeed, better than one. They find that ideas build on ideas and that the products of cooperative thought are usually much better than the products of independent thought.

SUMMARY

The Inclusion Process has provided not only focused instruction in some key thinking skills, but, more importantly, a model for cooperative improvement in metacognitive thinking that students can call upon in any challenging thinking situation. In developing a real understanding of some thinking skills, students are better able to apply these skills. As they move from knowing to true understanding, they come to see cognition and metacognition as intrinsically related and integral to true learning. Moreover, their development as both autonomous and interdependent lifelong learners has begun.

As one middle school student stated in response to a question on the value of the Inclusion Process model, "Well, it was discovering that there were hidden thinking paths in my mind and that these paths can be made clearer if I can share them with others and they don't seem to have any end. It is very exciting to discover that my mind can do so much!" Indeed it is!

NOTES

1. For samples of additional focus lessons see PDK Fastback #236 (Worsham & Stockton, 1986) or write to the Maryland Center for Thinking Studies (MCTS), Coppin State College, 2500 W. North Avenue, Baltimore, Maryland 21216.
2. For more examples of PAMS, write to MCTS (address in Note 1).

REFERENCES

Naisbett, J. (1984). *Megatrends*. New York: Warner.
Worsham, A. (1988, April). A grow as you go thinking skills model. *Educational Leadership*, pp. 56-57.
Worsham, A., & Stockton, A. (1986). *A model for teaching thinking: The inclusion process*. Bloomington, IN: Phi Delta Kappa.

6

The New School "Lecture"
Cooperative Interactions That Engage Student Thinking

Robin Fogarty and James Bellanca

The new "lecture" does not resemble the old lecture very much; in fact, the new "lecture" is really a myriad of interaction patterns. These authentic interaction models take the focus off the lecturer and put it squarely on the learner. From kindergarten classrooms to college lecture halls, educators are moving toward more involving models of instruction. The emergence of the new school "lecture" is unmistakable.

At one end of the spectrum of possibilities for cooperative interactions is the traditional stand-up teaching model. In this model the learner is viewed as a vessel to be filled. At the other end of the spectrum is a total group involvement model called the Human Graph, in which the learners actually move to spots on an imaginary graph that symbolize their position on an issue.

The shift from the most didactic teaching models to more intensely involving models is no easy task for teachers. Just as in any paradigm shift, major philosophical underpinnings are shaken. Yet, the move toward the new school "lecture," with its accent on student interactions, is made easier if seen as a gradual change. Student involvement is designed so that strategies increase student participation by degrees. In this way, teachers and students are able to adjust and adapt to the new model over time.

Surprisingly and almost unfailingly, once the philosophical shift begins, once teachers begin implementing cooperative interactions, the evidence of student motivation becomes so overwhelmingly visible that teachers are encouraged to try more. The momentum builds for both teachers and students, and before long "the new school lecture" becomes the norm in the classroom. By then, the novelty of the models is no longer the challenge. The challenge becomes choosing the most appropriate interactive designs for the target lesson; it is choosing a design in which the final focus rests on the learner, not on the lecturer.

AN OVERVIEW OF TWELVE COOPERATIVE INTERACTIONS

The many variables that come into play as one is selecting the most appropriate interactive strategy include time, space and facilities, level and behavior of students, number of students, purpose of the lesson, background and experiences of the students, support materials, and teacher expertise.

In the high-content, high-support, high-challenge classroom (see Figure 6.1), the overriding goal is intense student involvement and the subsequent transfer of learning across subject areas and into life situations. High content refers to rigorous disciplines such as the sciences, the humanities, and the arts; high support cites the expectation for cooperative interactions; and high challenge dictates the need for meaningful and thoughtful learner activities. By accumulating a repertoire of interactive strategies and coupling student involvement with information-processing models, the skillful teacher moves learning for all students to new depths. As one surveys the various interactive strategies, it becomes apparent that different strategies are appropriate for different classroom situations.

Figure 6.1. The New School Lecture

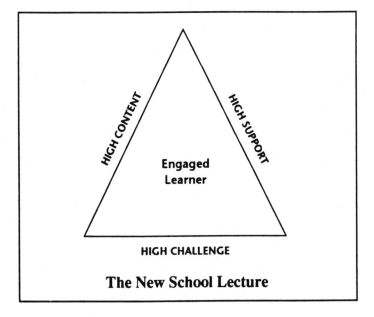

HIGH CONTENT

HIGH SUPPORT

Engaged
Learner

HIGH CHALLENGE

The New School Lecture

Twelve basic cooperative interaction models are presented at the end of this chapter. These models can be adapted to meet less-involving to more-involving teaching goals. For example, the strategies in Model 1, Lecture/Rhetorical Questioning, require minimal learner participation, while Model 8, Cooperative Learning: Groups, or Model 10, Forced Response: Wrap Around, engage the learner intensely due to the very nature and structure of the strategies.

The skillful teacher introduces increasingly engaging interactive models over time. As students become more adept in their social skills, the models are selected strictly for appropriateness. Initially, however, the models are subtly slotted into the lessons to familiarize students with the different interactions and to lead them toward involvement in the learning situation.

Each model included at the end of the chapter indicates the type of interaction, a source, and a lesson description. The prescription suggests when this particular model might be appropriate. A classroom *vignette* provides brief illustrations of the interactions that define the model. The brief *notes* are metacognitive cues or labels that explain the example under scrutiny.

Interactive models work with all levels—elementary, middle, high school, and college. Each of these particular examples features just one of the levels. Adjustments by the instructor are needed to tailor the examples for age, grade, and content appropriateness.

CONCLUSION

Based on current research and practice, the cooperative interaction designs that distinguish the new school lecture from the traditional seem to offer a positive and optimistic prognosis for future use in our nation's classrooms. By their very nature, cooperative learning strategies create a bubbling-up effect among both students and teachers. They somehow produce an energy that is at once contagious and self-propelling.

Teachers using cooperative interactions in the classroom say the positive effects on student motivation, achievement, and self-concept are so immediately visible and so astonishingly dramatic that the incentives are there for novices to do more. That's why cooperative learning has taken root in schools at the grass-roots level.

The designs for thoughtful interactions presented in this chapter provide a vigorous repertoire of instructional strategies. The seasoned practitioner will appropriately select from these strategies as opportunities occur in the instructional arena.

By varying the types of interactions and creating designs or variations on the themes presented, teachers provide a myriad of social and cognitive learning experiences for students. In turn, students reveal both their social skills and their thinking paradigms as they become involved in and responsible for their own learning.

The old lecture, according to John Gould, is "an occasion when you numb one end to benefit the other" (Peter, 1977, p. 101). The new school lecture, however, is more like a conversation. In a conversation, as Richard Armour suggests, "it is all right to *hold* the conversation for a time, but you should *let go of* it now and then" (p. 119). The new school lecture sees the teacher skillfully holding student attention and letting go of center stage, thus inviting thoughtful and engaging student conversations.

MODEL #1

Source	Type of Interaction
Perhaps "Professor Kingsfield" from *The Paper Chase*	# Lecture/Rhetorical Questioning

Description	
Traditional lecture or stand-up teaching in which interaction is a one-way broadcast, punctuated with occasional rhetorical questioning.	

(Suggested) Prescription	Lesson: Ethics of Medical Technology Level: College
Use with large groups and/or lots of information; punctuate with rhetorical questions throughout.	Methodology class at a university level in which 200 students attend an hour lecture twice a week as part of a required premed course.

Notes	Vignette: Lecture/Rhetorical Questioning
Lecture Input (or Teacher Talk):	*With the breakthroughs in medical technology, the options for life support systems are increasing at a rapid rate.*
Rhetorical Question	*How do you think that affects us?*
Lecture Input (or Teacher Talk):	*It seems quite straightforward to make a technical decision. But one must consider all the implications of that decision.*
Rhetorical Question	*Haven't we all faced a dilemma such as this?*

88

MODEL #2

Source	Type of Interaction
Hunter, 1983	**Signaling and Direct Questioning: Surveying**

Description	
Traditional lecture format interrupted every five to seven minutes; a posed question that requires a physical signal from students (raised hands) or a single student response that may require some elaboration.	

(Suggested) Prescription	**Lesson: Biology/DNA** **Level: Grade 10**
Use to make lecture slightly more interactive (à la interactive video model) so students are hooked momentarily—at least interacting with a physical response or a one-student in-depth answer.	As the high school biology teacher punctuates his DNA lecture with signaling questions, he deliberately weaves direct questions into the lecture for occasional in-depth student responses.

Notes	Vignette: Signaling and Direct Questioning
Signaling	*How many agree? Disagree?*
Direct question	*David, tell us why you agree with the text. You believe the assumptions are true.*
Student response	*Well, I'm not sure, but I was connecting this idea to . . .*

MODEL #3

Source	Type of Interaction
Weaver & Cotrell, 1986	**Turn To Your Partner And...** **(TTYPA)**

Description	
An informal strategy used throughout an input sequence in which two students discuss ideas discussed in the lecture.	

(Suggested) Prescription	Lesson: Down Memory Lane — Level: Grade 8
Use to punctuate a lecture, a film or a reading. After 7-8 minutes of straight talk, students need to be actively cued and engaged.	This informal, quick interaction in which students turn to a partner and dialogue briefly on a specifically directed task is used effectively as students are guided to model both cognition and metacognition in a lesson on thinking.

Notes	Vignette: TTYPA
Lecturer	*Metacognition is thinking about your thinking. Let me demonstrate.*
TTYPA	*Turn to your partner and recite a piece you know by memory. Then, switch roles and listen to your partner's memorized piece.*
Student #1 response	*Four score and seven years ago . . .*
Student #2 response	*We the people of the United States . . .*
Lecturer	*That's called cognition.*
TTYPA	*Now, TTYPA tell each other how you learned that piece by heart so well that you could say it today.*
Student response	*I learned by repeating . . .*
Lecturer	*Thinking about how you learned is called metacognition.*

MODEL #4

Source	Type of Interaction
Bloom & Broder, 1950 Whimbey, 1975	**Paired Partners: Think Aloud**

Description	
A problem solver talks his way strategically through a problem. A partner monitors his progress with cues and questions. Both reflect on problem-solving patterns.	

(Suggested) Prescription	Lesson: Math Problem Solving Level: Grade 6
Use over time to develop metacognitive, think-aloud tracking of student behaviors.	One partner thinks aloud as he/she solves a problem. The monitor cues the thinking with appropriate questions as the problem solver works systematically through the math calculations.

Notes	Vignette: Paired Partners
Teacher:	*With partners, solve this story problem using the think-aloud strategy.*
Problem solver: Thinks aloud and says everything that occurs to him/her in a systematic procedure.	*I'm going to add these two numbers. Then, I'll . . .*
Monitor: Asks leading questions to elicit the inner reasoning.	*Why are you doing that? Are you expecting a larger number or a smaller number than the original?*
Problem solver: Elaborates and catches another thought for a new strategy.	*Because the question calls for a total, I'm thinking the number, of course, will be larger and therefore I will add or multiply. Hmm, could I multiply here?*

91

MODEL #5

Source	Type of Interaction
Lyman & McTighe, 1988	**Dyads: Think/Pair/Share**

Description	
Partners are cued to think first with the use of wait time. Then pairs of students share their thoughts with each other. After pairing, students may share in the whole class.	

(Suggested) Prescription	**Lesson: The Non-Listening Game** Level: Grade 3
Use when formal wait time is needed for student internalization and connection making; use any time thoughtful articulation will help students understand.	To teach the social skill of active listening needed for cooperative interactions, the Non-Listening Game is used. By exaggerating the opposite behavior, students more readily focus on the desired behavior.

Notes	**Vignette: Think/Pair/Share**
Initial activity	Following a partner interaction for which a "listener" is asked to exhibit *non*-listening behaviors to the "speaker," the teacher instructs students:
Think alone	*Think about the things the listener did that signaled* no *listening.* (Wait 3-10 seconds)
Pair/share	Listener: *I looked away.* Speaker: *You interrupted me.* Listener: *I felt bad because I knew I wasn't paying attention. It was rude.* Speaker: *I wanted to quit talking to you.*

MODEL #6

Source	Type of Interaction
Rowe, 1969 Costa, 1986	**Triads: Observer Feedback**

Description	
Partners practice a designated interaction while a third-party observer records and reports feedback data.	

(Suggested) Prescription	Lesson: Fat and Skinny Questions Level: Grade 11
Use when a partner interactions can be extended or elaborated by objective observer feedback.	To teach students to use higher order questions, the teacher introduces the concept of fat and skinny questions and then asks student trios to practice their question-asking.

Notes	Vignette: Triads: Observer Feedback
Teacher targets behavior to look for.	*Observers, I will be noting FAT and Skinny questions. FAT questions will be those that elicit elaborated answers with examples and details. Skinny questions will be those that get "Yes, No, Maybe So" answers.*
Question asked (Recorded as a FAT question.)	*Interviewer: How do you compare and contrast democracy to socialism?* *Interviewee: Similarities might include ___ while differences include ___.*
Question asked (Recorded as a Skinny question.)	*Interviewer: Which do you prefer?* *Interviewee: The former!*
Question asked (Recorded as a FAT question.)	*Interviewer: Imagine justifying your choice. What might you say?*

93

Source	Type of Interaction
Fogarty & Opeka, 1988	**2-4-8: Tell/Retell**
Description	
Partners tell their own stories. Then they retell a partner's story. The pairs double—2-4-8.	
(Suggested) Prescription	**Lesson: Show and Tell** **Level: Grade 1**
Use to structure active listening in a partner sharing or for a quick gathering of lots of ideas.	In a typical primary classroom, "show and tell" time is structured carefully for both speaking and listening skills.
Notes	**Vignette: 2-4-8**

Notes	Vignette
2 Partners share show and tell items. (A)(B)	A: *This is my skin from a snake. I found it on the hiking path. It was there in the sunshine. I think the snake wiggled out of it while he was getting a suntan.* B: *I brought my favorite Transformer®. My dad couldn't figure it out. I had to help him. It's pretty tricky if you don't know much about them.*
4 A tells B's, B tells A's C tells D's, D tells C's (A)(B) (C)(D)	A: *"B" brought the Transformer® that his dad couldn't figure out.* B: *"A" found a snake's skin while he was hiking.* C: *"D" brought photographs of his birthday party at the pizza place.* D: *"C" forgot her show and tell but she told me about her ride in the row boat.*
8 Each tells a new story. 88 oo oo	A: *"C" forgot hers but she rode in a row boat.* B: *"D" has pictures of the pizza place.* C: *"B" can transform his Transformer®.* D: *"A" has the skin of a snake.*

MODEL #8

Source	Type of Interaction
Johnsons, 1986 Slavin, 1983 Kagan, 1988	**Cooperative Learning: Groups**

Description	
Three to five learners, heterogeneously grouped for an academic task. Key elements for formal cooperative groups include positive interdependence, individual accountability, group processing, social skills and face-to-face interactions.	

(Suggested) Prescription	Lesson: Prediction (BET) Level: Grade 7
Use to engage students intensely in the processing activities needed for learning for transfer.	Cooperative groups are used in a Directed Reading Thinking Activity (DRTA) to predict and justify what students think will happen next in a story.

Notes	Vignette: Cooperative Learning: Groups
Checker checks for understanding:	*Does everyone understand? We will use BET.*
Teacher monitors	Base on facts Express possibilities Tender a bet on what we think will happen next in the story entitled "The Dinner Party."
Encourager:	Encourages response in turn:
Teacher monitors	• *I think it's a murder mystery because of the title.* • *I think it's about cannibals. There will be a twist.* • *Maybe it's about animals having a tea party. This is from school, you know.*
Encourager: Group consensus	*Let's write down the cannibal idea because it's so different.* *What do the rest of you think?*
Recorder:	Writes down group answer.

Source	Type of Interaction
Fogarty & Bellanca, 1987	**Traveling Clusters: People Search**

Description	
Students are prompted with questions to move about and find someone who . . . Informal clusters form as students select new partners in their search for answers to the questions.	

(Suggested) Prescription	Lesson: People Search Level: Grade 12
Use as ice-breaker, as pre-learning strategy to activate prior knowledge or as a review of important concepts prior to a test.	A lesson used as a pre-learning strategy to "stir up" prior knowledge about thinking skills. The cue sheet starts the student interaction.

Notes	**Vignette: People Search**
Prompted by sheet	Using: FIND SOMEONE WHO... 1. Can classify friends 2. Can name problem-solving steps 3. 4. 5.
Students move about and talk to each other.	Student A: *I think I can classify friends into four groups.* Student B: *Great. Go ahead.* Student A: *The good, the bad, the ugly and best friend.* Student B: *Super. Maybe, I can help you with the steps to problem solving. First, decide on the real problem...*
Students move on to newly forming clusters of 2, 3 or 4 students	Student A: *Thanks. Talk to you later.*

96

MODEL #10

Source	Type of Interaction
Howe & Howe, 1975	**Forced Response: Wrap Around**

Description	
Round-robin style, students respond in turn to a lead-in statement cued by the teacher.	

(Suggested) Prescription	Lesson: Analogies Level: Grade 5
Use to anchor individual thoughts or give a quick reading of the group.	At the close of the lesson, students are asked to compare thinking to an animal. After jotting down some ideas, a verbal wrap around the room is used to share the ideas.

Notes	Vignette: Wrap Around
	Wrapping around the room, each student responds in turn...
Response of student #1	*Thinking is like a frog because it hops around in your mind.*
Teacher	[Signals next student without judging each response.]
Student #2	*Thinking is like an elephant, because it's heavy on your mind.*
Teacher	[Nods.]
Student #3	*Thinking is like a horse, because both can throw you.*
Student #4	*Thinking is like the cat family because it helps to be in a group.*
Student #5	*Thinking is like a monkey because you can fool around with both.*
Student #6	*Thinking is like a chicken, because both can lay an egg!*
etc.	

MODEL #11

Source	Type of Interaction
Fogarty & Bellanca, 1987	**Total Group Response: Human Graph**

Description	
Students advocate an opinion by standing at designated spots on an imaginary axis. This human graph is a living, breathing graph that can change as students change positions.	

(Suggested) Prescription	Lesson: Equity Level: Grade 9
Use to take a quick but highly visible reading of the group members' feelings on an issue, idea or concept.	Used to introduce a unit on Equity Issues, the teacher structures an agree/disagree statement for sampling "public opinion."

Notes	Vignette: Human Graph
Present graph format	
Teacher cues for graphing interaction:	*Indicate how strongly you agree or disagree:*
Students move on graph	
Sample reasons from students	*I agree strongly. Think about the pioneer women and the hardships they had to overcome.*

98

MODEL #12

Source	Type of Interaction
Aronson, 1978 Sharan and Sharan, 1976	# Group Investigation: # The Ultimate Jigsaw

Description	
Each member has a piece of the puzzle; responsibility is divided; to get the whole picture, or all the information, the separate pieces must be reassembled or synthesized into the completed puzzle by the various group members	

(Suggested) Prescription	Lesson: Geographic Regions Level: Grade 4
Use when groups are socially sophisticated or to build individual responsibility within the team.	In a fourth grade classroom, groups of three students are given regions of the U.S. to investigate and research. The group is ultimately responsible to know all three regions and will "teach each other." Students with the same topic help each other master it before presenting it to their groups.

Notes	Vignette: The Ultimate Jigsaw
Teacher	*Ones, take the Eastern seaboard. Twos, research the midsection of the country. Threes, gather information about the western portion of the United States.*
Student #1	*I'm going to start in the library.*
Student #2	*I need to define my area.*
Student #3	*This is great. I love the West.*

99

REFERENCES

Aronson, E. (1978). *The jigsaw classroom.* Beverly Hills, CA: Sage Publications.

Bloom, B., & Broder, L. (1950). *Problem solving process of college students.* Chicago: University of Chicago Press.

Clarke, J., Wideman, R., & Eadie, S. (1990). *Together we learn.* Toronto: Prentice Hall.

Costa, A. (1986). *Teaching for intelligent behavior.* Unpublished syllabus (3rd ed.).

Dalton, J. (1985). *Adventures in thinking.* Melbourne, Australia: Thomas Nelson Australia.

Fogarty, R., & Bellanca, J. (1987). *Patterns for thinking—patterns for transfer.* Palatine, IL: Skylight.

Fogarty, R., & Opeka, K. (1988). *Start them thinking.* Palatine, IL: Skylight.

Howe, L., & Howe, M. (1975). *Personalizing education: Values clarification and beyond.* New York: Hart.

Hunter, M. (1983). *Reinforcement.* El Segundo, CA: Tip.

Johnson, R., & Johnson, D. (1986). *Circles of learning: Cooperation in the classroom.* Alexandria, VA: Association for Supervision and Curriculum Development.

Kagan, S. (1988). *Cooperative learning: Resources for teachers.* San Juan Capistrano, CA: Resources for Teachers.

Lyman, F., & McTighe, J. (1988, April). Cueing thinking in the classroom: The promise of theory-embedded tools. *Educational Leadership*, p. 7.

Peter, L. J. (1977). *Peter's quotations: Ideas for our time.* New York: Bantam.

Reid, J., Forrestal, P., & Cook, J. (1989). *Small group learning in the classroom.* Scarborough, Australia: Chalkface Press.

Rowe, M. B. (1969). Science, silence and sanctions. *Science and Children, 6,* 11–13.

Sharan, S., & Sharan, Y. (1976). *Small group teaching.* Englewood Cliffs, NJ: Educational Testing Publications.

Slavin, R. E. (1983). *Cooperative learning.* New York: Longman.

Weaver, R., & Cotrell, H. (1986, Summer). Using interactive images in the lecture hall. *Educational Horizons, 64*(4), 180–185.

Whimbey, A., & Whimbey, L. (1975). *Intelligence can be taught.* New York: Innovative Science.

7

Some Thinking Skills
and Social Skills That Facilitate
Cooperative Learning

*Richard D. Solomon, Neil Davidson,
and Elaine C. L. Solomon*

It is the third day of school and Ms. Emerson wants to place her ninth grade English class into self-selected heterogenous cooperative learning groups. Each student is given a handout (see Figure 7.1).

Before permitting her students to complete the handout, Ms. Emerson states, models, and records her responses on an overhead transparency while saying:

> I'm going to write my complete name on the top line and my first name in the circle with the 1 in it. Now, let me see, what circles do I belong to? Well, one circle that I'm in, and many of you are also in, is the female circle. Notice that I am writing *female* in one of my circles. Now, here is a circle that I'm in that no one in our class is also a member of—I run marathons. (Ms. Emerson writes *marathon runner.*) Another circle I'm in that a few of you also belong to is the circle of *African-Americans*. Now, while I am completing the rest of my circles, I want you to think about the circles that you belong to. Which circles do you probably have in common with several members in our class? Which circles do you share with just a few of your classmates? Do you belong to a special circle in which you might be the only representative from our class? Record that also. Now take three minutes to think about and record the circles to which you belong.

After completing their circles diagrams, the students are invited to stand up and walk around the room with their "circles" data in hand. At this time, they are studying the different circles to which their classmates belong. They may briefly dialogue with their peers. Their objective,

Figure 7.1. Circles Handout

THE CIRCLES OF

_____

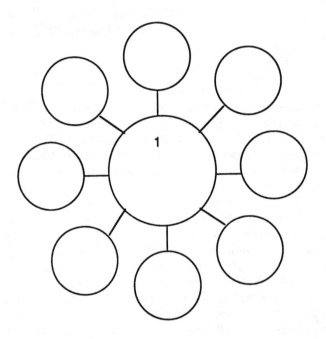

INSTRUCTIONS:
1. Write your name on the line at the top of the page, and your first name in the circle with the number 1 in it.
2. In the smaller circles write the name of different groups to which you belong. Ex. female, Catholic, feminist, Korean, swimmer, etc.
3. Walk around and find a partner whose circles are least like yours.
4. Walk around and find a pair whose circles are different from both of yours.

however, is to find a person in class where circles are least like their own. This person will later become their learning partner.

After the students are paired with their learning partners, they are instructed to discover as much as they can about their new partner during a three-step interview. One person speaks while the other partner listens. Then they switch roles. After they exchange information with their learning partner, they select another pair, and the four of them become a learning team or quad. In a structured manner, they each tell their quad what they had discovered about their learning partner.

After sharing the data in quads, Ms. Emerson asks what social skills were needed to do the circles activity and the three-step interview. Before getting an individual response, she gives her students 15 seconds of think-and-write time to reflect and record some of the social skills used during this team formation activity. In round robin fashion each team member shares a new social skill needed to participate in the circles activity. If members cannot identify a new social skill, they may pass. If members share a social skill that was not on their original list, they may add that skill to their list.

We elaborated upon this lesson to show how some thinking skills and social skills could facilitate a cooperative learning activity before, during, and after the event. Table 7.1 lists some of the thinking skills, thinking processes, and social skills that could be applied to facilitate this lesson.

We define these skills and processes as follows:

1. A cognition is an internal thought; it can be regarded as an inner form of speech or self-talk.
2. A *thinking skill* is a special way of arranging or modifying internal data or cognitions.
3. A *thinking process* describes a sequence of cognitions and thinking skills that, when strung together, becomes a pattern or way of thinking available for use.
4. A *social skill* is an intrapersonal, interpersonal, or intragroup means of communicating.

To be sure, some ninth graders could have completed the entire circles activity without the teacher pausing to model some of the thinking skills and social skills needed. Our years of teaching experience, however, give us strong evidence that some students do not possess the social and thinking competencies to participate successfully in certain cooperative learning activities. Many of these children seem to learn best when they are cognitively, emotionally, and behaviorally prepared for a

Table 7.1. Thinking Skills, Thinking Processes, and Social Skills Students Can Apply During the Circles Cooperative Learning Lesson

ACTIVITY	THINKING SKILLS AND THINKING PROCESSES	SOCIAL SKILLS
1. The teacher states, models and records the groups to which she belongs.	To recall the types of data shared by the teacher.	To listen to the data (e.g. facts, concepts and experiences) of another person.
2. The teacher gives her students 3 minutes of individual wait time to think about and record on their circle's handouts the groups to which they belong.	To classify data.	To state to oneself a concept (i.e. the circles to which one belongs).
3. Students stand up, walk around the room and study the circles' diagrams of their peers. They may briefly dialogue with their class-mates. Their objective is to find a person whose circles are least like their own.	To compare and contrast data. To determine whose circles are least like theirs. To formulate open and closed questions. To silently practice (rehearse) asking open and closed questions. To probe To decide what data to share. To decide how to share that data. To silently practice sharing data.	To ask open and closed questions. To probe to determine whose circles are least like theirs. To verbally share data.
4. Each student selects a learning partner.	To formulate an invitational question (i.e. would you be my learning partner?)	To invite a person to join a group. To gracefully accept an invitation to join a group.
5. Learning partners exchange data during an interview structure.	To decide what data to share and withhold. To decide which questions to ask. To decide which social skill(s) to apply. To silently practice the social skills (e.g. sharing data, asking open and closed questions, paraphrasing, probing, respectful listening, using appropriate body language).	To share data (e.g. facts, concepts, experiences, preferences, informed opinions, and feelings). To ask open and closed questions. To paraphrase. To probe. To respectfully listen. To apply appropriate body language.

new pedagogical method such as cooperative learning. That is, they need to

1. Know what to expect
2. Know what they are about to do
3. Feel comfortable about their part and what is about to happen

4. Practice and have command of the thinking and social skills that facilitate the new instructional strategy

Later in the chapter we will describe a seven step instructional model for teaching students the thinking skills and social skills of cooperative learning. For now let us address some of the thinking skills and social skills that can facilitate cooperative learning activities.

THE FOURTH R

Many of the social skills and related thinking skills that can facilitate cooperative learning are included as a part of the curriculum that we have termed the "Fourth R" (Solomon, 1987a, 1987b). To avoid any confusion we note that the Fourth R has also been identified as reasoning (Bossone, 1982; Dawson, 1982), resolving conflict (National Association for Mediation in Education), responsibility, respect, resourcefulness, and responsiveness (Evans, Corsini, & Gazda, 1990), religion (Johnson, H. C., 1986), and retention (Holmes, 1983).

The Fourth R represents the core intrapersonal, interpersonal, and intragroup *relationship* competencies that facilitate cooperative learning. The Fourth R may also be defined as:

- The social skills and procedures that facilitate group discussion and process.
- The part of the school curriculum that teaches students how to effectively communicate their thoughts and feelings.
- The part of the school curriculum charged with the responsibility of teaching students to appreciate self and get along with others.
- The medium that communicates the three Rs of reading, writing, and arithmetic.

Level One: The Intrapersonal Competencies

The intrapersonal competencies are the thinking skills and processes that access the internal data (cognitions) that exist within the individual. Each student has at least six types of intrapersonal data from which to personally draw. These are defined below:

1. *Factual data.* The name given for a generally accepted bit of data. Examples: chair, table, lamp, chalkboard.

2. *Conceptual data.* The name given for some abstract data. Examples: furniture, beauty, value, usefulness.
3. *Preferential data.* A decision to choose one bit of data over another. Example: I'd rather sit in a recliner than in a straight back chair.
4. *Informed Opinion data.* A decision and the rationale for choosing one bit of data over another. Examples: I'd rather sit in a recliner than a straight back chair because it is more comfortable. I'd rather sit in a straight back chair than a recliner when I am typing because it is more practical.
5. *Experiential data.* An event that one has personally engaged in or witnessed or has encountered through others. Example: I remember the time that I visited my grandmother and she let me rock back and forth in her rocking chair.
6. *Feelings data.* A positive, negative, or ambivalent emotion. Example: *I felt so loved* by my grandmother when she gave up her special rocking chair and let me use it. One time my teacher caught me cheating on a test and she made me sit in a chair in the back of the room (experience). Boy, was I *embarrassed!*

These intrapersonal competencies help the learner get in touch with the rich source of data that resides internally. As students get in touch with their intrapersonal data, they begin to recognize a new source of power that they possess—the power to access their thoughts, feelings, beliefs, values, experiences, and visions. They also realize that they possess the power to share with others or withhold from them this rich source of information. The specific content of a student's intrapersonal data is of paramount importance. The intrapersonal data are the cognitive and emotional components of a child's self-concept. The implication here is that students who have ownership of their internal data will be more likely to develop a positive self-concept, and, in turn, will be more likely to interact with others successfully and participate in cooperative learning groups. Marzano, Peckering, and Brandt (1990) describe this cognitive affirmation, this realization of personal empowerment through access to one's internal data, as the first dimension of learning. It is the first type of thinking needed to develop a positive attitude toward learning. Many other thinking processes are described by Marzano et al. (1988).

Level Two: The Interpersonal Relationship Competencies

The Level Two competencies include the social skills and related thinking skills needed for interpersonal communication.

Level Two relationship competencies include a behavioral and cognitive component. Students now learn different ways of sharing their intrapersonal data with others, and the appropriate social context for sharing that data. Here is a list of some of the interpersonal relationship competencies.

1. To share six types of intrapersonal data (see Level One) and listen to the data of others
2. To engage another person in conversation. This includes finding the free information that two people have in common, asking open questions and clarifying questions, probing, paraphrasing, checking for understanding, summarizing, respectful and active listening, and knowing how to start, maintain, and terminate a conversation. This also includes knowing how to apply nonverbal behaviors that show acceptance and respect for another person such as taking turns, using eye contact, open hand gestures, leaning toward the speaker, etc.
3. To give and receive constructive positive, negative, and corrective feedback, and to validate another person
4. To ask for assistance and to give assistance in a caring and nonthreatening way
5. To handle peer criticism and to say no and not feel guilty
6. To achieve consensus in pairs and to resolve interpersonal conflict

Note, this is a partial listing of a continually expanding set of interpersonal relationship competencies that can facilitate cooperative learning. Other researchers and staff developers (Johnson, Johnson, Holubec, & Roy, 1984; Johnson & Johnson, 1990; Dishon & O'Leary, 1984, 1990; Kagan, 1989) have their own lists of interpersonal social skills.

Level Three: The Intragroup Relationship Competencies

Developing the thinking and social competencies for interpersonal communication is necessary but may not be sufficient to help some students work in small cooperative groups. Thus, it is necessary to teach some students a third set of intragroup relationship skills, the Level Three competencies of the Fourth R. Students who are taught level Three relationship competencies do not simply acquire a set of intragroup social skills. They spend considerable time discussing, problem solving, and generalizing when it is appropriate to use these group-processing skills in social contexts. With this in mind, the intragroup relationship competencies include the ability to

1. Identify the roles that people play in groups
2. Help a group share information in an orderly fashion in which each member is heard and respected
3. Diagnose and apply an appropriate intervention so that the individuals and the group can satisfy their task, maintenance, and ego needs
4. Help a group envision and formulate its mission and goals, and set its standards and norms for participant behavior
5. Help a group become a team
6. Help a group evaluate both its maintenance needs and task performance
7. Help a group surface its hidden agenda items, creatively brainstorm alternative solutions to its challenges, and resolve intragroup or intergroup conflict
8. Help a group make decisions through such strategies as consensus seeking, polling, and majority voting
9. Help initiate, maintain, and bring closure to a group process

For example, let's revisit the interview structure in which the students exchanged data from their respective circles diagrams. Table 7.2 lists some of the internal cognitions, data, or inner speech that the students may generate and a set of core social/relationship skills that could facilitate the interview. Please note how the internal cognitions provide support and information for applying the social skills.

To sum up, we have identified some of the potential cognitions, internal data, social skills, and related thinking skills that could facilitate a simple cooperative learning structure such as the interview. Many additional social skills and thinking skills/processes would be needed to complete a complex multistructured cooperative lesson.

A SEVEN STEP INSTRUCTIONAL MODEL

As cooperative learning practitioners we have found that the following seven step instructional model is a helpful guide for teaching students some of the thinking skills and social skills that facilitate cooperative learning activities. Several of the steps can also be found in a related model given by Beyer (1987).

1. State the rationale for the thinking skill or social skill.
2. Describe or define the thinking skill or social skill.
3. Model or demonstrate the thinking skill or social skill.

Table 7.2. Some Internal Cognitions and Social Skills Involved in Interviewing

The assigned task is to interview one's learning partner for a Three-Step Interview.

POSSIBLE INTERNAL COGNITIONS (what is or can be said to oneself prior to applying a social skill for the interview)	SAMPLE SOCIAL SKILLS (what is or can be verbally and/or nonverbally expressed to the person with whom one is speaking)
What are we supposed to be doing now? What am I supposed to say? Who should speak first? Perhaps I should wait till he/she speaks. I have nothing important to say. I may say something foolish. What social skill could I use now?	
I could ask him/her an open question such as....	Ask open questions: e.g. "What exactly are we supposed to be doing?", "What would you like to know about me?" "Tell me about the music you like."
I could share some of my data on the handout	Share data: e.g. "I love to listen to Skid Row and Guns and Roses...great heavy metal groups."
I could paraphrase him/her after s/he speaks.	Paraphrase: e.g. "You say you love heavy metal music..."
I could probe.	Probe: e.g."What is heavy metal?" "How is it different from hard rock?" "What makes it so great?"
I could respectfully listen and then ask a question.	Respectful listening (paraphrasing and non-judgmental probing): e.g. "You said that you love heavy metal because of its loud and powerful sounds. Tell me what your parents say about your choice of music."
Should I give him/her some constructive positive feedback?	Give constructive positive feedback: e.g.. "I like the way that you defended your opinion about..."
I must remember to use good body language.	Using appropriate body language: e.g. eye contact, leaning forward, smiling, nodding, not interrupting

4. Have learners identify the indicators of the thinking skill or social skill.
5. Have learners participate in a guided practice of the thinking skill or social skill after which constructive feedback is provided.
6. Invite learners to reflect on the performance and/or applicability of the thinking skill or social skill.

7. Have the learners practice the thinking skill or social skill independently.

We should note that the order for steps one, two, and three can be
modified. At times, we will give the rationale after the definition and
demonstration. At other times, we demonstrate a thinking or social skill,
offer a definition, and then ask the learners to generate a rationale. For
purposes of simplicity, we will discuss the instructional model in the
order that appears above.

Teaching a Thinking Skill

A third grade reading teacher wants her students to know how to
apply causal thinking in preparation for a future cooperative learning
activity. Here is a suggested strategy.

1. *State the rationale for the thinking skill.* The teacher explains the
difference between natural and social causes. He explains that when you
throw a ball straight up, it should return to the ground due to the force of
gravity. There is a natural cause and effect relationship between throw-
ing the ball (cause) and its returning to the earth (effect). If you should
throw a ball at a stranger passing by on the street, you may get a host of
social effects. He/she may catch it, throw the ball back to you, run away,
or perhaps even chase you. These latter effects are not inevitable consequences; they are plausible social effects. Natural causes and effects obey
the laws of nature while social causes and effects follow the less precise
whims of human nature.

The teacher then gives another example. She tells the students that
sometimes before reading it is fun to predict what might happen to the
characters in a story. The teacher then facilitates a class discussion regarding why it is important to understand cause and effect relationships.

2. *Describe or define the thinking skill.* The teacher defines causal
thinking as follows: Given an event (cause), the student will be able to
identify what might follow from it (effect).

3. *Model or demonstrate the thinking skill.* The teacher first poses
this question: What would your school life be like if you could not speak?
The teacher then explains that one way to demonstrate or indicate a
thinking skill is to make a drawing of one's thoughts. The teacher then
draws and explains the consequence map that appears in Figure 7.2.

4. *Invite the learners to identify the indicators of the thinking skill.*
After presenting the consequence map, the teacher engages students in a
discussion in which the following questions are addressed:

Figure 7.2. A Consequence Map

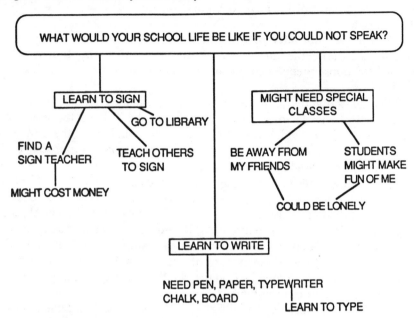

After studying the consequence map, can you identify some events
    that are the causes of other events?
Which events are the causes?
Which events are effects?
Are certain effects also causes of other events? Which ones are they?
Can you generate any other possible effects not shown on the conse-
    quence map?
Do the stated effects plausibly or logically follow from the given
    cause?
Which effect or effects are most likely to occur?

The ability to draw a consequence map and then correctly answer the
above questions are indicators that the students have command of this
thinking skill.

5. *Have learners participate in a guided practice of the thinking skill
after which constructive feedback is also provided.* The students are
invited to create their own consequence maps within cooperative groups.
The teacher places students into groups of four (quads) and assigns each

quad one of the enumerated problems: What would your school life be like if you could not (a) hear, (b) walk, (c) see, (d) read, (e) write, or (f) compute?

Two quads are later paired and discuss each other's consequence maps by answering the questions given above in step 4. The students who studied the consequence map of their peers can report their conclusions to the class.

During the activity, students are encouraged to give constructive feedback to their classmate in the pair. Example: "I liked the way you quickly figured out which were the causes and which were the effects!"

6. *Invite learners to reflect on the performance and applicability of the thinking skill*. Students are encouraged to reflect on this thinking skill by completing these sentence fragments: "A cause is . . ." "An effect is . . ." "A difference between a cause and effect is . . ." "When I do cause-and-effect thinking I must remember to . . ." Their answers can be shared in pairs, quads, or with the entire class. If desired, the teacher can engage the class in a discussion on the importance of identifying and understanding the possible social consequences of one's behavior. This data generated by the class could then be organized into a cognitive map providing the rationale for causal thinking.

7. *Have the learners practice the thinking skill independently*. Throughout the year the students can apply this thinking skill as they engage in cooperative learning and other instructional strategies, or encounter life situations involving causality.

Teaching a Social Skill

Recall that a social skill is an intrapersonal, interpersonal, or intragroup means of communicating. Let us assume that an 11th grade social studies teacher is ready to prepare her students to participate successfully in small group discussions of controversial issues. Prior to forming cooperative groups, she wants to be certain that her students know how to listen respectfully to each other. Respectful listening is a complicated social skill. It actually combines the two relationship skills of paraphrasing and probing. In addition, respectful listening involves giving the person with whom you are speaking specific nonverbal body cues expressing acceptance. In teaching the social skill of respectful listening, the seven-step model can be applied as follows:

1. *State the rationale for the social skill*. The teacher uses a think-pair-share structure (Lyman, 1981) to generate reasons why students need to listen respectfully to each other.

2. *Describe or define the social skill.* The teacher defines respectful listening as a combination of paraphrasing and nonjudgmental probing.

3. *Model or demonstrate the social skill.* The teacher asks for a volunteer to assist in demonstrating the relationship skill of *respectful listening* and also to demonstrate *disrespectful listening*. The teacher and a student volunteer may need a few minutes to practice the demonstration before presenting it to the class. Before the demonstration the students are asked to listen for the verbal behaviors of the teacher and to observe the nonverbal behaviors of the teacher. A sample demonstration of *respectful listening* follows (note that the listener applying this skill does not overtly disagree with the speaker, even if the views expressed are considered offensive):

Teacher: Tyrone, recently more than a half a million American soldiers served in the Persian Gulf, some of whom were women. Some people believe this is the right time for the Congress to pass an equal rights amendment. I wonder if you wouldn't mind telling your classmates your thoughts and feelings about having a special amendment to the Constitution guaranteeing equal rights for women?

Student: Sure, no problem . . . I'm against an equal rights amendment. Just because a few women who had something to prove went to the Persian Gulf, well . . . that doesn't mean anything. Women in this country have it made. Why change things? They don't have to work. They can stay home and watch soap operas, while their husbands bring home the money and fight the wars. This equal rights amendment business is the idea of a bunch of radical feminists who hate men.

Teacher: So let me see if I understand what you are saying. You believe an equal rights amendment is unnecessary because women in our country already have a great deal going for them. They don't have to get a job and they don't have to serve in the military. You also believe that the supporters of this amendment are a group of radical feminists who despise men. (*Paraphrase.*) Is this your position?

Student: Yes.

Teacher: Well, let me ask you this question. There is some evidence that women in our country who are doing the same job as their male counterparts are receiving less money. What are your thoughts about this practice? (*Probe.*)

Student: Well, just because a women has the same job title as a man, that doesn't mean that she's doing the same job. My dad tells me that in the place where he works there's a lady who refuses to carry heavy packages and do the dirty work, but she wants to get the same wages as my dad. Do you think that's fair? I don't!

Then the teacher and the student demonstrate *disrespectful listening*. The dialogue begins as before with the teacher's question and the student's first response. Suddenly, the teacher interrupts Tyrone, saying:

Teacher: Do you realize how narrow-minded you sound? Don't you care about women's issues? If you were married or had a daughter, wouldn't you want her to get paid as much as any man? You don't really believe this stuff, do you?

Student: Of course, I believe in what I said. Women have it made in our country. . . .

Teacher: (*interrupting*) I guess we all know where you're coming from. You're a male chauvinist! You can sit down now. Thanks for your point of view.

4. *Have learners identify the indicators of the social skill*. The teacher then asks the students to identify and contrast the specific verbal and nonverbal behaviors the teacher demonstrated during respectful and disrespectful listening.

5. *Have learners participate in a guided practice of the social skill after which constructive feedback is provided*. The students may be placed in quads. One pair practices respectful listening on some controversial topic while the second pair observes them. After the guided practice, the observers can share feedback on how well the social skill was applied and, perhaps, what could be done to improve the application of the skill. Time permitting, each member of the quad can practice demonstrating the skill and sharing feedback.

6. *Invite learners to reflect on the performance and/or applicability of the social skill*. In round-robin fashion the students can describe what they were thinking and feeling when they were practicing respectful listening. Each quad could also generate circumstances in which this particular skill could facilitate small group discussions. This data could then be presented to the entire class.

7. *Have the learners practice the social skill independently*. Students can use respectful listening whenever topics are discussed in pairs, in small cooperative groups, with the entire class, or out of class.

Teaching a Cooperative Structure

Round-robin brainstorming is a cooperative structure. It assumes that students can individually brainstorm. With round-robin brainstorming, students take turns sharing their responses to a question posed by the teacher or member of their learning team. The rules for round-robin brainstorming are described below.

Let us suppose that a fourth grade science teacher wants to teach her students the round-robin brainstorming cooperative structure. Here is one possible strategy that uses the seven-step model to teach the structure.

1. *State the rationale for the cooperative structure.* The teacher explains the rationale behind round-robin brainstorming as follows:

> Round-robin brainstorming gives all students a chance to participate or respond to a question posed by me or a student, generate many different responses to a question, and practice some social skills such as listening, respecting the ideas of others, and waiting one's turn.

2. *Describe or define the cooperative structure.* The teacher explains *his or her rules* for the round-robin brainstorming cooperative structure, which are as follows:

- Think about the question posed by me or a member of the class.
- One person states an answer to herself and then to the group. (The person may pass if she has no answer to share.)
- The next person to the left states an answer. Try your best to state a new or different answer to the question posed. You may piggyback on others' ideas. You are free to share as wild an idea as you like. You will not be criticized for your ideas.
- The procedure continues: take turns responding until you have no more new answers, or you have reached the time or number limit set by me, the class, or the quad.

During round-robin brainstorming students may not put others down, praise or criticize students' ideas or suggestions, or answer out of turn. Evaluation of ideas occurs only after brainstorming is completed.

3. *Model or demonstrate the cooperative structure.* First the teacher posts her rules for round-robin brainstorming on the chalkboard and asks three volunteers to demonstrate the cooperative structure with the

teacher. The teacher then poses a question to her three volunteers such as: "How many different flowers can you name? Let's see if we can come up with 15 different kinds of flowers. Let's first take 15 seconds of silent thinking time; you may record your answers privately if you wish." After the think time has elapsed, the student to the left of the teacher shares his or her response to the question and the procedure for taking turns continues.

4. *Have learners identify the indicators of the cooperative structure.* After the structure is demonstrated to the class, the teacher records these questions on the chalkboard. (The teacher could also write these questions prior to the demonstration so that the students watching can participate in a focused observation.)

> Did the participants have time to think about the question posed by the teacher?
> Did each member have an opportunity to state his/her answer?
> Did members take a turn in the proper order?
> Did members interrupt other students?
> Did members put others down?
> Did members praise or criticize the ideas of others?
> Did the members achieve their goal? Why or why not?

The participants and the class use these questions as a springboard to begin discussion of this cooperative structure.

5. *Have learners participate in a guided practice of the cooperative structure in which constructive feedback is also provided.* Suppose the class is divided up into seven quads. Each quad is assigned to use round-robin brainstorming for one of these problems that the teacher poses: Name as many animals as you can that (a) swim, (b) crawl, (c) fly, (d) hop, (e) come out at night, (f) eat only meat, (g) eat only plants. Each quad then practices the round-robin brainstorming process and reflects on the procedure by discussing its responses to the questions listed under step 4.

6. *Invite learners to reflect on the performance and applicability of the cooperative structure.* The teacher engages the class in a discussion regarding how well the students followed the steps of round-robin brainstorming. A subsequent class discussion could address when this cooperative structure could be used outside of the classroom.

7. *Have the learners practice the structure independently.* Throughout the year, the teacher can introduce round-robin brainstorming as needed.

Discussion

The examples above have shown the use of the seven-step model in teaching thinking skills, social skills, and cooperative structures. There is a synergistic relationship among thinking skills, social skills, and cooperative learning. Certain thinking skills and social skills facilitate cooperative learning activities, while many cooperative learning activities reinforce these same thinking and social skills. Many students already bring to the classroom those prerequisite thinking skills and social skills that facilitate cooperative learning. However, other students seem to require prior modeling of the necessary thinking and social skills. If certain students are consistently stumbling in their participation in cooperative learning, due to lack of thinking skills and social skills, they may need additional time to observe those skills modeled, to practice and refine them.

This relationship between cooperative learning, the thinking skills, and social skills is not merely mutually supportive and self-reinforcing; it also can lead to the acquisition of more complex thinking skills and social skills, and the learning of new and more complex cooperative structures. Let us be more specific.

As students develop an elementary set of thinking skills (i.e., the ability to access their internal data of facts, concepts, preferences, informed opinions, experiences, and feelings) and a basic set of interpersonal social skills (i.e., the ability to share and exchange data, to identify free information, paraphrase, probe, ask open questions, and listen respectfully), they gain confidence and competence in working in dyads. In time students will be able to participate in larger cooperative groups. These cooperative groups in turn provide the learners with the opportunity to practice more sophisticated thinking skills (e.g., round-robin brainstorming, generating causes and effects, hypothesizing, categorizing, deducing and inducing, and problem solving) and more complex intragroup social skills (e.g., establishing group norms and standards, giving and receiving positive and negative feedback, achieving consensus). Concomitantly, as students master simple cooperative structures such as think-pair-share, roundtable, round-robin, and numbered heads together, they can eventually learn to participate successfully in the more complex cooperative structures such as partners, expert jigsaw, group investigation, and co-op co-op (see Kagan, 1989). Additionally, these rich, complex cooperative structures offer students the arena or laboratory in which to practice the higher order thinking skills and the most challenging social/relationship skills. In short, cooperative learning activities reinforce and enhance the use of thinking skills and social skills. The thinking skills and social skills can facilitate participation in cooperative learning activities.

SUMMARY

We believe that most if not all students can enjoy the academic and affective gains associated with cooperative learning. This is in part true because many students already possess the thinking skills and social skills required to participate in simple cooperative structures. We suspect, however, that those gains would be enhanced if students in need of certain prerequisite thinking skills and social skills had an opportunity to learn those competencies before engaging in the more complex cooperative learning activities. In sum, we support the following propositions:

- Cooperative learning activities give students an opportunity to apply a set of varied thinking skills and social skills.
- More complex cooperative structures require more sophisticated and elegant thinking skills and social skills.
- Some students do not possess the thinking skills and social skills required to participate successfully in complex cooperative learning activities. These students need an opportunity to learn the thinking skills and social skills for group cooperation and group processing.
- The Fourth R, the relationship competencies, can provide students with many of the social skills and related thinking skills that facilitate cooperative learning activities.
- A seven step instructional model for teaching students thinking skills and social skills is a useful pedagogical approach.

REFERENCES

Beyer, B. (1987). *Practical strategies for the teaching of thinking*. Boston: Allyn and Bacon.

Bossone, R. M. (1982). The fourth r: Reasoning. *Proceedings of the Conference of the University/Urban Schools National Task Force*. San Juan, Puerto Rico.

Dawson, G. G. (1982). *Developing reason as the fourth r*. Report of the Joint Council on Economic Education, New York.

Dishon, D., & O'Leary, P. W. (1984). *A guidebook for cooperative learning: A technique for creating more effective schools*. Holmes Beach, FL: Learning Publications.

Dishon, D., & O'Leary, P. W. (1990). Social skills and process "in a nutshell." *Cooperative Learning, 10*(3), 35–36.

Evans, T. E., Corsini, R. J., & Gazda, G. M. (1990). Individual education and the 4 r's. *Educational Leadership, 48*(1), 52–56.

Holmes, C. T. (1983). The fourth r: Retention. *Journal of Research and Development in Education, 17*(1), 1–6.

Johnson, D. W., & Johnson, R. T. (1990). Social skills for successful group work. *Educational Leadership, 47*(4), 29–33.

Johnson, D. W., Johnson, R. T., Holubec, E. J., & Roy, P. (1984). *Circles of learning.* Alexandria, Virginia: Association for Supervision and Curriculum Development.

Johnson, H. C. (1986). The fourth r—the final taboo? *Journal of Teacher Education 37*(3), 17–20.

Kagan, S. (1989). *Cooperative learning: Resources for teachers* (rev. ed.). San Juan Capistrano, CA: Resources for Teachers.

Lyman, F., Jr. (1981). The responsive classroom discussion: The inclusion of all students. *Mainstreaming Digest.* College Park: University of Maryland Press, 114–119.

Marzano, R. J., Brandt, R. S., Hughes, C. S., Jones, B. F., Presseisen, B. Z., Rankin, C. S., & Suhor, C. (1988). *Dimensions of thinking: A framework for curriculum and instruction.* Alexandria, VA: Association for Supervision and Curriculum Development.

Marzano, R. J., Peckering, D. J., & Brandt, R. (1990). Integrating instructional programs through dimensions of learning. *Educational Leadership, 47*(5), 17–24.

McCabe, M. E., & Rhodes, J. (1988). *The nurturing classroom.* Willits, CA: ITA Publications.

National Association for Mediation in Education (NAME) publishes a newsletter entitled *The Fourth R*; NAME promotes the thinking of conflict resolution skills in schools.

Solomon, R. D., & Solomon, E. C. (1987a). *The handbook for the fourth r: Relationship skills* (rev. ed., Vol. 1). Columbia, MD: National Institute for Relationship Training.

Solomon, R. D., & Solomon, E. C. (1987b). *The handbook for the fourth r II: Relationship skills for group discussion and process* (Vol. 2). Columbia, MD: National Institute for Relationship Training.

8

Encouraging Thinking Through Constructive Controversy

David W. Johnson and Roger T. Johnson

> Have you learned lessons only of
> those who admired you, and were tender
> with you, and stood aside for you?
>
> Have you not learned great lessons
> from those who braced themselves
> against you, and disputed the passage
> with you?
>
> *Walt Whitman, 1860*

In an English class students are considering the issue of civil disobedience. They learn that in the civil rights movement, individuals broke the law to gain equal rights for minorities. In numerous literary works, such as *Huckleberry Finn*, individuals wrestle with the issue of breaking the law to redress a social injustice. Huck wrestles with the idea of breaking the law in order to help Jim, the runaway slave. In order to study the role of civil disobedience in a democracy, students are placed in a cooperative learning group of four members. The group is then divided into two pairs. One pair is given the assignment of making the best case possible for the constructiveness of civil disobedience in a democracy. The other pair is given the assignment of making the best case possible for the destructiveness of civil disobedience in a democracy. In the resulting conflict, students draw from such sources as the *Declaration of Independence, Civil Disobedience*, by Henry David Thoreau, *Speech at Cooper Union, New York*, by Abraham Lincoln, and *Letter from Birmingham Jail*, by Martin Luther King, Jr. to challenge each other's reasoning and analyses concerning when civil disobedience is, and is not, constructive.

Such intellectual "disputed passages" create a high level of reasoning, thinking, and metacognition when they occur within cooperative learning groups and when they are carefully structured to ensure that students manage them constructively. Cooperation, controversy, cognition, and metacognition are all intimately related. Cooperative learning provides the context within which cognition and metacognition best take place. The interpersonal exchange within cooperative learning groups, and especially the intellectual challenge resulting from conflict among ideas and conclusions (i.e., controversy), promotes critical thinking, higher level reasoning, and metacognitive thought. Within this chapter cooperative learning is defined and its impact on cognition and metacognition is discussed. The nature of controversy and its effects on higher level reasoning and critical thinking are then addressed.

WHAT IS COOPERATIVE LEARNING?

Cooperation is working together to accomplish shared goals and *cooperative learning* is the instructional use of small groups so that students work together to maximize their own and each other's learning. Within cooperative learning groups, students are given two responsibilities: to learn the assigned material and make sure that all other members of their group do likewise. Their success is measured by a fixed set of standards. Thus, a student seeks an outcome that is beneficial to himself or herself *and* beneficial to all other group members.

Simply placing students in groups and telling them to work together does not in and of itself promote higher achievement and higher level reasoning. There are many ways in which group efforts may go wrong (Johnson & Johnson, 1989). In order to be productive, cooperative learning groups must be structured to include the essential elements of *positive interdependence*, in which each member can succeed only if all members succeed, *face-to-face promotive interaction*, during which students assist and support each other's efforts to achieve, *individual accountability* to ensure that all members do their fair share of the work, the *interpersonal and small group skills* required to work cooperatively with others, and *group processing* (in which groups reflect on how well they are working together and how their effectiveness as a group may be improved).

Cooperative learning may be contrasted with competitive and individualistic learning. In a *competitive* learning situation, students work against each other to achieve a goal that only one or a few students can attain. Students are graded on a curve, which requires them to work faster and/or more accurately than their peers. Thus, students seek an outcome that is personally beneficial but detrimental to all other students in the class. In an *individualistic* learning situation, students work by themselves to accomplish learning goals unrelated to those of the other students. Individual goals are assigned, students' efforts are evaluated on a fixed set of standards, and students are rewarded accordingly. Thus, the student seeks an outcome that is personally beneficial and ignores as irrelevant the goal achievement of other students. In both competitive and individualistic learning situations, the interpersonal exchange so necessary to cognition and metacognition tends not to take place.

COOPERATION'S IMPACT ON COGNITION AND METACOGNITION

Working cooperatively can have profound effects on students' achievement and level of reasoning (Johnson & Johnson, 1989). During the past 90 years, over 600 studies have been conducted on cooperative, competitive, and individualistic efforts. Cooperative learning experiences promote higher achievement than do competitive and individualistic learning (effect sizes of 0.66 and 0.63 respectively). In addition to the mastery and retention of material being studied, achievement is indicated by the quality of reasoning strategies used to complete the assignment, the generation of new ideas and solutions (i.e., *process gain*), and the transfer of what is learned within one situation to another (i.e., *group-to-individual transfer*). The superiority of cooperative over competitive and individualistic learning increases as the task is more conceptual, requires more problem solving, necessitates more higher-level reasoning and critical thinking, needs more creative answers, seeks long-term retention, and requires more application of what is learned (Johnson & Johnson, 1989).

Many of the studies relating cooperative learning experiences and achievement have focused on quality of reasoning strategy, level of cognitive reasoning, and metacognitive strategies. Studies on both Piaget's cognitive development theory and Kohlberg's moral development theory have indicated that the transition to higher level cognitive and moral reasoning is promoted more frequently by cooperative than competitive or individualistic experiences (effect sizes = 0.79 and 0.97 respectively) (Johnson & Johnson, 1989). We conducted a series of studies on the impact of cooperative, competitive, and individualistic efforts on higher level reasoning with Linda Skon and Barbara Gabbert (Gabbert, Johnson, & Johnson, 1986; Johnson, Skon, & Johnson, 1980; Skon, Johnson, & Johnson, 1981). In our studies we used tasks that could be solved using either higher level or lower level reasoning strategies. We found that more frequent discovery and use of the higher level reasoning strategies occurred within cooperative learning situations than occurred

within competitive or individualistic ones. In a categorization and retrieval task, for example, first grade students were instructed to memorize 12 nouns during the instructional session and then to complete several
retrieval tasks during the testing session the following day. The 12 nouns
were given in random order and students were told to (1) order the nouns
in a way that makes sense and aids memorization and (2) memorize the
words. Three of the words were fruits, three were animals, three were
clothing, and three were toys. Eight of the nine cooperative groups
discovered and used all four categories, and only one student in the
competitive and individualistic conditions did so. Even the highest-
achieving students failed to use the category search strategy in the competitive and individualistic conditions.

WHY COOPERATION AFFECTS COGNITION
AND METACOGNITION

Within performance situations considerable advantage may go to
individuals who (1) engage in critical thinking and higher level reasoning
and (2) know what thinking strategies they are using and how to modify
them in order to improve performance. There are a number of reasons
why cooperative learning promotes the cognitive and metacognitive
activity required to achieve.

First, the expectation that one will have to summarize, explain, and
teach what one is learning impacts the strategies used. The way students
conceptualize material and organize it cognitively is different when they
are learning material to teach to others than when they are learning
material for their own benefit (Annis, 1979; Bargh & Schul, 1980; Murray,
1983). Material to be taught to collaborators is learned by using higher
level strategies more frequently than is material being learned for one's
own use.

Second, the discussion within cooperative learning situations promotes more frequent oral summarizing, explaining, and elaborating of
what one knows (Johnson & Johnson, 1989). These tasks are necessary for
the storage of information into the memory (through further encoding
and networking) and the long-term retention of the information. Such
oral rehearsal provides a review that seems to consolidate and strengthen
what is known and to provide relevant feedback about the degree to
which mastery and understanding have been achieved. In one of the
earliest studies on this issue, Johnson (1971b) found that a person's understanding and level of reasoning about an issue are enhanced by the
combination of explaining one's knowledge and summarizing and para-

phrasing the other person's knowledge and perspective. Subsequently, vocalizing what is being learned is more strongly related to achievement than is listening to other group members vocalize (Johnson, Johnson, Roy, & Zaidman, 1985), summarizing the main concepts and principles being learned increases achievement and retention (Yager, Johnson, & Johnson, 1985), and both explaining relevant information and disagreeing with another group member are positively related to individual achievement (Vasquez, 1989). These and other studies support the conclusion that meaning is formulated through the process of conveying it. It is while students are orally summarizing, explaining, and elaborating that they organize and systematize cognitively the concepts and information they are discussing.

Third, cooperative learning groups are nourished by heterogeneity among group members. As students accommodate themselves to each other's different perspectives, strategies, and approaches to completing assignments, divergent thinking and creative thinking are stimulated. Learning experiences are enriched by the exchange of ideas and perspectives among students from high, medium, and low achievement levels, handicapped and nonhandicapped students, male and female students, and students from different cultural, ethnic, and socioeconomic backgrounds (Johnson & Johnson, 1989).

Fourth, in most cooperative learning situations students with incomplete information interact with others who have different perspectives and facts. In order to understand all the relevant information and the variety of perspectives and create a synthesis based on the best reasoning and information by everyone involved, students must (1) attempt actively to understand both the content of the information being presented and the cognitive and affective perspectives of the person presenting the information and (2) be able to hold both their own and other people's perspectives in mind at the same time. Cooperative experiences have been found to promote greater perspective-taking ability than do competitive or individualistic experiences (effect sizes = 0.57 and 0.44 respectively), and perspective taking results in better understanding and retention of others' information, reasoning, and perspectives (Johnson, 1971a; Johnson & Johnson, 1989). This evidence indicates that having information available does not not ensure that it will be utilized. Utilization depends on students' ability to understand their own and each other's perspectives.

Fifth, within cooperative learning groups members externalize their ideas and reasoning for critical examination. As a result, there tends to be considerable peer monitoring and regulation of members' thinking and reasoning. Exploration of ideas is stimulated and focused by groupmates.

Individuals working by themselves more frequently get lost in wild-goose chases. Individuals generally have difficulty monitoring their own cognitive activity. Within a cooperative group, however, each member can monitor the reasoning of other members and help enhance their understanding of the issue or material. In essence, the cooperative experience serves as a training ground for metacognitive skills that are transferable to individual learning.

Sixth, within cooperative learning groups, members may give each other feedback concerning the quality and relevance of contributions and how to improve one's reasoning or performance. Typically, personalized process feedback (as opposed to terminal feedback) is given continuously as part of the interaction among group members. In cooperative learning groups feedback is received from fellow group members and discussed face-to-face in ways that make clear its personal implications.

Seventh, perhaps the most powerful mediator of all is the controversy (i.e., conflicts among the ideas, opinions, conclusions, theories, and information of members) resulting from the involved participation in cooperative learning groups (Johnson & Johnson, 1987).

NATURE OF CONTROVERSY

A social studies teacher asks students to think about what problems people faced in hunting and gathering societies. Immediately, Jim states that the major problem was how to hunt better so they could have more food. Jane disagrees. She says the major problem was how to store food so it would last longer. Jeremy tells both Jim and Jane that they are wrong; the major problem was how to domesticate the wild grains that grew in the area so that the people would be less dependent on hunting. Jim, Jane, and Jeremy begin to argue forcefully, bringing out the facts supporting why each thinks he or she is right.

Using academic conflicts for instructional purposes is one of the most dynamic and involving yet *least-used* teaching strategies. Although creating a conflict is an accepted writer's tool for capturing an audience, teachers often suppress students' academic disagreements and consequently miss out on valuable opportunities to capture their own audiences and enhance learning.

Controversy exists when one student's ideas, information, conclusions, theories, and opinions are incompatible with those of another, and the two seek to reach an agreement. Structured academic controversies are most often contrasted with concurrence seeking, debate, and individualistic learning. For instance, students can inhibit discussion to avoid any disagreement and compromise quickly to reach a consensus while they discuss the issue (concurrence-seeking). Or students can appoint a judge and then debate the different positions with the expectation that the judge will determine who presented the better position (debate). Finally, students can work independently with their own set of materials at their own pace (individualistic learning).

Over the past 15 years, we have developed and tested a theory about how controversy promotes positive outcomes (Johnson, 1979, 1980; Johnson & Johnson, 1979, 1985, 1987). Based on our findings, we have developed a series of curriculum units on energy and environmental issues structured for academic controversies. We have also worked with schools and colleges throughout the United States and Canada to field-test and implement the units in the classroom. We will review these efforts by discussing the process of controversy, how teachers can organize and use it, and the advantages of using controversy to enhance learning and thinking.

HOW STUDENTS BENEFIT

When students interact, conflicts among their ideas, conclusions, theories, information, perspectives, opinions, and preferences are inevitable. Teachers who capitalize on these differences find that academic conflicts can yield highly constructive dividends. Over the past 15 years, we have conducted a systematic series of research studies to discover the consequences of structured controversy (Johnson & Johnson, 1979, 1985, 1987, 1989; Johnson, Johnson, & Smith, 1986). Compared with concurrence-seeking, debate, and individualistic efforts, controversy tends to result in

- Greater student mastery and retention of the subject matter being studied as well as greater ability to generalize the principles learned to a wider variety of situations. In a meta-analysis of the available research, Johnson and Johnson (1989) found that controversy produced higher achievement than did debate (effect size $= 0.77$), individualistic learning (effect size $= 0.65$), and concurrence seeking (effect size $= 0.42$).
- Higher quality decisions and solutions to complex problems for which different viewpoints can plausibly be developed. If students are to become citizens capable of making reasoned judgments about the complex problems facing society, they must learn to use the higher level reasoning and critical-thinking processes involved in effectively

solving problems, especially problems for which different viewpoints can plausibly be developed. To do so, students must enter empathically into the arguments on both sides of the issue and ensure that the strongest possible case is made for each side, and arrive at a synthesis based on rational, probabilistic thought. Participating in structured controversy teaches students of all ages how to find high quality solutions to complex problems.

- More frequent creative insights into the issues being discussed and synthesis combining both perspectives. Controversy increases the number of ideas, quality of ideas, creation of original ideas, the use of a wider range of ideas, originality of expression in problem solving, the use of more varied strategies, and the number of creative, imaginative, novel solutions.
- Greater exchange of expertise. Students often know different information and theories, make different assumptions, and have different opinions. Within any cooperative learning group, students with a wide variety of expertise and perspectives are told to work together to maximize each member's learning. Many times students study different parts of an assignment and are expected to share their expertise with the other members of their group. Conflict among their ideas, information, opinions, preferences, theories, conclusions, and perspectives is inevitable. Yet such controversies are typically avoided or managed destructively. Having the skills to manage the controversies constructively, and knowing the procedures for exchanging information and perspective among individuals with differing expertise, are essential for maximum learning and growth.
- Greater accuracy in understanding the perspectives of others.
- Greater task involvement reflected in greater emotional commitment to solving the problem, greater enjoyment of the process, more feelings of stimulation and enjoyment.
- More positive relationships among participants and greater perceived peer academic support.
- Higher academic self-esteem.

In addition to these outcomes, *there are a number of critical-thinking skills required by the controversy structure.* Students must develop at least four sets of conceptual skills to prepare a "best case" presentation of an assigned position, based on evidence (Johnson & Johnson, 1987).

1. Students must collect, analyze, and present evidence to support a position. This involves:
   a. Researching, gathering, and collecting all facts, information, and experiences available and relevant about the issue being studied.

b. Analyzing and organizing the information into a position statement or claim, a listing of all supporting evidence, and a coherent, reasoned, valid, and logical rationale (this requires conceptual analysis and the use of inductive and deductive reasoning).
c. Presenting the position with vigor, sincerity, and persuasiveness
while keeping an open mind. Students must present and advocate the position in a way that takes into account who the audience is and how they may be persuaded.
2. Students must evaluate and criticize the opposing positions. Students
critically analyze the opposing position and challenge and attempt to
refute it based on the rules of logic and evidence. At the same time,
students rebut attacks on their position. This requires a continual
reconceptualizing of both positions and determining when faulty information or faulty reasoning is being presented.
3. Students are required to see the issue from both perspectives.
4. Students make tentative conclusions based on a synthesis and/or integration of the best evidence from both sides. This requires probabilistic thinking (i.e., knowledge is available only in degrees of certainty)
rather than dualistic thinking (i.e., there is only right and wrong and
authority should not be questioned) or relativistic thinking (i.e., authorities are sometimes right, but right and wrong depend on your
perspective). It also requires considerable divergent as well as conver-
gent thinking. Such cognitive skills are valuable contributors to creative problem solving.

PROCESS THROUGH WHICH CONTROVERSY AFFECTS HIGHER LEVEL REASONING

The hypothesis that intellectual challenge promotes higher level reasoning, critical thinking, and metacognitive thought is derived from a
number of premises:

1. When individuals are presented with a problem or decision, they have
an initial conclusion based on categorizing and organizing incomplete
information, their limited experiences, and their specific perspective.
2. When individuals present their conclusion and its rationale to others,
they engage in cognitive rehearsal, deepen their understanding of their
position, and discover higher level reasoning strategies.
3. Individuals are confronted by other people with different conclusions
based on other people's information, experiences, and perspectives.

4. Individuals become uncertain as to the correctness of their views. A state of conceptual conflict or disequilibrium is aroused.
5. Uncertainty, conceptual conflict, and disequilibrium motivate an active search for more information, new experiences, and a more adequate cognitive perspective and reasoning process in hopes of resolving the uncertainty. Berlyne (1966) calls this active search *epistemic curiosity*. Divergent attention and thought are stimulated.
6. By adapting their cognitive perspective and reasoning through understanding and accommodating the perspective and reasoning of others, a new, reconceptualized, and reorganized conclusion is derived. Novel solutions and decisions are detected that are, on balance, qualitatively better.

When teachers structure controversies within cooperative learning groups, students are required to research and prepare a position (reasoning both deductively and inductively); advocate a position (thereby orally rehearsing the relevant information and teaching their knowledge to peers); analyze, evaluate critically, and rebut information; reason deductively, inductively, and probabilistically; take the perspective of others; and synthesize and integrate information into factual and judgmental conclusions that are summarized into a joint position to which all sides can, hopefully, agree.

Controversies are resolved by engaging in the discussion of the advantages and disadvantages of proposed actions aimed at synthesizing novel solutions. In controversy there is advocacy and challenge of each other's positions in order to reach the highest possible quality decision based on the synthesis of both perspectives. There is a reliance on argumentative clash to develop, clarify, expand, and elaborate one's thinking about the issues being considered.

STRUCTURING ACADEMIC CONTROVERSIES

An example of a controversy on environmental education is as follows. The teacher assigns students to groups of four and asks them to prepare a report entitled "The Role of Regulation in the Management of Hazardous Waste." There is to be one report from the group representing the members' best analysis of the issue. The groups are divided into two-person advocacy teams, with one team being given the position that "more regulations are needed" and the other team being given the position that "fewer regulations are needed." Both advocacy teams are given articles and technical materials supporting their assigned position. They are then given time to read and discuss the material with their partner and to plan how best to advocate their assigned position so that (1) they learn the information and perspective within the articles and technical reports, (2) the opposing team is convinced of the soundness of the team's position, and (3) the members of the opposing team learn the material contained within the articles and technical reports. To do so, students proceed through five steps.

First, students *research the issue, organize their information, and prepare their positions.* Learning begins with students gathering information. They then categorize and organize their present information and experiences so that a conclusion is derived. Second, the two advocacy teams actively *present and advocate their positions.* Each pair presents their position and reasoning to the opposition, thereby engaging in considerable cognitive rehearsal and elaboration of their position and its rationale. When the other team presents, students' reasoning and conclusions are *challenged by the opposing view* and they experience *conceptual conflict and uncertainty.* Third, students engage in a general discussion in which they *advocate their position, rebut attacks on their position, refute the opposing position, and seek to learn both positions.* The group discusses the issue, evaluates critically the opposing position and its rationale, defends positions, and compares the strengths and weaknesses of the two positions. When students are challenged by conclusions and information that do not fit with their reasoning and conclusions, conceptual conflict, uncertainty, and disequilibrium result. As a result of their uncertainty, students experience *epistemic curiosity* and, therefore, students actively (1) search for more information and experiences to support their position and (2) seek to understand the opposing position and its supporting rationale. During this time students' uncertainty and information search are encouraged and promoted by the teacher. Fourth, students *reverse perspectives* and present the opposing position. Each advocacy pair presents the best case possible for the opposing position. Fifth, the group of four reaches a consensus and prepares a group report. The emphasis during this instructional period is on students *reconceptualizing* their position and *synthesizing* the best information and reasoning from both sides. The group's report should reflect their best-reasoned judgment. Each group member then individually takes an examination on the factual information contained in the reading materials.

For the past several years we have been training teachers and professors throughout North America in the use of structured academic controversies. Structured academic controversies are now being used at the

University of Minnesota in engineering, psychology, and education courses. They are being used in elementary and secondary schools in the United States and Canada. The basic format follows. A more detailed description of conducting academic controversies may be found in Johnson, Johnson, and Smith (1986) and Johnson and Johnson (1987).

Structure the Academic Task

The task must be structured cooperatively and so that there are at least two well-documented positions (e.g., pro and con). The choice of topic depends on the interests of the instructor and the purposes of the course. Topics on which we have developed curriculum units include the following and many others: What caused the dinosaurs' extinction? Should the wolf be a protected species? Should coal be used as an energy source? Should nuclear energy be used? Should the regulation of hazardous wastes be increased? Should a canoeing area in certain boundary waters be a national park? How should acid precipitation be controlled?

Prepare Instructional Materials

Prepare the instructional materials so that group members know what position they have been assigned and where they can find supporting information. The following materials are needed for each position:

1. A clear description of the group's task
2. A description of the phases of the controversy procedure and the interpersonal and small group skills to be used during each phase
3. A definition of the position to be advocated with a summary of the key arguments supporting the position
4. Resource materials (including a bibliography) to provide evidence for the elaboration of the arguments supporting the position to be advocated

Structure the Controversy

The principle requirements for a successful structured controversy are a cooperative context, skillful group members, and heterogeneity of group membership. These are structured by

1. *Assigning students to groups of four.* Divide each group into two pairs. A high reader and a low reader may be assigned to each pair. The responsibility of the pair is to get to know the information supporting

their assigned position and prepare a presentation and a series of persuasive arguments to use in the discussion with the opposing pair.

2. *Assigning pro and con positions* to the pairs and giving students supporting materials to read and study. A bibliography of further sources of information may also be given. A section of resource materials may be set up in the library.

3. *Highlighting the cooperative goals* of reaching a consensus on the issue, mastering all the information relevant to both sides of the issue (measured by a test), and writing a quality group report on which all members will be evaluated. Also highlight the group reward—each group member will receive five bonus points if all score 90 percent or better on the test.

Conduct the Controversy

1. Assign each pair the tasks of

- Learning their position and its supporting arguments and information
- Researching all information relevant to their position
- Giving the opposing pair any information found supporting the opposing position
- Preparing a persuasive presentation to be given to the other pair
- Preparing a series of persuasive arguments to be used in the discussion with the opposing pair

They research and prepare their position, presentation, and arguments. Students are given the following instructions:

Plan with your partner how to advocate your position effectively. Read the materials supporting your position. Find more information in the library reference books to support your position. Plan a persuasive presentation. Make sure you and your partner master the information supporting your assigned position and present it in a persuasive and complete way so that the other group members will comprehend and learn the information.

2. Have each pair present its position to the other. Presentations should involve more than one media and advocate persuasively the "best case" for the position. There is no arguing during this time. Students should listen carefully to the opposing position. Students are told: "As a pair, present your position forcefully and persuasively. Listen carefully

and learn the opposing position. Take notes, and clarify anything you do not understand."

3. Have students openly discuss the issue by freely exchanging their information and ideas. For higher level reasoning and critical thinking to occur, it is necessary to probe and push each other's conclusions. Students ask for data to support each other's statements, clarify rationales, and show why their position is a rational one. Students evaluate critically the opposing position and its rationale, defend their own positions, and compare the strengths and weaknesses of the two positions. Students refute the claims being made by the opposing pair, and rebut the attacks on their own position. Students are to follow the specific rules for constructive controversy. Students should also take careful notes on and thoroughly learn the opposing position. Sometimes a "time-out" period needs to be provided so that pairs can caucus and prepare new arguments. Teachers encourage more spirited arguing, take sides when a pair is in trouble, play devil's advocate, ask one group to observe another group engaging in a spirited argument, and generally stir up the discussions. Students are instructed to

> Argue forcefully and persuasively for your position, presenting as many facts as you can to support your point of view. Listen critically to the opposing pair's position, asking them for the facts that support their viewpoint, and then present counterarguments. Remember that this is a complex issue, and you need to know both sides to write a good report.

4. Have the pairs reverse perspectives and positions by presenting the opposing position as sincerely and forcefully as they can. It helps to have the pairs change chairs. They can use their own notes, but may not see the materials developed by the opposing pair. Students' instructions are: "Working as a pair, present the opposing pair's position. Be as sincere and forceful as you can be. Add any new facts you know. Elaborate their position by relating it to other information you have previously learned."

5. Have the group members drop their advocacy and reach a decision by consensus. Then they

- Write a group report that includes their joint position and the supporting evidence and rationale. Often the resulting position is a third perspective or synthesis that is more rational than the two assigned. All group members sign the report, indicating that they agree with it, can explain its content, and consider it ready to be evaluated.

- Take a test on both positions. If all members score above the preset criteria of excellence, each receives five bonus points.
- Process how well the group functioned and how their performance may be improved during the next controversy. Teachers may wish to structure the group processing to highlight the specific conflict management skills students need to master.

Students are instructed to

> Summarize and synthesize the best arguments for *both* points of view. Reach consensus on a position that is supported by the facts. Change your mind only when the facts and the rationale clearly indicate that you should do so. Write your report with the supporting evidence and rationale for your synthesis that your group has agreed on. When you are certain the report is as good as you can make it, sign it. Organize your report to present it to your entire class.

Teach Students Conflict Skills

No matter how carefully teachers structure controversies, if students do not have the interpersonal and small-group skills to manage conflicts constructively the controversy does not produce its potential effects. Students should be taught the following skills.

1. Emphasize the mutuality of the situation and avoid win-lose dynamics. Focus on coming to the best decision possible, not on winning.
2. Confirm others' competence while disagreeing with their positions and challenging their reasoning. Be critical of ideas, not people. Challenge and refute the ideas of the members of the opposing pair, but do not reject them personally.
3. Separate your personal worth from criticism of your ideas.
4. Listen to everyone's ideas, even if you do not agree with them.
5. First bring out all the ideas and facts supporting both sides and then try to put them together in a way that makes sense. Be able to differentiate the differences between positions before attempting to integrate ideas.
6. Be able to take the opposing perspective in order to understand the opposing position. Try to understand both sides of the issue.
7. Change your mind when the evidence clearly indicates that you should.

8. Paraphrase what someone has said if it is not clear.
9. Emphasize rationality in seeking the best possible answer, given the available data.
10. Follow the golden rule of conflict—Act toward your opponents as you would have them act toward you. If you want people to listen to you, then listen to them. If you want others to include your ideas in their thinking, then include their ideas in your thinking. If you want others to take your perspective, then take their perspective.

SUMMARY

To promote students' higher level reasoning, critical thinking, and metacognition it is necessary to carefully structure the two steps of (1) cooperation among students and (2) academic controversy within the cooperative groups. Cooperation, controversy, cognition, and metacognition are all intimately related. Cooperative learning provides the context within which cognition and metacognition best take place. They are stimulated by the interpersonal exchange within cooperative learning groups. To ensure that higher level reasoning, critical thinking, and metacognition take place, students need the intellectual challenge resulting from conflict among ideas and conclusions.

Cooperative learning needs to be carefully structured to include positive interdependence, face-to-face promotive interaction, individual accountability, the appropriate use of interpersonal and small-group skills, and processing how effectively the group has functioned. Under these conditions, cooperative learning results in higher achievement, more frequent use of higher quality reasoning strategies, the generation of new ideas and solutions, and more frequent metacognitive thinking than do competitive or individualistic learning situations. Within cooperative learning groups there is a process of interpersonal exchange that involves teaching what one learns to groupmates, explaining and elaborating what is being learned, being exposed to diverse perspectives and ideas, taking others' perspectives, externalizing ideas and reasoning, and feedback. Perhaps most important is that intellectual conflict occurs within cooperative groups.

Controversy exists when one student's ideas, information, conclusions, theories, and opinions are incompatible with those of another, and the two seek to reach an agreement. Controversy, compared with concurrence-seeking, debate, and individualistic efforts, results in higher achievement, higher quality decisions and problem-solving, more creative thinking, higher level reasoning and critical thinking, greater perspective-taking accuracy, greater task involvement, more positive relationships among group members, and higher academic self-esteem.

These outcomes occur as a result of the structured process of controversy. Students make an initial judgment, present their conclusions to other group members, are challenged with opposing views, become uncertain about the correctness of their views, actively search for new information and understanding, incorporate others' perspectives and reasoning into their thinking, and reach a new set of conclusions. While this process sometimes occurs naturally within cooperative learning groups, it may be considerably enhanced when teachers structure academic controversies. This involves dividing a cooperative group into two pairs and assigning them opposing positions. The pairs then develop their position, present it to the other pair, listen to the opposing position, engage in a discussion in which they attempt to refute the other side and rebut attacks on their position, reverse perspectives and present the other position, and then drop all advocacy and seek a synthesis that takes both perspectives and positions into account. Participation in such a process requires a set of social and cognitive skills. To promote higher level reasoning, critical thinking, and metacognitive skills, teachers are well advised to first establish cooperative learning and then structure academic controversies.

REFERENCES

Annis, L. (1979). The processes and effects of peer tutoring. *Human Learning, 2*, 39–47.

Bargh, J., & Schul, Y. (1980). On the cognitive benefits of teaching. *Journal of Educational Psychology, 72*, 593–604.

Berlyne, D. (1966). Notes on intrinsic motivation and intrinsic reward in relation to instruction. In J. Bruner (Ed.), *Learning about learning* (Cooperative Research Monograph No. 15). Washington, DC: U.S. Department of Health, Education and Welfare, Office of Education.

Gabbert, B., Johnson, D. W., & Johnson, R. (1986). Cooperative learning, group-to-individual transfer, process gain, and the acquisition of cognitive reasoning strategies. *Journal of Psychology, 120*, 265–278.

Johnson, D. W. (1971a). Effectiveness of role reversal: actor or listener. *Psychological Reports, 28*, 275–282.

Johnson, D. W. (1971b). Role reversal: A summary and review of the research. *International Journal of Group Tensions, 1*, 318–334.

Johnson, D. W. (1979). *Educational psychology.* Englewood Cliffs, NJ: Prentice-Hall.

Johnson, D. W. (1980). Group processes: Influences of student–student interaction on school outcomes. In J. McMillan (Ed.), *The social psychology of school learning* (pp. 123-168). New York: Academic Press.

Johnson, D. W., & Johnson, R. (1979). Conflict in the classroom: Controversy and learning. *Review of Educational Research, 49,* 51-61.

Johnson, D. W., & Johnson, R. (1985). Classroom conflict: Controversy versus debate in learning groups. *American Educational Research Journal, 22,* 237-256.

Johnson, D. W., & Johnson, R. (1987). *Creative conflict.* Edina, MN: Interaction Book Company.

Johnson, D. W., & Johnson, R. (1989). *Cooperation and competition: Theory and research.* Edina, MN: Interaction Book Company.

Johnson, D. W., & Johnson, R., Roy, P., & Zaidman, B. (1985). Oral interaction in cooperative learning groups: Speaking, listening, and the nature of statements made by high-, medium-, and low-achieving students. *Journal of Psychology, 119,* 303-321.

Johnson, D. W., & Johnson, R., & Smith, K. (1986). Academic conflict among students: Controversy and learning. In R. Feldman (Ed.), *The social psychology of education* (pp. 199-231). Cambridge, MA: Cambridge University Press.

Johnson, D. W., Skon, L., & Johnson, R. (1980). Effects of cooperative, competitive, and individualistic conditions on children's problem-solving performance. *American Educational Research Journal, 17,* 83-94.

Murray, F. (1983). *Cognitive benefits of teaching on the teacher.* Paper presented at American Educational Research Association Annual Meeting, Montreal.

Skon, L., Johnson, D. W., & Johnson, R. (1981). Cooperative peer interaction versus individual competition and individualistic efforts: Effects on the acquisition of cognitive reasoning strategies. *Journal of Educational Psychology, 73,* 83-92.

Vasquez, M. (1989). *The impact of cooperative versus traditional instruction on the acquisition of knowledge of naval air-traffic controller trainees.* Unpublished doctoral dissertation, University of Minnesota, Minneapolis.

Yager, S., Johnson, D. W., & Johnson, R. (1985). Oral discussion, group-to-individual transfer, and achievement in cooperative learning groups. *Journal of Educational Psychology, 77,* 60-66.

The Touchstones Project
Learning to Think Cooperatively

*Howard Zelderman, Geoffrey Comber,
and Nicholas Maistrellis*

> You don't want to just butt heads with other people. If you don't, they
> may give you something you need, something you can use later.
>
> 12th-grade student

Effective action in the modern world requires cooperation among
persons of diverse abilities, expertise, temperament, and background.
This is equally true in scientific, political, corporate, and social settings.
Corporate actions have political and social consequences that can't be
ignored. Scientific discoveries that don't have immediate social, political,
and moral implications are rare, especially in the biological field. Politicians and even ordinary citizens are being called upon every day to judge
the legitimacy and propriety of technical procedures that prolong life or
reverse the effects of infertility. Even rarefied theoretical fields like
cosmology and particle physics have immediate political and social consequences, since the experiments they require involve colossal expendi-
tures of public money.

If we consider a global problem, such as how to reverse the deteriora-
tion of the environment, the degree of cooperation required among experts
from different disciplines is truly extraordinary. It is not simply a matter of
pooling information. It is, rather, a matter of bringing diverse points of
view and talents together to define and construct the human world.

COOPERATIVE THOUGHT VERSUS SOLITARY THOUGHT

We are called on every day to make judgments that cut across
ordinary lines of expertise. We cannot make these judgments by ourselves. The day of the solitary thinker, as exemplified in Descartes's "I
think, therefore I am" or Rodin's *Thinker*, is for the most part gone. This
is not simply because of the sheer proliferation of information; data

banks and computers can handle this. It is rather because in the real world the divisions of different disciplines are disappearing. There hardly exists an important modern problem that isn't multidisciplinary and therefore requires for its solution a collective judgment.

However, in order to learn to judge collectively, we must learn to think cooperatively. Cooperative thinking is not presently stressed in schools, where teaching and learning is largely, if not exclusively, governed by the model of a teacher informing, and students individually receiving.

This model of teaching and learning becomes the exclusive model as students diverge from one another in their various skills and interests. The very students who are successful in our schools, and who, therefore, are expected to confront and deal with the kinds of problems emergent in a technological world, become increasingly less able to achieve this. Their skills become increasingly compartmentalized. The finesse and subtlety needed to approach a poem and the rigor and precision displayed in mathematical concerns remain isolated from one another even when the same student can do both. Our students never learn the strengths and deficiencies of various approaches, or experience how these diverse methodologies can be focused on the same concern.

Recently, we have seen an increase among educators in the desire to think cooperatively. However, this desire does not, by itself, lead to cooperative thought. Cooperative thinking is a skill that must be learned and practiced. Such practice is a crucial aspect of Touchstones discussion classes. The first aim of Touchstones discussion classes is to challenge students' compartmentalized skills.

Successful students prepare for class, learn from teachers, do well on tests, and apply what they have learned to new contexts. From another perspective, each of these strengths often involves a corresponding weakness. Such students falter when they feel unprepared; they are made uneasy when a teacher's approval is not forthcoming. They are often at a loss when there is uncertainty about whether a problem has an answer, and they can be intellectually distressed when previous models or precedents cannot be extrapolated to deal with a new situation. In other words, such students lack the skills that would enable them to think on the basis of inadequate information, without experts, where a solution to a problem does not have a definite shape or there are no previous models. Yet these are precisely the conditions that increasingly characterize our intellectual, social, and political world and force us to develop the skill we have called cooperative thought. Our students have no experience and practice in responding to the very situations that will confront them. The skill to respond responsibly is one result of the Touchstones Project.

THE TOUCHSTONES PROJECT

The Touchstones Project presently involves approximately 100,000 students in 25 states. The project sites range from inner-city schools in Hartford, Baltimore, Philadelphia, and Albuquerque to schools in suburban areas like Prince William County, Virginia and Greenwich, Connecticut, to schools in rural areas in Alabama, New Mexico, and Arizona. Students from the entire spectrum of social and economic backgrounds participate in both public and private schools. These students range from the highly gifted to those in at-risk programs and special educational classes. Extensive research with students in a Pittsburgh High School (Miller, 1990) as well as teachers' and students' reports from around the country indicate that after one year of Touchstones experience, students:

1. Realize that radically different approaches can illuminate an issue, problem, or task
2. Can cooperate with other students whose backgrounds, perspectives, and skills are different from their own
3. Can explore a problem where what counts as a solution is unclear, and allow the exploration to remain open-ended or devise strategies for a possible solution
4. Can think in conditions in which no one is an expert and that are characterized by "inadequate" information and intellectual uncertainty

The Touchstones Project develops these skills by bringing together specifically chosen texts and a specially designed discussion format.

Touchstones discussion classes generally meet once a week for a full class period. (In some schools there are two meetings per week.) There is no preparation for the class. A text from one of the four Touchstones volumes is read by the students at the start of the class. These texts are short and require no more than 6 to 8 minutes to read. The absence of outside preparation achieves a number of purposes. All students are placed on an equal footing. The brief allotted reading time results in the members of the group noticing different aspects of the text, so they are forced to depend on one another. Since the students do not feel entirely comfortable with their degree of mastery of the text, they also need to draw on their own experience to supplement their understanding. In addition, it is made clear early in the process that the teacher is not an authority on the content and so the discussion will not lead to a predetermined right answer.

The Touchstones Texts

The texts used in the Project are the four volumes of the Touchstones series (Comber, Maistrellis, & Zeiderman, 1985–1988). Volume 1 is also now available in a Spanish translation. The texts were field tested in various sites with students in grades 7 to 12 and adults. They have been used with participants of all skill and ability levels from special education and at-risk groups to highly gifted students to teachers, college students and faculty, and corporate executives. The materials were all edited by the creators of the Project. Different stages of the Project require different kinds of texts. To form a group in which people learn how to take responsibility for opinions and begin to think cooperatively, noncontemporary classics are most useful. In the second year, students increasingly make their own intellectual presuppositions explicit. Texts from other cultures and by minorities and women are most suitable as a tool to develop these skills in the discussion process. In the final stage, students begin to think cooperatively about their own concerns. This is fostered by pairs of texts in which a noncontemporary work and a contemporary work are juxtaposed in the treatment of a concern.

Touchstones Volume 1 is used by all students in their first year of work with Touchstones, whether these are middle or high school students. If the project is implemented beyond a one-year sequence of meetings, students use the other volumes in succeeding years. All the volumes are similar in approximate length of text. They differ in regard to the diversity of authorship and complexity.

Touchstones texts all fuse various degrees of familiarity and strangeness with regard to their fundamental presuppositions. This fusion is necessary to achieve the skills developed by the Project and dictates the use of noncontemporary works. Current works—newspaper or magazine articles or recent fiction and essays—manifest the same presuppositions as the students. They are, therefore, initially of no use in enabling students to discern their own intellectual presuppositions. What they assume is so familiar that our own assumptions remain invisible. The texts chosen for Touchstones, on the other hand, deal with recognizable concerns—revenge, happiness, geometrical figures—but in ways that are no longer familiar or obvious. In other words, the texts do not fit into our current categories of subject matters. Since these current categories determine our students' methodological approaches, the use of these texts enables students to get some distance from their own approaches to look at them and explore their strengths and weaknesses. The texts function as devices for the students to discern their own habits of thought.

The discussion format and the texts reinforce one another to develop the skills of cooperative thought. Since the texts are equally familiar and strange to all the participants, including the teacher, there are no experts on the issues that emerge. The issues need to be explored rather than settled. This encourages and requires a discussion format. Since the texts do not fit into the current divisions of subject matter, they require that the perspectives, skills, and approaches both of differing groups of students and apparently competing subject matters be employed in a complementary fashion to engage with the text. Some typical examples of texts from *Touchstones Volume 1* will clarify the approach.

A short excerpt from *About Revenge*, by Francis Bacon, deals with a subject well known to all the students but approaches it from a conceptually alien direction:

> Whatever is past is gone and can't be changed. Wise people know they have enough to do in the present and with whatever might happen in the future. They don't spend their time taking revenge. People who spend their time worrying about past injuries just waste their time. Also, no person hurts another person just to hurt him. Rather, it is done for his profit or his own pleasure or his honor or for some other reason he might have. So why should I be angry with someone for loving himself better than he loves me? Suppose someone hurts me because he is evil. Isn't that just like a thorn or briar which scratches me because it can't do anything else? (p. 5)

His reasons for being against individual acts of vengeance are practical rather than ethical. He is concerned about the effect the desire for revenge has on the soul of a person, not on whether a rule is being broken. The important issue for him is that the desire for revenge, especially when it becomes an obsession, corrupts the person who feels it. The students expect to be preached at, but aren't. Such a text requires that the students work together to reconceive a type of experience all of them take for granted. Another text is a passage from Euclid's *Elements*. As a text on geometry, this engages the interest of students who are comfortable and skilled at mathematics. However, Euclid's approach differs radically from that of our mathematics textbooks—it is not an axiomatic system—and his language is not what one ordinarily finds in mathematics textbooks. In order to deal with this text other skills that are rarely, if ever, present in a mathematics class are required. These are precisely the skills that characterize investigating a poem: interpretation, attention to use of images, and exploration of self-contained structure of rules.

These two selections are typical examples of how Touchstones texts act as distorting mirrors through which the students can discern their intellectual presuppositions and approaches. In the piece by Bacon, a familiar experience must be removed from the conceptual orientation familiar to all of us and reconceived. The Euclid text takes a different direction. Conventional subject categories must be surrendered and new hybrid strategies developed. These approaches make cooperative thought possible and can only emerge in a cooperative discussion format.

Students with diverse skills find they require one another to focus on the blend of familiarity and strangeness in each text. The student skilled in the analysis of poems can help the mathematically skilled student to think in conditions of uncertainty, where answers are better or worse rather than right or wrong. The mathematically skilled student can assist the others by teaching them to look for general principles underlying their thought and insisting on rigor in the approach. Although these texts both require and make discussion possible, they cannot create the skills necessary to discuss and think cooperatively. A specific approach involving large-and small-group exercises, explicit attention to the dynamical features of group discussion, and the utilization of degrees of interplay between students' experience and a text are necessary to create cooperative discussion skills.

Touchstones Discussions

Touchstones discussions are designed for groups ranging from 4 to 32 students. The optimum class size is 14 to 28 students. At the smaller range, the size of the class encourages the teacher to continue in the dominant role that characterizes regular classes. If the teacher remains aware of this danger, this problem is avoidable. The problems with having too many students—more than 30—are more difficult. Since the group sits in a circular arrangement, two difficulties emerge. Regular classrooms are often not large enough to accommodate a circular arrangement of 30-plus chairs and, therefore, another room must be used for this activity. In addition, the circular arrangement of the chairs can encourage private side conversations. These break the public character of the discussion activity and can create severe classroom management problems for the teacher.

The creation of a cooperative discussion group faces four issues that are dealt with through the first year in seven-week stages. These are specifically addressed by Zeiderman (1989). In the first stage, students must learn to speak to one another without the mediation of the teacher. This involves developing the skill of thinking about a subject, text, or issue without anyone claiming expertise and authority. This is achieved by the use of texts that encourage students to feel that their own experience is enough to make them sufficiently knowledgeable to speak.

The second issue and stage emerges once the teacher is no longer viewed as the focus of activity. The teacher's central position will generally be taken over by a few highly dominant students. The task now is to enable all students to view themselves as potential speakers. Once students do see themselves as potential speakers, they still tend to address their remarks only to certain other members of the group. In the second stage of the Touchstones activity, the students, through small-group exercises, discussions, and discussions about discussions, learn to focus on the dynamic relations of dominance, passivity, and disrespect for others that characterize any emergent discussion group, and to change these behaviors. These exercises will be elaborated later.

Once the students have realized that issues and problems can be discussed without an expert present and they have all started to act as potential speakers, they must in the third stage learn the skill of listening. Generally, all of us hear what we wish to hear or what we expect to hear. The students must now learn to hear what another speaker wished to say. In the first two stages the text played a role subordinate to the process. Now the texts and process take on equally important and interdependent functions. Students must learn to hear what other students say even if they disagree. They must learn to hear what an author has said even if initially this appears false or impossible. With the third stage, occurring in weeks 15 to 22 of the first year, the skills of cooperative thinking can become more central features of this activity.

In the first three quarters of the year, the students learn to take the initiative in the discussion but the format of the class is prearranged. In the fourth stage, students also begin to take on these responsibilities. They explore how to select a class period design that will enable the group to initiate cooperative inquiry. The students learn how to manage a discussion group. They learn when and how as leaders to intervene, and select the texts to be read (generally from Touchstones but in two sessions they prepare the materials themselves). They determine whether and what kind of small-group work will precede the full-group discussion and choose, if they feel it is necessary, exercises to assist the class pursue its discussion. In this last stage, they have taken on both the responsibility and the initiative for their cooperative thinking.

A group of ninth graders in the 28th week of Touchstones were allowed to choose a topic for discussion. Five very vocal students advocated a discussion on teenage sex and persuaded the rest of the class. The other students, however, insisted that these five take responsibility for planning and leading the discussion. The group of leaders met twice to design the format. By the next week's meeting, they had realized how volatile such a subject was and how difficult it would be to discuss it without getting into arguments and disagreements about it. They therefore designed a format focusing on small-group work, which was to last for half the class period. The task they assigned the small groups was to consider the difficulties of such a discussion and strategies to avoid these. They then brought the class together to hear their reports and moved into a discussion on the topic lasting about 15 minutes. These students had learned to recognize that a topic they wished to discuss would fractionalize a group and devised an approach that made cooperation possible.

Cooperation is a skill that must be learned. In Touchstones classes, this skill is developed by small-group work and large-group exercises focused on the particular impediments to cooperation. From the very first meeting of the year, it is important for the teacher to convey to the students that the Touchstones' activity is theirs. However, this is at first merely a piece of information. It becomes a reality as the students take increased responsibility for the direction of the class. This occurs in small-group work and also in large-group discussions about the problems and successes of the group which are encouraged throughout the year.

Structure of a Touchstones Class

A typical Touchstones class has a number of segments, each designed to encourage the students to take ownership of the activity and to learn to cooperate. The class generally lasts for 40 to 45 minutes. Students enter the classroom, move the chairs into a large circle, and choose where and next to whom they sit. The books are then distributed. The text to be discussed is read aloud and then silently. Students are then given time to write down a question they feel would be interesting to discuss. Next, students work in small groups of three to five members, either assisting one another in reformulating their individual questions, devising a group question, or discussing how to approach a text as if they were to lead the discussion. The small-group work is always composed of task-oriented activites requiring cooperation. When the class reconvenes, the groups report their results to the class. A Touchstones class occurring about 10 weeks into the year raises the cooperative task to a different level. In this meeting, the students are divided into two groups. For the first 10 to 12 minutes one of the groups will discuss a text while the other group sits in an outside circle and uses a student observation sheet. The observers keep track of the speech incidents, determine the reason for silences if these occur, and evaluate the discussion itself—giving a grade and justifying it. In the second segment of the class, the groups switch roles and go through the same process. In the last 12 minutes of the class, the entire class is reunited. The students in the outer circle present their reports, propose recommendations for class improvements, and discuss these. At this stage the students begin to cooperate, not only on specific tasks, but also on the issue of how to deal with those areas where the group is failing to cooperate.

The roles of the students change drastically as the year progresses. Though the students are told that the teacher is not the source of answers in the discussion and that they can initiate the questions and the discussion, their habits and expectations about a classroom activity carry over into the first Touchstones classes. They address their remarks to or through the teacher and expect their answers to be right or wrong. As this changes, the students take on greater responsibility for the initiation of the discussion, the directions for improvement, and eventually for the leadership itself. The goal of the first year in regard to the students' role is that in the last seven classes they, in groups of 3 to 6, will choose the text and lead the large group discussion. A crucial moment in this transformation of roles occurs in the 22nd week. The students spend one session working on the issues involved in leading discussions. They receive a handout describing 10 typical situations that can arise in a discussion and that require a leader to decide whether and how to intervene. As exhibited in the two samples shown below, each situation is followed by three possible interventions by the leader.

1. There is five-second period of silence.
   a. Ask another question.
   b. Call on a student to speak.
   c. Wait a little longer to see if a student will speak.
2. Some members of the group keep talking to their neighbors.
   a. Tell them to stop and remind them of the ground rules.
   b. Ask them if they would like to say what they just said to the whole group.
   c. Pretend not to notice it. (p. 157)

The students choose among options, give reasons for their choices, and discuss the benefits and defects of the possible interventions. Following this class, the students take on the role of leader that the teacher has modeled through the year.

The Touchstones Discussions Leader

The most complex aspect of the Touchstones process is the role of the teacher as discussion leader. The teacher-leader is neither the source of authority on the content of the text, nor the judge of the value or correctness of the student's opinions. Nor is the teacher simply a mere observer of the process. The teacher remains a teacher but with different goals and responsibilities. The teacher's goal is to enable the students to conduct the discussion themselves by the end of the first year. To achieve this, teachers continually make decisions about whether and how to intervene.

The teacher-leaders are prepared to conduct Touchstones discussions through participating in a one-day workshop, or by viewing a 5½-hour video training tape. These sessions clarify the goals and problems of Touchstones discussions outlined as the four stages of the first year. Teachers then use the *Guide for Leading Discussions Using Touchstones* (Vol. 1) (Zeiderman, 1989) as a reference when conducting the classes. In the *Guide*, classes are divided into the small-group work and large-group discussions. During the periods of small-group work, teachers often act as they would in regular classes. They monitor that the groups stay on task, and assist each group by giving suggestions and by clarifying and explaining the task.

Once the large group discussion begins, however, the teacher's role shifts. At first the teacher uses the text to invite students to consider common experiences such as, for example, "getting even" when discussing Bacon's *About Revenge*. This is done to allow the students' own expertise to free them from dependence on the teacher's opinion and to maximize participation. In the early stages, teachers withhold approval of particular remarks. This forces students to realize that the success or failure of the activity depends on them. The teacher manages the situation in order, eventually, to turn over that responsibility to the students. The teacher's response to silences is an instructive example. In a regular class, a period of silence following a teacher's question is a danger signal. The teacher will generally allow silence to last for about 6 to 7 seconds before reformulating what was asked. In a Touchstones discussion an initiating or opening question can be greeted by silence, or an active discussion can suddenly stop and turn into silence. A Touchstones teacher-leader will generally allow a silence to continue for 10 to 15 seconds before considering an intervention.

A 15-second period of silence is painful for both leader and students. In a regular class, silence is viewed as the teacher's problem. However, in Touchstones classes, silence is seen by the leader both as a problem and an opportunity for the entire class. By not breaking the silence, the leader makes it clear that the problem of silence is everyone's responsibility. In addition, a leader will also view silence as an opportunity.

Often the student who breaks the silence is one who has had difficulty participating.

CONCLUSIONS

Evaluation

The evolution of a group and of the student's discussion skills can be studied, or the effects of participation on individual students in non-Touchstones environments—i.e., transferability of skills—can be investigated. Extensive documentation has been collected concerning groups and individual changes within the Touchstones format. Video histories of classes, in-depth interviews of students and teachers, teacher reports and studies of teacher/student participation, student/student collaboration, have all been collected. When teachers have adapted the recommended Touchstones format in conducting Touchstones classes, the studies show

1. A marked increase in student participation, initiative, and collaboration
2. Increased demands among students for evidence to support an opinion
3. Participation by students who are generally reticent about speaking in class approximately equals the activity of those who aren't
4. High activity by students of all skill levels who are generally disaffected

The issue of transferability studies is quite complicated. The means are being sought to determine which skills developed in Touchstones by groups and by individuals transfer into other school environments. One problem is that the format of regular classes often does not leave room for the skills of questioning and cooperating to become apparent. We are trying to deal with this by keeping teachers who are not leading Touchstones discussions informed about the project's methods and goals. In addition, it is not clear that an evaluation instrument presently exists that can quantify listening and questioning skills, or can determine successful collaboration in problem solving. Also, there is little general confidence about what is evaluated by the various critical-thinking tests and just how these might be utilized to determine the effects of participation in Touchstones. Attempts to clarify the difficulties in order to devise a useful evaluation instrument are currently being made in Maryland, Connecticut, Alabama, and New Mexico.

Student Responses

The three following vignettes show the evolution of skills and changes in attitudes typical among Touchstones students. In a Hartford magnet school where fairly skilled seventh graders participate, a class of 22 students was discussing a text from Euclid on geometrical straight lines. A highly skilled math student began asserting a typical textbook definition of a straight line. Another student, who is strong in English but never speaks in math class, interrupted. He told the math student that the words he was uttering were not his and then directed the group to the consideration of the quite different definition of a straight line given by Euclid. This student then led the class in a discussion comparing the two definitions. The results of this class were that a student alienated from mathematics found an entry into that subject, that a mathematically proficient student could recognize the need for developing skills enabling care and attentiveness to language, and that the whole class could become more reflective about what many were taking for granted.

A different kind of incident occurred in a Pittsburgh High School in a year-end discussion in which students discuss the Touchstones Project itself. Many of the students described their increased self-respect, ability to communicate, and sense of empowerment. A student described how he felt when he caused someone else to change an opinion. However, following this assertion he continued, "But what's really weird is when someone else changes *your* mind. When that happens, it kind of makes you feel whole." When he finished, many students in the group agreed. What is surprising is not that a discussion format empowered students; one would expect that. What is surprising is that having one's own mind changed by another student was not viewed as a diminution of empowerment. In other words, collaborative thinking was seen as a further instance of one's own strength of thought.

A third incident in Pittsburgh illustrates another form of empowerment. A class of 10th and 11th graders who are functionally nonreaders were discussing the scene in Homer's *Iliad* in which Priam came to retrieve Hector's body from Achilles. The students' access to the text was mediated by the leader's reading aloud of the text. The text was initially an object of fear, as are all writings for these students. Although Touchstones is not primarily a reading project, the discussion format makes the text less fearful. In this discussion, the students spent much of their energy trying to decide about a purely factual matter in the text. The teacher tried once to straighten them out, but they ignored his attempt. He wisely backed off and allowed them to handle the problem themselves. Finally, one student and then others slowly and laboriously read passages from the text to settle the matter. It didn't. However, what it did reveal is that a discussion format in which students take one another seriously enables them to confront their intellectual fears. Fear—and most students feel it toward some subject or necessary skill—can be mastered only when students realize the urgency of their need and feel the confidence necessary to attempt to satisfy it. This recognition and confidence develops in Touchstones discussions.

The Touchstones Project is only a first step in realizing large-group cooperative thought. As students develop these skills, it becomes possible to apply them in concrete ways in regular classes. Occasions should be sought where discussion skills and cooperative exploration can be utilized in the various subject areas. Facts, techniques, and many skills can be acquired by means of lecture, presentation, practice, and cooperative learning strategies. However, students most fully appropriate the framework that gives order, import, and significance to information and grasp the long-range purposes that bestow life on specific skills through the cooperative thinking and exploration that occurs in discussion. In a technological world, Descartes's solitary *cogito* must surrender its primacy to cooperative thought.

REFERENCES

Comber, G., Maistrellis, N., & Zeiderman, H. (Eds.) (1985–1988). *Touchstones* (Vols. 1–3). Annapolis, MD: CZM Press.

Miller, S. (1990, April). *Critical thinking in classroom discussion of texts: An ethnographic perspective.* Paper presented at the annual meeting of the American Educational Research Association, Boston.

Zeiderman, H. (1989). *A guide for leading discussions using Touchstones* (Vol. 1). Annapolis, MD: CZM Press. [Touchstones volumes and the *Guide for Leading Discussions* are available from CZM Associates Inc., 48 West St., Suite 104, Annapolis, MD 21401]

10

Cooperating for Concept Development

Linda Hanrahan Mauro and Lenore Judd Cohen

The development of conceptual knowledge is a lifelong process that begins at an early age and continues in both school and everyday life. Concepts enable us to categorize and classify knowledge and experience; by developing concepts, we provide frameworks for our continued learning. The teaching of concepts may well be the most important teaching we do.

Teachers, teacher educators, and staff developers have for years both used and advocated the use of two particular models of teaching that are especially effective in the teaching of concepts. The models of teaching known as concept attainment and concept formation offer three major strengths.

1. Students are active participants in the process of attaining and forming concepts.
2. Critical thinking occurs as students participate in the natural processes of comparing and contrasting examples.
3. Metacognitive skills are developed as students reflect on the ways in which they use examples and nonexamples to develop conceptual understanding.

These models have been used successfully with diverse sets of learners, across grade levels and content areas, in a variety of settings, and with concepts varying in degrees of difficulty.

The two scenarios presented below provide glimpses of two different teachers teaching two different concepts to students at two different grade levels. The first scenario describes the beginning of a concept attainment lesson; the second scenario portrays a concept formation lesson in progress.

- *Scenario 1.* All eyes are on the teacher, who stands well prepared and encouraging before his sixth-grade language arts class. He has carefully planned the day's writing lesson. His goal is to develop further among his students the concept of descriptive writing; he has chosen to do so inductively. Clear examples and nonexamples of the concept have been printed on large pieces of construction paper. One at a time, in preselected order, the teacher displays on the front blackboard first an example and then a nonexample of good descriptive writing. In the area designated "examples," the teacher hangs a sentence strip printed with, "Hunched over against the cold, the old man crept cautiously down the lonely street." In the "nonexamples" area, the teacher puts, "The man walked down the street." He displays another example: "The table was littered with crumbs, and the sink was stacked with dirty dishes," and then a nonexample: "The kitchen was a mess." The teacher asks his students to silently compare and contrast examples and non-examples in order to determine characteristics of good descriptive writing. Several examples into his lesson, the teacher pauses and sur-veys his class. Orlando is intently scrutinizing examples; Andrea looks confused; the entire third row reveals only noncommittal faces. The teacher proceeds with his lesson by reaching for his next best example. In the back of the room, a hand begins to wave wildly, and before she can be reminded to hypothesize privately, Karen blurts out, "I get it! I get what you mean!" and proceeds to describe her ideas. Karen has critically evaluated the examples and developed an understanding of the concept. Unfortunately, no one else in the class has yet reached that point.
- *Scenario 2.* Across town at the high school, the social studies teacher's overall instructional goal is for her students to better understand the concept of emigration. She asks students to brainstorm groups of people throughout history who have left their homelands for other countries. David calls out, "People came here from England. And from Ireland. And people are coming here now from Central America and the Persian Gulf." The teacher writes David's suggestions on the board and nods to Maria, whose hand is waving eagerly. "Soviet Jews are moving to Israel," Maria suggests. "And some Americans left the U.S. for Canada during the Vietnam War." Again, the teacher writes the student-generated ideas on the board. Two or three other students provide examples, but then the room quiets down and only David and Maria continue to offer ideas. In the next step of her lesson, the teacher asks students to group the examples into categories or classes. Students quietly contemplate the list of examples and record their attempts at categorization. Several students, including David, group the list by

geographic areas; others do it according to chronological periods; still others consider the reasons for the emigration. Maria works and reworks several possible classification systems. A fair number of students have blank papers before them. The lesson is rich with critical thinking . . . for Maria. But what about the others?

Concept attainment and concept formation are motivational and effective strategies for teaching concepts, but when used in a traditional sense, as in Scenarios 1 and 2, a variety of potential problems can occur. A more powerful use of these models occurs when the sequence of instructional steps is adapted to incorporate cooperative structures. A cooperative approach to the development of concepts further increases student participation in learning, establishes a mutually beneficial attitude toward critical thinking, ensures that all students more fully understand the concepts, and provides opportunities for students to mutually develop metacognitive processes.

BACKGROUND ON THE TEACHING OF CONCEPTS

The concept attainment and concept formation models of teaching are based on the notion that the natural learning process involves the learner in a continual act of categorization. As learners, we consider the examples of phenomena and experience that we encounter and then, through comparison and contrast, we develop broader conceptual understandings. In concept attainment lessons, the teacher first selects a concept to teach and then carefully structures examples and nonexamples designed to lead students to attain the concept; thus, students participate in the natural process of comparing and contrasting in order to learn. Concept formation differs in that a concept is formed rather than attained; in response to the teacher's facilitating questions, students generate examples, compare and contrast attributes of these examples, and eventually formulate an underlying concept.

Concept Attainment

The concept attainment teaching model as described by Joyce and Weil (1986) requires meticulous advance planning. Teachers collect 12 to 20 examples and nonexamples of the concept to be taught and then sequence them according to their power and clarity. During the activity itself, teachers present the carefully ordered examples, record students' hypotheses, prompt students when appropriate, and provide additional examples as needed. They guide analysis of the hypotheses, help to clarify the concept once it is attained, and facilitate a discussion of students' thinking strategies. Table 10.1 presents the basic syntax of the concept attainment model of teaching.

Concept Formation

Concept formation is an inductive teaching model designed by Hilda Taba (1967) to teach a specific thinking strategy. In this model, the eliciting questions asked by the teacher are the key to the lesson's effectiveness. The teacher asks a question that results in a student-generated listing of examples or ideas. Next, the students work to form groupings and categories of their listed items. Conceptual understanding develops as the students label and define their categories. See Table 10.2 for an outline of the syntax of the concept formation teaching strategy.

Difficulties with the Concept-Teaching Scenarios

The teachers in the scenarios presented earlier in this chapter are attempting to teach concepts. In Scenario 1, the teacher is using the concept attainment model to teach the concept of descriptive writing. In Scenario 2, the teacher is using the concept formation model to teach the concept of emigration. In each case the teachers might have planned a didactic instructional approach to the concept; they could have named the concept, presented a definition, further explicated the attributes of the concept, and then provided their own examples. Instead, they chose to develop conceptual understanding inductively by using concept attainment and concept formation.

The two scenarios are representative of dozens of classroom lessons we have observed and taught over the years. The strengths of the inductive approach are hinted at in both scenarios. Students participate actively in a categorizing activity that reflects the process of learning in a natural environment. The students are generally motivated and eager; these classroom activities are of interest to them. Skilled teacher questioning leads to critical thinking on the part of the students. These scenarios are glimpses of essentially good lessons, but they could be better.

Consider the first scenario. The teacher is well prepared; the students are attentive. The initial step of the concept attainment activity is proceeding smoothly . . . until Karen's enthusiastic outburst. True, skilled teachers can structure lessons so that such incidents are infrequent, and skilled teachers can smoothly respond to such interruptions and proceed with the lesson. But once a student has publicly proclaimed her under-

Table 10.1. Syntax of the Concept of Attainment Model

SEQUENCE OF PHASES	TEACHER BEHAVIOR
1. Present goals and establish set	Explains the goals of the lesson and gets students ready to learn
2. Present examples and non-examples	Presents examples and nonexamples
3. Compare and contrast	Emphasizes the comparison of the examples and contrasting with the nonexamples
4. Identify concept	Has students state the essential characteristics of the concept; concept is identified
5. Test attainment and justify	Provides additional examples; students individually test the concept to see if new examples fit their understanding and justify their answers; students generate own examples and nonexamples
6. Analyze and evaluate	Helps students analyze their thinking process and evaluate the effectiveness of their strategies

Adapted from Jantz, 1988; Joyce and Weil, 1986

standing of the concept, two unfortunate results can occur: (1) students still contemplating examples feel intimidated or slow, and (2) students as yet unsure of the concept latch on to the disclosed idea as their new hypothesis to be tested. Most of us who have used the concept attainment model have had students like Karen and scenarios like the one described.

Even without the unexpected interruption, similar occurrences can take place within a concept attainment lesson. Karen may hypothesize

Table 10.2. Syntax of the Concept Formation Model

SEQUENCE OF PHASES	TEACHER BEHAVIOR
1. Listing	Asks students a question that generates a list of objects and ideas
2. Grouping	Asks students to group the objects into classes
3. Labeling	Asks students to label the various classes of objects
4. Processing	Asks students to analyze the criteria they used for listing the items

Adapted from Jantz, 1988; Joyce and Weil, 1986

more privately, but some of her peers may still be all too aware that Karen has developed a hypothesis while they remain undecided. And more often then we know, our quieter or more tentative students, no less involved in concept building, may for one reason or another withhold ideas from group consideration. At worst, an atmosphere of competition leading to feelings of failure can develop; at best, good ideas may go unnoticed and unshared.

Scenario 2, the concept formation lesson, is similar in that its premise is sound and the general strategy effective. Again, however, several concerns can be raised. The first step in this model of teaching involves the listing of student-generated examples. When done orally, as in the scenario, a small number of students may dominate the activity by participating more fully than others. When the listing is done individually, some students may generate more or better examples than their peers. And the effectiveness of the second step in concept formation lessons, the categorizing, is in many ways dependent on the quantity and quality of the list of examples generated in step one. In Scenario 2, there may be students who feel like outsiders during this lesson on emigration. Unable to generate many examples, and unsure if their grouping strategies are appropriate, these students may not reap the full benefit of the opportunities for critical thinking. Maria is the only student in this scenario who actively compares and contrasts examples and classification strategies. Hopefully, the teacher in this scenario will proceed in the lesson to encourage the interaction of students' ideas for grouping, but too often we neglect the learning opportunities offered by the concept formation model of teaching.

The challenges faced by the teachers in these two scenarios are not insurmountable. Good teachers are able to establish classroom atmospheres of trust and respect; they are able to facilitate risk taking and hypothesis generating on the part of their students; they are able to encourage an active exchange of student ideas. Planned carefully and implemented well, the concept attainment and concept formation models of teaching are exciting and effective approaches to instruction. Through the critical thinking stimulated by these two models, students develop and expand their conceptual understandings.

What can we do as teachers to enhance the potential of these two models of teaching? How can we increase the likelihood that all of our students will participate fully in activities that involve critical thinking? How can we improve the depth and breadth of our students' conceptual understandings? It is our contention that concept attainment and concept formation are more powerful models of teaching when they are adapted to include planned structures and procedures for cooperative learning.

REASONS FOR TEACHING CONCEPTS COOPERATIVELY

There are three major reasons for teaching concepts cooperatively. The first is the development of a sense of classroom collaboration and interdependence as students work together to attain and form concepts. In "traditional" approaches to concept attainment, an uncomfortable edge of competitiveness can develop as students attain concepts at different rates and with varying degrees of success. The second reason for utilizing cooperative learning techniques is that students attain a higher level of concept development; by sharing ideas and jointly formulating categories, students expand and elaborate on their initial understandings of the concept. A third major advantage of cooperation in concept development involves the improvement of students' metacognitive strategies. When students hypothesize and problem-solve together during concept attainment and formation, they learn from one another alternative approaches to critical thinking.

Collaboration and Interdependence

The development of conceptual understanding is not only an intellectual goal but also a social one. The very process of categorizing phenomena and experiences implies an interdependent relationship in the development of concepts. Moreover, the possibilities for human communication and mutual respect increase as we expand the conceptual frameworks through which we view the world. What better way to promote respect for others and their ideas than to provide opportunities for working together in the exploration of conceptual understandings? What better way to fully explore the meaning or meanings of a concept than to share ideas with one another?

In the two scenarios we have been discussing, it is possible that students will compete with one another to make comparisons and formulate categories more quickly or more accurately. Students like Karen and Maria may relish the challenge of concept attainment and concept formation lessons, but their enthusiasm and quickness may be at the expense of their classmates' participation and learning. By intentionally including cooperative learning structures within the teaching of concepts, we enhance the possibility of developing mutual understandings of concepts.

A sense of collaboration and interdependence develops when students jointly generate or consider examples and then cooperate with one another to formulate hypotheses and categories. Students gain respect for others' ways of knowing and thinking as they mutually attain and form concepts.

Extension and Elaboration of Conceptual Understanding

Understanding a concept requires complex thinking. It involves the critical skills of comparison and contrast as well as the ability to categorize. When cooperative structures are used in the teaching of concepts, students extend their understanding by adding to their own thinking the ideas of their peers. Group members provide one another with additional possibilities for examples, hypotheses, and strategies. In addition, student thinking is challenged and elaborated on as students explain to one another the sources and reasoning behind their hypotheses.

In Scenarios 1 and 2, students are generally asked only to develop their own personal lines of inquiry. These individual attempts at concept development are less extensive and less elaborate than they would be if the teacher had employed cooperative learning. David had but one focus as he grouped and categorized the examples of emigration in Scenario 2; had he worked in conjunction with other students, he would certainly have seen that multiple grouping possibilities exist.

Concept attainment and concept formation lessons are excellent activities for critical thinking; add cooperative structures to them and the level of complexity increases, enhancing both the texture and depth of thinking.

Alternatives for Problem Solving and Metacognition

An important step in concept attainment and concept formation is the analysis of thinking. How did a student approach the categorizing? At what point were hypotheses generated? Were multiple ideas considered?

At the end of the typical concept attainment and concept formation lessons, students are asked questions designed to encourage reflection and metacognition. Some students, like Karen in Scenario 1 and Maria in Scenario 2, may be eager to describe their critical approaches to the learning task; others, like those in Scenario 1 who have not yet formulated a hypothesis, might not want to disclose their tentativeness. Seldom in the typical lesson do students have opportunities to hear descriptions of other students' problem-solving strategies, much less to see them in action. By working cooperatively in the development of conceptual understanding, students gain in-process understandings of alternative metacognitive strategies. For example, in cooperative versions of the scenarios, Orlando could share his initial hypotheses and then listen as Karen describes the ways in which she is comparing the lesson's exemplars and nonexemplars; David and Maria could exchange their reasoning in the development of systems for classifying examples.

STRUCTURES AND STRATEGIES FOR COOPERATION

A wide variety of cooperative learning techniques discussed in other chapters of this volume and elsewhere (Johnson, Johnson, Holubec, &

Roy, 1984; Kagan, 1990; Slavin, 1983) are excellent for use in the teaching of concepts. The concept attainment and concept formation approaches to concept development can be easily adapted to include the following simple cooperative learning structures:

- *Think-Pair-Share.* Think-Pair-Share (Lyman, 1990) is a strategy that utilizes the principle of "all before one"; that is, all students are engaged in thinking before any one student is called upon. In Think-Pair-Share, the teacher asks a question and then allows at least 3 to 5 seconds of wait time (Rowe, 1974) while all students are thinking. A preestablished signal is given, and students are asked to "pair" with their partners to share questions, answers, or ideas. When each student in the class has had the opportunity to interact within a pair, the teacher gives the signal again. Now, with the full attention of the group, the teacher calls on several students to "share" their thinking. Thus, by the time students are called on by the teacher, all students have had time for thinking and interacting (for an extended discussion of Think-Pair-Share, see Chapter 11 of this volume).
- *Numbered Heads Together.* In Numbered Heads Together (Kagan, 1990), three or more students are grouped together for the purpose of assisting one another in learning some information. Each student in the group must actively participate by giving ideas, teaching, and learning the information because any one of the group can be called upon later to represent the group. For example, in a group of four, each student is assigned a number from one to four; student discussion begins and continues until a predetermined time. Students discuss the issue and make sure that all group members understand and can respond. The teacher then calls a number and asks group members with that number to answer a particular question or to share the group's ideas.
- *Group Discussion with Roles.* A small group of 4 to 6 students is given a particular topic, question, or problem that requires brainstorming, analysis, synthesis, problem solving or decision making. Each student in the group is given a particular role to perform. For example, the initiator begins the group discussion; the recorder writes down the ideas expressed by team members; the encourager offers words of encouragement to group members; the resource person gathers any materials needed to complete the group task; and the reporter shares the group's ideas, solutions, or decisions with the entire class.
- *Round-robin.* Four or five students are seated around a table. A question, problem, or concept is posed to them. Students contribute ideas orally in turn, clockwise or counterclockwise.

- *Roundtable.* A small group of students seated around a table is presented with a question, problem, or conceptual issue. Each student in the group has a different color marker or crayon. Brainstorming on the assigned topic is done in writing as one piece of paper is rotated around the table from one team member to the next. When students are unable to think of other ideas to record, they ask a team member for assistance or they "pass." The paper is passed around until either the time limit has expired or until all group responses are recorded. The group's reporter shares the team's responses with the rest of the class.
- *Interview.* Two students interview one another; one is the interviewer, the other is the speaker. The interviewer listens to the speaker and may ask a series of questions related to a particular topic. A time limit is given so that the pair reverses roles after a specified period. Two pairs can then join to do a Round-robin, with each student sharing the partner's response with the other pair.
- *Team Concept-Webbing.* Small groups of students work together to generate a diagram of their ideas surrounding a particular concept. The concept is placed in the middle, then spokes protrude out from the center, and each idea is placed on a spoke or web.
- *Think-Pair-Question/List/Web.* These are adaptations of the previous strategies. Students are given independent think time and then pair to share their questions, lists, or webs.

Table 10.3 lists cooperative learning structures that are especially conducive to the various phases of the syntax of the concept attainment model of teaching. Suggested cooperative learning structures for enhancing the syntax of the concept formation model appear in Table 10.4.

INTEGRATING COOPERATIVE LEARNING WITH CONCEPT TEACHING

This section of the chapter provides explanations and examples of how to incorporate cooperative structures into concept formation and concept attainment lessons. Think-Pair-Share, Group Discussions with Roles, and Numbered Heads Together are suggested structures for concept attainment lessons; Think-Pair-Share, Team Concept-Webbing, Roundtable, Interview, Numbered Heads Together, and Round-robin are possible strategies for adapting the syntax of the concept formation model. Two lessons that integrate cooperative learning and concept teaching are described.

Table 10.3. Syntax for Concept Attainment and Cooperative Learning

SEQUENCE OF PHASE	TEACHER/STUDENT BEHAVIOR	COOPERATIVE OPTIONS
1. Present goals and establish set	Explains the goals of the lesson and gets students ready to learn	Think-Pair-Question
2. Present examples and nonexamples	Presents both examples and nonexamples	Think-Pair-List or Think-Pair-Web
3. Compare and contrast	Emphasizes the comparison of examples and contrasting with nonexamples	Think-Pair-Share
4. Identify concept and agreement	Has students state the essential characteristics of the concept in pairs	Think-Pair-Share or Group Discussion
5. Test attainment and, justify	Provides additional examples; students test the concept and justify their answers	Think-Pair-Share Group Discussion Numbered Heads Together
6. Analyze and evaluate	Helps students analyze their thinking processes and evaluate the effectiveness of their strategies	Think-Pair-Share Group Discussion Numbered Heads Together
7. Demonstrate understanding through independent practice of the concept	Has students independently create or find additional examples	Think-Pair-Share Group Discussion following the independent practice

162

Table 10.4. Syntax for Concept Formation and Cooperative Learning

SEQUENCE OF PHASE	TEACHER/STUDENT BEHAVIOR	COOPERATIVE OPTIONS
1. Listing	Asks students a question a question that generates a list of objects or ideas	Think-Pair-Share Roundrobin Roundtable Interview
2. Grouping	Asks students to group the objects into classes	Think-Pair-Share Group Discussion Team Concept Webbing Numbered Heads
3. Labeling	Asks students to label the various classes of objects	Think-Pair-Share Group Discussion
4. Processing	Asks students to analyze the criteria they used for listing the items	Think-Pair-Share Interview Roundrobin Group Discussion Numbered Heads

Cooperating for Concept Attainment

Let's return again to Scenario 1, in which a teacher is using concept attainment to teach characteristics of good descriptive writing. The teacher in Scenario 1 can easily revise the original plan and teach a concept attainment lesson in which the students cooperate for concept development (refer to Table 10.3). Phase 1 of the syntax of concept attainment can remain the same as in the original scenario; the teacher presents goals and establishes the focus for the lesson. Directions for the concept attainment lesson are given, and students are asked to compare and contrast examples silently as Phase 2 proceeds. After several pairs of examples are shown, the teacher begins a cooperative version of Phase 3;

Think-Pair-Share is used. After individual students have written down their preliminary hypotheses, they pair with a partner to discuss their thinking. Karen has already considered several possibilities and is eager to tell someone what she has determined; Orlando has developed one hypothesis that, when shared with Karen, seems to be on the same track as her thinking. In another pair, Andrea resolves her confusion by listening to her partner's ideas. The teacher presents several additional examples for the pairs to consider before she instructs each pair to join another pair for a group sharing of ideas. Using Group Discussion with Roles, the students discuss and record their ideas. The teacher calls on the reporters from each foursome to present their group hypotheses to the rest of the class. One group thinks specificity is important in descriptive writing; another group reports its belief that descriptive writing contains adjectives and adverbs; a third group focuses on visual images. Group results are compared and contrasted and characteristics of good descriptive writing are tentatively agreed upon. Numbered Heads Together is employed in Phase 5 as the teacher provides the group with examples for testing and justifying the hypothesis; the teacher calls on "numbered" group representatives to check for understanding. As part of Phase 6, the teacher asks questions about the students' thinking processes; the groups of four discuss the ways in which they considered examples to attain the concept. The Numbered Heads Together structure is again utilized to stimulate a whole-class discussion of problem-solving strategies. In the final phase of the model, Phase 7, the teacher returns to the use of Think-Pair-Share. He instructs individual students to write a descriptive sentence that contains the characteristics of the concept attained during the lesson. Students then exchange examples in their pairs and help one another revise their sentences and improve them for whole-class sharing.

This version of the scenario contains the same instructional objective, uses the same materials, and follows the same basic syntax as Scenario 1 presented earlier. The difference here is that the teacher has increased the participation level of the students and provided opportunities for shared learning. By utilizing cooperative structures within the lesson, the teacher has increased the likelihood that all students will have opportunities for critical thinking. Note that the lesson could also be presented with repeated use of only one cooperative structure: Think-Pair-Share.

Cooperating for Concept Formation

The following is a detailed description of a lesson that combines the concept formation model of teaching and cooperative learning structures (refer to Table 10.4). Like the lesson on emigration in Scenario 2, this elementary school social studies lesson begins with specific examples familiar to the students and builds toward larger conceptual understanding.

Prior to the lesson, a third-grade teacher thoughtfully considers academic ability, gender, and multicultural diversity as she divides her students into representative groupings of four. She has two sets of goals for this lesson, one is academic, the other social. Her students are beginning a geographical study of the United States, and she wants them to begin thinking about state locations, characteristics, similarities, and differences. Moreover, she wants them to do so in a spirit of cooperation. She selects concept formation as a strategy because it stimulates critical thinking.

After the teacher has assigned and seated her students in groups, the first part of the concept formation activity is done independently. The teacher asks her students to think about the specific names of the states that comprise the United States. She writes the word *states* on the chalkboard and draws a circle around it. She instructs her students to do the same and then to create a web of sample states. She allows approximately 30 seconds to complete this task, expecting that most children will list at least four states. "Listing," which is Phase 1 of the concept formation model, has begun. While the students are working independently, the teacher goes from group to group distributing four different color markers and a large sheet of chart paper. At the end of the allotted time the teacher calls "time."

The students are now ready to begin the second activity in this phase of the lesson. The teacher explains the Roundtable process and the Quiet Zone Signal (Kagan, 1990) to her class. (In the Quiet Zone procedure, the teacher signals the class for quiet by a raised hand. The students who see this signal then raise their hands, become quiet, alert their group members, and look up at the teacher. Once the class is quiet the teacher continues with the next set of directions.) Each child in the group chooses a different color marker. The sheet of paper rotates clockwise from child to child. Using their independently generated webs as a reference, the children take turns writing down the names of different states. If the point is reached at which a child is unable to think of another state's name, the rest of the group assists and the child records the suggested state on the sheet of paper. The teacher sets a time limit of approximately two minutes for the Roundtable activity, hoping that in that time each group will generate a list of states. While the students participate in Roundtable, the teacher walks around to each group and monitors the activity. At the end of the allotted time, or when each group has approximately 16 states, the teacher gives the preestablished Quiet Zone Signal.

In Grouping, the second phase of this concept formation lesson, the teacher asks the students to look at the lists they have generated and think about how they might group the various states. After a minute of individual think/write time, the teacher gives specific roles to each child in each group for the Group Discussion with Roles. Group members count off from one to four; no. 1 in each group is the recorder and takes down on chart paper the ideas that are generated, no. 2 is the initiator who begins the activity and makes sure each person has an opportunity to participate, no. 3 will later report the group's action to the whole class, and no. 4 will act as the facilitator, encouraging and reflecting on the cooperation and the consensus building in the group. The teacher begins the Group Discussion with Roles by challenging the groups to come up with a method for categorizing their lists of states. Once the group discussions have begun, the teacher monitors the social and academic progress of her students by rotating from group to group. As she wanders, she notes that the groups are considering geography, state size, climate, beginning letters, and states group members have visited. When appropriate, the teacher facilitates the group activity by asking: What are some ways in which we can put these states together? Which states belong together? What are your reasons for putting these states together in this way? Are there other relationships among the states that would justify organizing them into different groupings? Why does this state go there? The activity has a definite deadline so that students know how much time they have.

After using the Quiet Zone Signal and gaining the attention of the entire class, the teacher begins Phase 3, Labeling, by asking the students to consider silently the groupings on the chart paper and to begin to think of possible labels or category headings for these groupings. She gives 30 seconds of individual think time and then begins group discussion again. The students continue in their previously assigned group roles; the teacher monitors the activity. The group's task is to reach consensus regarding group labels. After approximately two minutes, the teacher calls for group reports. Group reporters share their group's thinking with the rest of the class.

Phase 4 of the concept formation lesson begins after each group has reported its labeling ideas. The teacher then asks the class to reflect on the exercise. The following three questions are put on an overhead or the chalkboard:

1. What criteria did you use for grouping the states the way in which your group did?
2. What was going through your mind as you were grouping the states?
3. How did your group arrive at consensus?

Time is provided for individual consideration and reflection of these questions.

The teacher divides the groups of four into two pairs to conduct an Interview consisting of these questions. Group member no. 1 interviews no. 4, and after one minute no. 4 interviews no. 1; group members no. 2 and no. 3 follow the same procedures.

After the interviews are completed, the group gets back together and a Round-robin is implemented. Group member no. 4 shares the information learned from no. 1 with the group, no. 1 shares the information from no. 4, and no. 3 and no. 2 share the information learned from each other. The teacher monitors the timing of the Round-robin and gives the Quiet Zone Signal when the activity has ended. Group member no. 3, the group reporter, shares one or two group learnings with the rest of the class. The teacher concludes the concept formation lesson by asking students to compare and contrast the various groups' ideas and processes.

In this lesson, elementary school students have reviewed their prior knowledge of the states, considered various ways in which state can be compared and contrasted, and improved their metacognitive strategies as they reflected on their proposed state groupings. Each step of this concept formation lesson involves cooperative structures, thus enabling the students to share ideas and learn from one another. The secondary school lesson on emigration, described in Scenario 2, can be altered in similar ways. High school students can develop a conceptual understanding of emigration while simultaneously developing a sense of classroom collaboration.

SUMMARY

Concept development, cooperation and mutual respect, and critical thinking and problem solving should be essential goals of all classroom teachers. Instructional strategies and structures that promote these goals lead to personal, social, and academic gains for our students. In this chapter we describe concept attainment and concept formation, proven models of teaching concepts. We emphasize the impact of integrating cooperative learning techniques into the syntax of these models. An atmosphere of cooperation and mutual respect develops in the classroom, and the possibilities for critical thinking and problem solving are expanded. Two strong models of teaching become even more effective when students cooperate for concept development. "As one piece of iron sharpens another, so too do two students sharpen each other" (Chama, 3rd century).

REFERENCES

Arends, R. I. (1988). *Learning to teach.* New York: Random House.

Chama, R. (3rd century). Taanit 7A. In *Babylonian Talmud* (27:17).

Jantz, R. (1988). Teaching concepts for higher-level thinking. In R. I. Arends, *Learning to teach* (pp. 318–360). New York: Random House.

Johnson, D. W., Johnson, R. T., Holubec, E. J., & Roy, P. (1984). *Circles of learning.* Alexandria, VA: Association for Supervision and Curriculum Development.

Joyce, B., & Weil, M. (1986). *Models of teaching* (2nd ed.). Englewood Cliffs, NJ: Simon and Schuster.

Kagan, S. (1990). *Cooperative learning: Resources for teachers.* San Juan Capistrano, CA: Resources for Teachers.

Lyman, F. T. (1981). The responsive classroom discussion: The Inclusion of all students. In A. Anderson (ed.) *Mainstreaming Digest.* College Park: University of Maryland Press, pp. 109–113.

Lyman, F. (1990). Concept Development Structures: Think-Pair-Share. In S. Kagan, *Cooperative learning: Resources for teachers.* San Juan Capistrano, CA: Resources for Teachers.

Rowe, M. B. (1974). Wait-time and rewards as instructional variables: Their influence on language, logic, and fate control. *Journal of Research in Science Teaching, 11,* 291-308.

Slavin, R. (1983). *Cooperative learning.* New York: Longman.

Taba, H. (1967). *Teacher's handbook for elementary social studies.* Reading, MA: Addison-Wesley.

11

Think-Pair-Share, Thinktrix, Thinklinks, and Weird Facts
An Interactive System for Cooperative Thinking

Frank T. Lyman, Jr.

A classroom is a psychologically and logistically complex social and intellectual ecosystem in which all elements are in dynamic relationship with one another. Understanding and manipulating these elements to create maximum student response is crucial to the teaching of thinking and cooperation. This chapter is about the inclusion of all learners in an interactive, responsive, cooperative, thinking environment. It is about the journey of the mind in the classroom.

Crucial classroom elements are

Wait time (the space for thought)
Cooperative learning (the sharing of thought)
Cognitive mapping (the shaping of thought)
Context cueing (the referents for thought)
Problematics (the fuel of thought)
Theory making (the ownership of thought)
Thinking symbols (the sharing of metathought)
Signaling (the cueing of thought)

The chapter will show the interaction of these crucial elements within four central teaching/learning strategies: Think-Pair-Share, Thinktrix, Thinklinks, and Weird Facts. The framework is Think-Pair-Share as a central vehicle for classroom interaction; Thinktrix, or Thinking Matrix, for shared metacognition; Thinklinks, or cognitive mapping, for the generation and organization of thought; and Weird Facts, or conceptual incongruity, for the drive to know. All the strategies and built-in elements are generic—usable in kindergarten through graduate school in all content areas.

THINK-PAIR-SHARE AS A CENTRAL VEHICLE

Think-Pair-Share (Lyman, 1981, 1989) is a multimode, cooperative learning strategy that incorporates wait time, pair learning, and signaling. Whereas the traditional lecture/recitation model consists strictly of listening and sharing in the large group, in the listen-think-pair-share cycle students listen, always think for at least 3 seconds (wait time 1), interact with a partner, and sometimes participate in large group sharing, during which they again think for at least 3 seconds after each student speaks (wait time 2). The strategy is also a vehicle for numerous other structured, or "scripted,"[1] response possibilities in the share mode such as vote (thumbs up, thumbs down), show (fingers or objects), and choral speak (everyone shares at once), as well as for cognitive and social variations or "scripts" within the think and pair modes.

There are many variations of Think-Pair-Share. In a truly responsive classroom discussion there can be no teacher or student question or request (stimulus) that is not followed by at least 3 seconds of think time before the answer or action (response). This invariable wait time pattern will have several positive outcomes (Rowe, 1986) and is achievable if both teacher and students are committed to it. The technical secret to its survival is keeping hands down during the pause and varying the "scripts"—for example, using visualization and cognitive mapping for the thinking. Motivating students to allow wait time can be achieved by having them consider the value of having time to think before anyone is recognized to share, or conversely by having them consider the negative effects of not having a chance to think first.

Once students and teachers have accepted and mastered the thinking segment, or mode, they are ready to build in the pair talk. As there are several ways to structure the think mode, so are there a variety of "scripts," or structurings, of the pair mode. For example, students can come to agreement, be ready to share the partner's idea, interview each other as experts, or complete a cognitive map together. These options may be cued on the wall. When Think-Pair-Share is in place and the teacher gives a signal for large group sharing in the share mode, most students will have a rehearsed response, even if they have not talked to a partner. Consequently, the sharing will be approached with more confidence and competence. It will be more focused, more elaborate, more representative of students' true level of knowledge, more responsive, in the sense that students listen to each other, and generally free of misbehavior. A key share mode maneuver is for the teacher to allow, after each student response, at least 3 seconds of wait time 2 (time after student response and before next comment) for everyone to think before hands are raised again. The pattern of the share mode then is think, share, think, share, think. . . . There are also ways to structure the share mode wait time 2 into "scripts"—for instance, by asking students to repeat mentally the response, to evaluate, create analogy, probe cause and effect, or rehearse mentally their original response and/or their newly crafted response.

None of the above possibilities of Think-Pair-Share can be realized if students believe they are in a race for teacher approval. If the students understand the reasons for the waiting, the pairing, and the scripting, and if the teacher notices them for their thinking and cooperating, they will take ownership of the process. Otherwise, they will continue to think that the only way they can do well is to win the hands-up race and talk the most. They will equate schooling with public speaking and take their place in the natural selection scheme of things, forcing the teacher to remain with the bimodal listen-share recitation model.

Consider the use of Think-Pair-Share in the following example. The fourth graders are learning rules for placing quotation marks in dialogue paragraphs. Each student finds examples of quotation marks in a book and tries to figure out why they are where they are. Having found and thought about several examples, the students then work with partners to derive a rule or rules for using quotation marks. When pairs are ready with formulated rules, the teacher puts the rule or rules on a chart. Students are then directed to go back to the books to test the rules, which they do first individually and then in pairs. When the rules are validated, the students are given *Aesop's Fables* scene outlines from which to role-play a dialogue. While two act, another pair transcribes the dialogue. After everyone has acted and transcripts are examined, individuals think, then pairs decide where to place the quotation marks, applying the rule. Finally, the teacher gives Think-Pair-Share signals to ask the students to discover how their minds worked during the activity. They decide that they have thought: Example to Rule to Example, as will be explained in the next section.

THINKTRIX FOR SHARED METACOGNITION

Why should the teacher be the high priest, the witch doctor of the mind, concealing a secret litany of teaching and learning? In a responsive, cooperative, and thinking classroom everyone should know how the mind works. This premise underlies the classroom use of a basic thinking typology known as Thinktrix[2] or Thinking Matrix (see Figure 11.1). The Thinktrix consists of seven fundamental thinking processes, or mind

Figure 11.1. Thinktrix

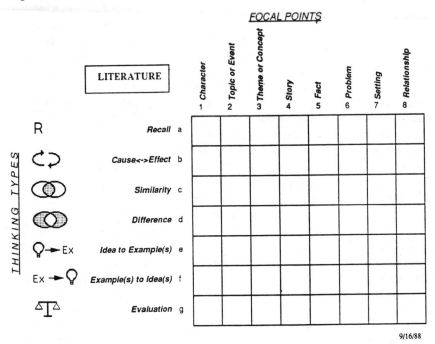

9/16/88

moves, on the one axis and content-specific focal points on the other axis. The thinking processes, or types, are recall, cause and effect, similarity, difference, idea to example (general to specific), example to idea (specific to general), and evaluation. They are represented by the symbols shown at the left of Figure 11.1.

Teaching the thinking types to children is not difficult, since the symbols represent the ways they think all the time. Generally, it works well to challenge the students to figure out the meaning of the symbols on cue cards or on the Thinktrix. The teacher uses the symbols to ask questions and shape answers on visual organizers, and when students become curious, the teacher helps them learn the meaning of the symbols inductively one by one. The more visual and kinesthetic the learning, the better: for example, teaching cause and effect by dramatic role playing and by using chains and tree roots to show the "shapes" of cause and effect. Once the symbols are understood, teacher and students use them to generate questions, make responses, and analyze thinking and writing. To cue the types, teacher and students can use various other tools, such as large and small wheels, manipulable cards and strips, and even hand signals.

Once the symbols are known, questions may be created or responses made from the thinking type alone, or the focal point (on the second axis) may be combined with the type to create a question (see Figure 11.2). For instance, a similarity question about a character might be: "How is the Karate Kid like Pinnochio?" Or a cause-and-effect question about a theme might be: "What causes prejudice?" To answer this complex cause and effect question, students would also have to use idea to example, example to idea, and similarity.

The seven thinking processes were distilled from a great variety of cognitive maps (Thinklinks) made by children, and have been field-tested since 1979 in Maryland classrooms. They have undergone an evolution in their use from teacher-question-generating cues only, to question-

Figure 11.2. Thinking Symbol Examples

R Recall	Tell the sequence of events in "Ransom of Redchief."
Similarity	How are the causes of the Revolution and the Civil War similar? What feelings does Pinnochio have that Wilbur also has? How is Johnny Dorset like Tom Sawyer?
Difference	How is a rhombus different from a parallelogram? How is a mammal different from a reptile?
Cause<->Effect	What are the effects of teasing? What do you think causes a rainbow? What would happen if the earth rotated only once a year? Why was Ahab wrong to push after Moby Dick?
Ex Idea to Example(s)	What are some examples of irony in "Ransom of Redchief?" From our list of stories, find some examples of friendship. Show some examples of the distributive property.
Ex Example(s) to Idea(s)	What are some character traits of Dorothy? What are the themes of The Karate Kid? From the evidence, what conclusion do you draw? From these examples make up a rule for use of quotation marks.
Evaluation	Was Ahab right or wrong to push on after the whale? What is, for you, the main theme of The Wizard of Oz?

response cues understood and used by students in grades 1 through 12 (Lyman, 1987; DePinto, 1988; Coley & Hoffman, 1990; Knight, 1990). They help students understand the basic moves of the mind, which make up the less accessible abstractions such as the levels in Bloom's *Taxonomy* (Bloom et al., 1956) or the commonly taught constructs such as prediction. Once understood, they can be used as cues to facilitate teacher- and student-generated questions; as response cues to enable students to operate cognitively upon data; as a metacognitive language to analyze steps and strategies for problem solving, decision making, inquiring, and creating; as a way to understand the structure and shape of written text and composition; and as cues to promote versatility and depth in oral discourse.

A scenario to exemplify the potential of the fully understood Thinktrix might be as follows: The teacher gives the students an assignment to make up several questions of different types and foci about the novel they are all reading. Using a two-sided game board matrix[3] (see Figure 11.3), pairs of students ask each other the questions, place a marker on the cells that indicate the type of questions, and answer and discuss the answers. The teacher moves from pair to pair, listening, reinforcing, and encouraging students to use a reference list of other stories to make connections. After the game board activity, individual students choose a question to answer in writing. Selecting an appropriate Thinklink, or cognitive map, prototype from 30 shapes posted on the wall (see Figure 11.4), each student graphically organizes the answer to the question. Then, using the Thinklink as a prewriting blueprint, the students write the answer to the question. When finished, the students share their diagrams and answers with partners, together labeling the types of thinking that were used in answering the questions. The teacher collects the papers, selects the best questions and answers, and has them typed up for a classroom publication. The above scenario could occur at least in part in grades 1 through 12.

Difficulties with the Thinktrix strategy, or reciprocueing,[4] include overlap when, for instance, an idea-to-example question requires analogical thinking, or when multiple types of thinking are required to respond to an evaluation question. Also, there is a continuum of complexity[5] within each thinking type such that a simple cause to effect question is far different from asking what causes prejudice. The latter question is classified cause and effect, but to respond to it, students must think idea-to-example, then example to causal idea, and then arrive at common causes by analogy, or similarity.

Another difficulty is that students who don't have a visual, kinesthetic concept of the types may depend exclusively on syntax to classify

Figure 11.3. Thinktrix Gameboard

THINK TRIX / Science	R / Recall	Cause and Effect	Similarities	Differences	Idea to Example(s)	Example(s) to Idea(s)	Evaluation	THINK TRIX / Science
Relationship								Relationship
Concept/ Principle/ Theory								Concept/ Principle/ Theory
System								System
Phenomenon								Phenomenon
Event								Event
Environment								Environment
Object								Object
Person								Person
THINK TRIX / Science	R / Recall	Cause and Effect	Similarities	Differences	Idea to Example(s)	Example(s) to Idea(s)	Evaluation	THINK TRIX / Science

Belinda Miller/Frank Lyman/Sam Pollack/Nancy Koza 1984-1990

Figure 11.4. Thinklink Prototypes

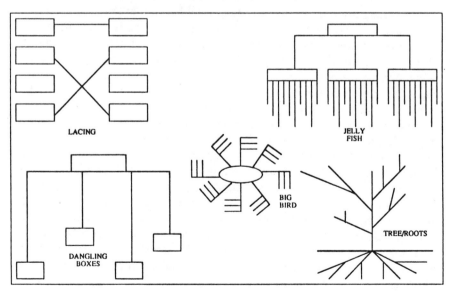

LACING

JELLY FISH

BIG BIRD

DANGLING BOXES

TREE/ROOTS

175

the question. For this reason it is not always wise to use lists of question starters for each type. A student who correctly types a hypothetical prediction question as cause and effect may get the associative clue from "What would happen if . . .?" and have no true understanding that the question is asking, "Given this changed cause, what would the effects be?"

A problem occurs when students associate the word "opinion" with the evaluation process. Since almost every response to any question is an opinion, it is inaccurate to use "opinion" only with evaluation. Evaluation is, in general, a critical weighing against a standard, but the more closely that evaluation is related to right or wrong, good or bad, justified or unjustified, the more useful it is as a cue to elicit question and response. Also, every evaluation question requires cause and effect or example-to-idea reasoning to answer.

Finally, the major difficulty with the Thinktrix is distinguishing between certain cases of idea-to-example and example-to-idea. Most cases are clear, such as when one asks for examples of symbiosis (idea-to-example), or for a classification of the pilot fish and the shark (example-to-idea). It is not as clear when the question is, "What are Pinnochio's character traits?" or "What are the economic problems caused by the Civil War?" In these two cases, the thinking is primarily from specific to general, but the question appears to begin with an idea. Since the unknowns are general, and the mind has to move from known specifics, the two questions are labeled example-to-idea.

Metacognition is crucial to critical thinking in that the aware thinker can more easily use the mind as a tool. The Thinktrix is a cognitive tool that allows students and teachers to know how they know, to dredge up and connect knowledge, to be knowledge makers. Through a shared metacognition the boundaries between student and teacher blur, structures of knowledge are built, and uncovering meaning becomes the achievable goal of a responsive classroom.

For example, in civics class, an 11th-grade student gives his opinion about the drug problem in his city. After he speaks there is a 10-second, hands-down silence. Another student gives a hand gesture signifying an analogy and procedes to draw a parallel to the alcohol problem during prohibition. After she speaks, she signals the other students to derive the most significant causal factor in the case she described. Her triple hand signal cues the students to think of causes, to evaluate by weighing them, and to write down an answer. After 1 minute, the student cues the others to justify their answers to partners for 60 seconds and try to reach agreement (the "consensus" script). The teacher then guides the sharing of ideas.

THINKLINKS FOR THE GENERATION
AND ORGANIZATION OF THOUGHT

Frequently utilized at all levels of schooling and in industry, cognitive mapping is a major medium for a responsive classroom. All thought has shape, and hence every response lends itself to a visual rendering. There are over 30 names for the graphic generation and organization of thought—one of the most popular names in a school setting is Thinklinks.[6] (When thinking is linked, thought will have been wrought.) The connecting of concept to example, cause with effect, structure to parallel structure (analogy) enables students to access and build structures of knowledge. The examples in Figure 11.4 are illustrative of some of the prototypical shapes of cognitive mapping.

Key factors in making thought-shaping a critical element of a responsive, cooperative classroom are modeling, metacognition, the cueing of prototypes, demonstrating utility, and student invention.

The teacher who organizes students' thoughts visually on charts or the blackboard will inductively communicate the cognitive mapping process to students. When they see example after example of "thought shapes," they will be eager to do the linking themselves. After the teacher has made the process seem to be an organic necessity for classroom discourse, the students can learn the shapes, and build their own repertoire.

Facilitating metacognition through a typology such as Thinktrix, the teacher helps the students classify questions and their thinking and select the Thinklink, or map shapes, that are most conducive to certain types of thinking. For instance, a chain or tree roots might be used for cause and effect reasoning. This combination of a concrete understanding of basic "moves" of the mind and the shapes that make the moves visible has far-reaching implications for the empowerment of learners.

Essential to this shape selection process is the cueing of the prototype shapes as well as the adding of new shapes as students invent them. Students are able to look at the wall cues, match shape to thinking type, and complete a cognitive map as a blueprint for discussion or written composition. This task can be completed by individuals or in cooperative learning groups of two or more.

It is important for students to comprehend the utility and versatility of cognitive mapping. They become excited about the process and convinced that it makes learning easier for them. One approach to motivating them is to allow them to create their own designs. When students are encouraged, they invent shapes, artistic embellishments, and color schemes that probably contribute to a deeper understanding of the ideas they are exploring. Also, students may come to believe that Thinklinks arise within them, rather than materialize out of thin air as many teacher initiatives seem to do. A student who has completed an original color-coded triangular concentric design showing analogous relationships among a poem, a painting, a song, and a story may now see that knowledge is constructed, not simply handed down.

Students should come to appreciate cognitive mapping as an efficient and creative means to various ends. If the teacher demonstrates that linked thinking as a "blueprint" can make written composition significantly less stressful and better, students will do the mapping even without being told. If they see that notetaking can be accomplished more efficiently and playfully in diagrammatic form, they will do it. If the teacher notices the quality of their thought shaping, they will want to generate and organize their thoughts in a visible manner. When they see what visual organization can do for rehearsing their ideas before speaking in a group, they will be anxious to spend their wait time doing a quick Thinklink. When they have done better on tests after studying in pairs from mapped notes, they will not resist organizing visually in preparation for tests. If they see the enhanced products and reinforcement resulting from generating and organizing their ideas in cooperative groups, they will want to shape thought cooperatively. In other words, though cognitive mapping is a tried and true universal strategy, students have to know what is in it for them; they must take ownership.

Cognitive mapping provides a meeting ground for prior knowledge and new knowledge. For teacher and student there is no better way to assess thinking than to "see" it, no better way to make use of knowledge than to shape it first. For too long we have been asking ourselves and students to come full blown with product, to cut out of whole cloth. Thinklinks take care of the framework, allowing the content to be released. The river flows within its banks.

"What is prejudice? What are the effects of teasing? How do people remember? What is a true friend? What is the value of making a mistake? Why do people fake? How do we learn from reading?" The seventh graders, well versed in creating theoretical propositions from relevant questions as well as in making up the questions themselves, choose a question, classify the type of thinking they will have to do (idea-to-example, cause and effect, analogy, or similarity), pick an appropriate cognitive map shape, or Thinklink prototype, begin scanning their prior knowledge from memory as well as from cued lists of familiar contexts, choose contexts/cases, derive causes, find common causes, and transcribe their findings onto the selected visual organizer (Thinklink). Once the individual students are well into this process, the teacher cues them to share their thinking with a partner, asking each other for additional ideas (the "add-on" script).

After ten minutes of paired discussion, the teacher, who has been moving around the room seeing and listening to the thought crafting, stops the pairs and praises the class on another session of effective "theory making." She then asks the individuals to select one of their recently completed Thinklinks and be ready to convert the organized thinking into a written composition the next day.

WEIRD FACTS

Having something worthwhile to think about is as crucial as any facilitating strategy for thought. The drive to know, or epistemic motivation (Berlyne, 1960), can be stimulated by conceptual incongruities or "weird facts." Whether these apparent anomalies be discrepant events, far-out theories, strange phenomena, paradoxes, puzzling questions, or mind-bending problems, they create an itch that must be scratched. When the mind is thus perplexed and fueled, it will persist in inquiry. Such problematics are a key ingredient in cooperative learning and thinking since they take the minds off the form and onto the content, away from self-consciousness and toward world consciousness. To be perplexed or astonished is to be ready to think and learn. Also, a calculated and consistent use of conceptual incongruity will open students up to each other as well as to inquiry, since nothing breaks the ice better than pair and square (four students) discussion of weird facts.

Third-grade students, seated with partners, can ponder deep sea fish with beacon lights, apes communicating with sign language, a pilot fish and a shark. Each child tries to astound the others with a weirder fact, creating an atmosphere resembling a joke-telling session. There is laughter, disbelief, questioning, a compulsion to share. One student, eager to outdo his partner, starts a string of analogies to the pilot fish and the shark; another hypothesizes how the ape can talk in sign; still another, impressed by a picture of a leaping armadillo, tells of the incredible exploits of her cat. One child, given a classification (example-to-idea) signal by his partner, attempts to label a weird fact by seeking its essence. Upon a cue from the teacher, the pairs team with other pairs to form squares, and one student shares his partner's fact with the other pair. Animated conversation ensues after the astonished listeners have finished laughing and doubting.

SUMMARY

Cooperative sharing, allowing thought space, shaping, connecting to referents, fueling through problematics, owning by constructing knowledge, meta-thought-sharing, and cueing: all these elements are part of a social, intellectual ecosystem and are crucial to a thinking, cooperative, minds-on classroom. When the key elements are combined within strategies such as Think-Pair-Share, Thinktrix, Thinklinks, and Weird Facts the resultant inclusive and responsive classroom is a safe haven for the mind's journey.

NOTES

1. "Scripting" is a term coined by Don Dansereau and associates in 1984. "Scripting" is defined by Dansereau as the "specification of processing roles and activities for interacting dyads." In this chapter, scripting is applied to other modes as well.

2. Coined by Tom Payne of the Howard County, Maryland, schools.

3. Invented by Belinda Miller.

4. Classification used by Thomasina DePinto of Carroll County schools and Joan Coley of Western Maryland College.

5. Developed by Sam Pollack of the Howard County, Maryland, schools.

6. A term coined by Tom Bruner in 1975, it is used widely in Howard County, Maryland, and throughout the state. The term describes a variety of diagrammatic thought shapes, some of which I first utilized with children in 1965 at Estabrook School in Lexington, Massachusetts.

REFERENCES

Berlyne, D. E. (1960). Toward a theory of epistemic behavior: Conceptual conflict and epistemic curiosity. In *Conflict Arousal and Curiosity*. Toronto: McGraw-Hill, pp. 283–303.

Bloom, B. S., Engelhart, M. D., Furst, E. J., Hill, W. H., & Krathwahl, D. R. (Eds.) (1956). *Taxonomy of educational objectives: The classification of educational goals. Handbook I: Cognitive domain*. New York: David McKay.

Coley, J. D., & Hoffman, D. M. (1990, April). Overcoming learned helplessness in at-risk readers. *Journal of Reading*, 497–502.

DePinto, T. (1988). Action research: a teacher's perspective. *Reading: Issues and Practices*, 5, 52–56.

Knight, J. E. (1990). Coding journal entries. *Journal of Reading*, 34(1), 42–47.

Lyman, F. T. (1981). The responsive classroom discussion: The inclusion of all students. In A. Anderson (Ed.), *Mainstreaming Digest*. College Park: University of Maryland Press, pp. 109–113.

Lyman, F. T., Lopez, C., Mindus, A. (1986). Thinklinks: The shaping of thought in response to reading. Unpublished manuscript.

Lyman, F. T. (1987). The think-trix: A classroom tool for thinking in response to reading. *Reading: Issues and Practices* (Yearbook of the State of Maryland International Reading Association Council, Vol. 4). Westminster: State of Maryland International Reading Association Council, pp. 15–18.

Lyman, F. T. (1989, September–October). Rechoreographing the middle-level minuet. *The Early Adolescence Magazine, 5*(1), *22–24.*

McTighe, J. and Lyman, F. T. (edited by Costa, A., Bellanca, J. and Fogarty, R.) (1992). Mind tools for matters of the mind. *If Minds Matter: A Forward to the Future*. Illinois: Skylight Publishing, Vol. 2, pp. 71–90.

Rowe, M. B. (1986). Wait time: slowing down may be a way of speeding up! *The Journal of Teacher Education, 31*(1), 43–50.

12

Graphic Organizers
Collaborative Links to Better Thinking

Jay McTighe

Think back to your own days as a student. Were you ever required to turn in an outline along with a paper you were assigned to write? If so, did you ever write your paper first and then construct your outline because it was required? I suspect that at least some of you are now chuckling with the recollection of this common coping strategy. Now for the really important question: Why is this so common when the purpose of the outline is to help us organize our thoughts in advance of our writing? The formal outline requires students to perform at least three important mental operations in advance of their writing—generating thoughts, organizing those ideas into logical clusters, and developing the sequence of the written presentation. While the formal outline apparently helps some students to organize their thoughts, many of us find it unnatural and unproductive. What does seem to work is the iterative method of writing itself. The very process of drafting and revising helps us to organize our ideas and information, clarify our thoughts, sharpen the internal logic of our paper, and arrive at an effective sequence. Following the completion of this writing process, the construction of the required outline was a relatively simple matter.

This is not meant to denigrate the importance of organization to effective writing; indeed, organization is a crucial component of effective thinking and its manifestation on paper. Rather, it is meant to raise a question about strategy; specifically, whether the formal outline is the most effective organizational method for all students.

In this chapter, we'll examine using a set of cognitive tools known as graphic organizers as an alternative to the formal outline for helping students organize information and ideas. We'll also explore ways to enhance the effectiveness of graphic organizers by integrating their use within a cooperative learning context.

FORMS OF GRAPHIC ORGANIZERS

Graphic organizers provide a visual, holistic representation of facts and concepts and their relationships within an organized frame. They have proven to be effective tools for enhancing thinking and promoting meaningful learning by helping teachers and students to

Organize information and ideas
Generate many ideas
Elaborate on ideas
Represent abstract or implicit concepts in more concrete and explicit
    forms
Illustrate the relationships between and among concepts
Relate new information to prior knowledge
Store and retrieve information
Assess thinking and learning

A variety of graphic organizer designs have been developed including the following:

- *Web*. The web features a central idea or topic located in the center of the design (see Figure 12.1). Related categories and supporting details branch out from the center. The web may be used as a vehicle for generating ideas (brainstorming) or as a means for summarizing newly learned material.
- *Sequence Chain*. The sequence chain may be used to depict the sequential flow of information, such as the progression of main events in a story (see Figure 12.2). It also illustrates the ordered steps in a process, such as the scientific method.
- *Story Map*. Since it provides a structural representation of a narrative, the story map may be used as a tool for analyzing a story (see Figure 12.3). It also assists students in developing and organizing ideas for an original story.
- *Main Idea Table*. This graphic organizer presents a main idea or generalization on the "table top," supported by the facts or details in the legs (see Figure 12.4). The "feet" may be used to document sources of information. The main idea table is especially effective as an organizer for expository or persuasive writing.
- *Character Map*. The map may be used to identify character traits through an analysis of behavior patterns displayed during various events (see Figure 12.5). In addition to serving as an analytical tool, the

Figure 12.1. Web

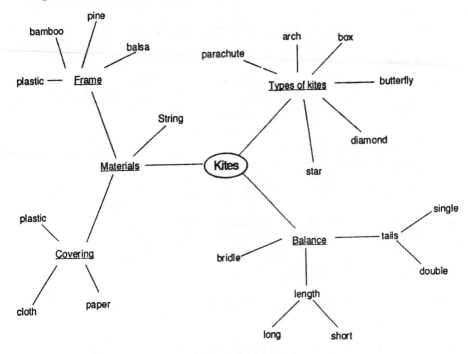

Figure 12.2. Sequence Chain for the Digestive Process

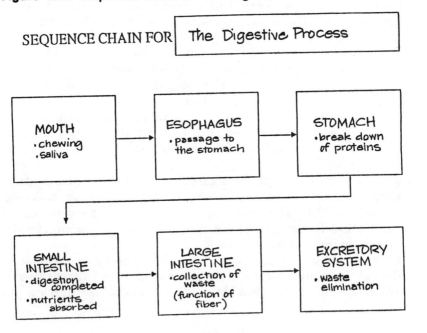

184

Figure 12.3. Story Map

Title: <u>A Christmas Present</u>

Setting:
> Time: Christmas Day - Christmas Day five years later
>
> Place: Sara Smith's house

Characters: <u>Sara Smith 5 yrs. old</u>   <u>GiGi, a pet monkey</u>

<u>Jelly Bean, a teddy bear</u>

<u>Spot, a dog</u>

Problem:
> Jelly Bean is Sara's favorite toy until she gets a new dog for Christmas. Then she doesn't pay any attention to Jelly Bean and he is upset.

Event 1 <u>Sara gets Jelly Bean for Christmas and loves him</u>
> very much.

Event 2 <u>Five years later Sara gets a dog for Christmas</u>

Event 3 <u>Jelly Bean cries every night and complains to GiGi</u>

Event 4 <u>GiGi tries to calm him down</u>

Event 5 <u>Spots runs away. Sara takes Jelly Bean on a picnic,</u>
> instead

Solution:
> Jelly Bean is happy because Sara learns that old things are just as good as new things.

Figure 12.4. Main Idea Table

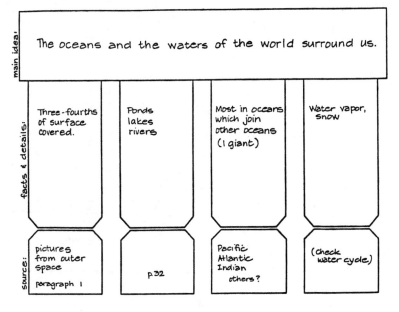

185

Figure 12.5. Character Map

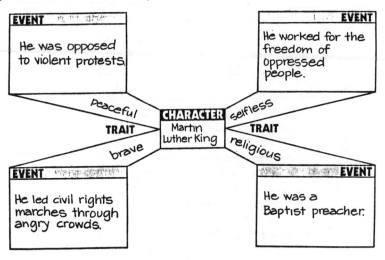

Figure 12.6. Attribute Wheel

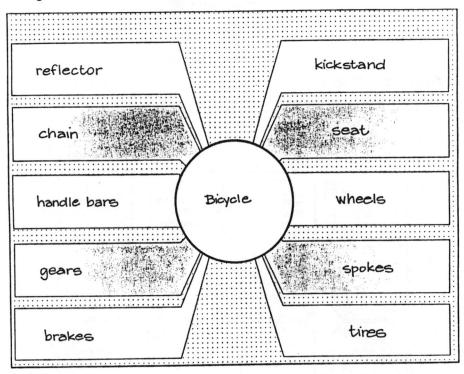

character map provides a framework for developing original characters as part of creative writing.

- *Attribute Wheel.* The attribute wheel provides a visual representation of analytical thinking (see Figure 12.6). The focus of the analysis (object, concept, system, etc.) is placed at the center or hub of the wheel while the major characteristics or attributes are listed on the spokes.
- *Decision-Making Model.* This thinking frame encourages students to identify problems, state goals, consider alternatives, evaluate pros and cons, reach a decision, and provide a rationale for their choice(s) (see Figure 12.7).

Figure 12.7. Decision-Making Model

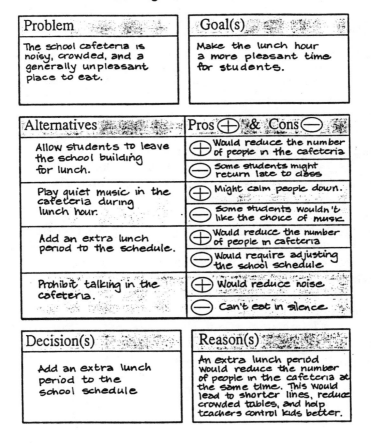

Figure 12.8. Venn Diagram

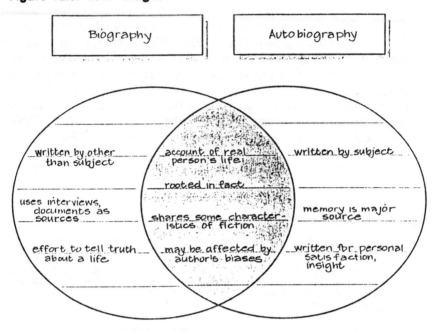

- *Venn Diagram.* The Venn diagram is used for comparing various dimensions or aspects of two objects, ideas, or concepts (see Figure 12.8). Similarities are listed in the intersection of the two ovals, while differences are placed in the nonoverlapping sections.

The selection of a particular form of graphic organizer is determined by the instructional purpose, the nature of the content, and the age and experience of the students with whom it will be used.

Graphic organizers may be used productively at any stage in the instructional process. They are effective when used *before* instruction to activate prior knowledge, to provide a conceptual framework for integrating new information, and to encourage student prediction. *During* instruction, they can help students to actively process and reorganize information. *After* instruction, graphic organizers may be used to summarize key points, encourage elaboration, help organize ideas for writing, provide a structure for review, and assess the degree of student understanding.

AN INSTRUCTIONAL PROCEDURE

Graphic organizers may be thought of as cognitive tools since they assist thinking. As with any new tool (or skill), a learning process including explicit instruction, modeling, guided practice, and independent application will facilitate the development of competence. Teachers wishing to develop the abilities of their students to use graphic organizers effectively are encouraged to refer to the following nine-step instructional procedure.

1. Develop an understanding of the concept of graphic organizers by discussing the importance of organizing information, various ways in which people organize information, and the benefits of using a visual organizer.
2. Introduce a specific graphic organizer by describing its form (e.g., Venn diagram—overlapping circles or ovals) and purpose (e.g., depicting comparative relationships).
3. Explain and demonstrate the use of the selected organizer with familiar information and then with new information or ideas.
4. Let students apply the graphic organizer for a specified purpose with familiar information and then with new information or ideas.
5. Have students reflect on the use of the graphic organizer by sharing student examples, evaluating the effectiveness of the organizer, and proposing variations.
6. Provide multiple opportunities for students to practice using the graphic organizer.
7. Provide feedback to students about their use of the organizer.
8. Once students have become proficient in the use of several graphic organizers, allow them to select their own organizers appropriate for specific purposes.
9. Encourage students to construct their own organizers.

Following such a procedure, students should be prepared for independent use of the graphic organizer.

LINK TO COOPERATIVE LEARNING

Cooperative learning may be broadly defined as any classroom learning situation in which students at all levels of performance work together in groups toward a common goal. Since cooperative learning engages students in the interactive processing of information and ideas, it complements naturally instructional approaches designed to develop student thinking skills. The link between collaborative classroom groupings and the use of graphic organizers is uniquely supportive, benefiting students in at least four ways:

1. Graphic organizers provide a focal point for group discussions by offering a common frame of reference for thinking.
2. The completed graphic organizer provides a "group memory" or tangible product of the group's discussion.
3. By working with a graphic organizer as part of a collaborative group, students are encouraged to expand their own thinking by considering different points of view.
4. The articulation of reasoning required by the use of a graphic organizer helps to render the invisible process of thinking visible for all participants.

FROM THEORY TO ACTION: CLASSROOM ILLUSTRATIONS

In this section, we'll take a glimpse at three lessons (at the elementary, middle, and high school levels) illustrating the application of three different graphic organizers. These lessons will provide examples of the use of graphic organizers within cooperative learning contexts. In each case, students have been taught, and have had experience applying, the specific graphic organizer being used in the lesson.

Lesson Example 1

Level: Elementary, grade four
Content: Social studies
Context: Students have reviewed the objective of the lesson—to arrive at a generalization about slavery—and are about to view a filmstrip on the topic.

Before viewing the filmstrip, the teacher:

1. Organizes the students into their cooperative learning teams (in this instance into heterogeneous groups of three)
2. Distributes one copy of the main idea table to each group (refer to Figure 12.4)

3. Instructs each group to look for specific facts about slavery that will be presented in the filmstrip and explains that these will be recorded on the "legs" of the table at a later time
4. Encourages students to take notes as they watch the filmstrip

Following the viewing, students are given approximately 5 minutes to discuss the filmstrip and to identify four facts about slavery. Once group agreement is reached, a designated recorder completes the main idea table by listing the four facts about slavery on the table legs. The teacher then refers the class to a large main idea table on the chalkboard. In succession, a spokesperson for each group is called upon to present one fact about slavery from their table. These are recorded on the board. Repetitive entries are omitted, and the class arrives at a synthesis of facts that are listed on the legs of the large table (see Figure 12.9).

The teacher then asks the students to determine the main idea, i.e., what generalizations can be made about a place that treats some of its people this way? Students are given several minutes to discuss this question in their learning teams and to arrive at a generalization supported by the facts. Each team records its "main idea" on a sentence strip using colored markers, the completed "main ideas" are posted on the board, and each team shares its generalizations about slavery with the class. A

Figure 12.9. Main Idea Table

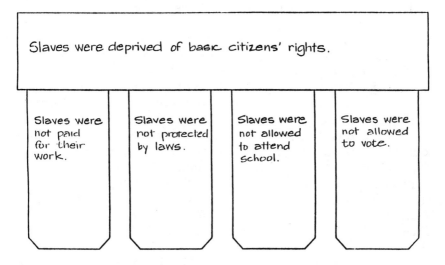

final class synthesis leads to the development of the general statement listed on the "table top" in Figure 12.9.

During the final activity of the lesson, students each develop one written paragraph about slavery using the information from the main idea table to guide their writing.

The main idea table is an especially effective organizer given the purpose of this lesson. Its shape represents visually the concept of generalization: a larger idea (the table) is supported by facts/details (the legs). Through the use of the organizer, the teacher was able to help students "see" the process of moving from specific facts/details to a more comprehensive and abstract main idea. The sharing of ideas in the learning groups actively involved students in the process of "constructing meaning" as they worked to make a generalization about slavery. In addition, the main idea table served as an excellent organizer for writing because it depicts the main idea and supporting details.

By providing each group of three students with only one main idea table, the teacher has reinforced a basic tenet of cooperative learning— positive interdependence. The single graphic organizer serves to focus the group's attention on the collaborative task.

Lesson Example 2

> *Level*:   Middle school science class
> *Content*: "Environments" unit
> *Context*: Students have just completed a reading from their textbook on deserts and tundras.

Utilizing the think-pair-share strategy (Lyman, 1989; see Chapter 11 of this volume), the teacher directs each student to list the characteristics of two harsh environments—the desert and the tundra—on the outside sections of a Venn diagram (refer to Figure 12.8). The students may refer to their textbook as they complete this activity during their 5-minute *think* time period.

At the end of the designated period, the teacher signals the students to *pair* with their designated partners and compare their Venn diagrams. The students are then instructed to complete the center section of the diagram by discussing the common attributes of the desert and the tundra. They are encouraged to think about and discuss the ways in which these two dissimilar environments are alike. Following the paired discussion, the teacher places a transparency of the Venn diagram on the overhead projector and signals the class to switch to the *share* mode. Students are then called on at random to help fill in the graphic organizer,

Figure 12.10. Venn Diagram

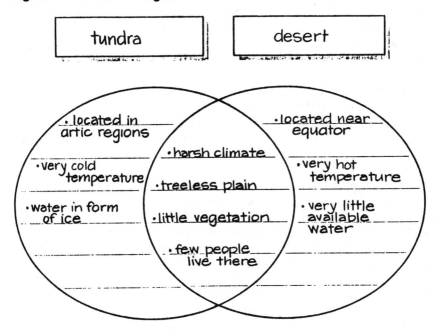

justifying their responses with information from the text and explanations of their reasoning. A completed class version of the diagram is shown in Figure 12.10.

For the final activity of the lesson students are asked to write a summary of the characteristics of a harsh environment, citing examples from the desert, the tundra, and any other harsh environment with which they may be familiar. Their completed diagram serves as a prewriting organizer. The written summaries are collected, reviewed by the teacher, and returned with comments.

The 30-minutes lesson actively involves all students in content reading, critical analysis of content material, paired discussion, and writing. While the textbook clearly describes the characteristics of the desert and the tundra, it does not explicitly present the similarities. The students are thus challenged to think more deeply about the concept of a harsh environment when they are asked to complete the center of the Venn diagram. The graphic organizer serves as a focal point for helping students organize information, discuss their findings, generalize the underlying concept, and organize their writing. The paired interaction and class

sharing encourage each student to contribute something to the completion of the diagram, while the writing assignment provides for individual
accountability.

Lesson Example 3

Level: High school English class
Content: American literature
Context: Students have read the play *Death of a Salesman* and have
           participated in a general class discussion during yester-
           day's class period.

At the beginning of the period, the teacher targets the objective of
the day—to analyze Willie Loman, the play's central character. He then
distributes copies of the character map (refer to Figure 12.5), giving each
student approximately 5 minutes to develop a preliminary character
sketch by making notes on the graphic organizer. Students work on this
activity individually, while referring to their anthologies.

At the conclusion of their individual thinking time, the students shift
to preassigned four-member heterogeneous learning groups. Group
members arrange their desks to form a square to promote eye contact
and to facilitate preparation of a group character map. Using their
individual maps as a starting point, the group members engage in a
discussion of the character traits of Willie Loman with the goal of reaching a group consensus. Since inferences about a character's traits are
developed through an analysis of the character's behavior in various
circumstances, the text serves as the reference point to guide the group's
discussion.

Following approximately 20 minutes of discussion and notetaking
on individual character maps, the teacher distributes a sheet of manila
drawing paper (28″ × 36″) to each group along with several colored
markers. Students select different colors with which to record their
specific contributions to the analysis. (*Note*: The use of a different color
by each student in the group encourages participation by all members
since the group map will visually reveal the degree of their involvement).
A group character map is then prepared (see example, Figure 12.11).

Upon completion, each group tapes its large map to a chalkboard or
wall. Given their own involvement in the character analysis, students are
eager to see the ways in which others interpreted the character's traits.
The teacher capitalizes on this heightened interest by concluding the
period with a "gallery walk" around the classroom to view the completed
maps. This brief tour provides students with a glimpse of the analyses of

Figure 12.11. Character Map

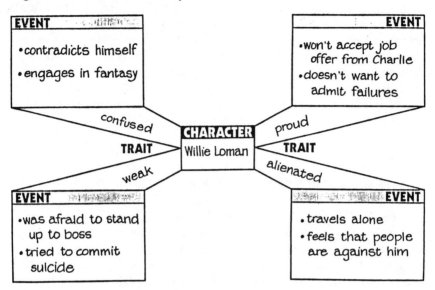

other groups in preparation for tomorrow's group presentations. The students leave the room with Willie Loman on their mind!

The following day, students meet in their learning groups and are given 7 minutes to prepare their oral presentation for the class. Each student in the group is responsible for discussing one trait from the group map. Desks are then arranged in a large horseshoe shape, and groups are randomly called to the center to present their character analysis to the class. Following the presentation, students may ask questions of the presenting group. This sequence continues until all groups have presented.

The final activity in this lesson involves the preparation of individual character analysis essays. Students complete their first draft for homework. They may refer to the notes on their individual character maps as well as the group map. The next day students meet in newly formed learning groups for peer response to their drafts. Peer responses are guided by the use of a praise-question-polish (P-Q-P) frame. In using the P-Q-P frame, students respond to the writing of other group members by presenting a summary of the strengths of the writing (praise), pose clarifying questions, and make suggestions for refining the piece (polish). The remainder of the period is devoted to revision, with final copies due on the following day.

During this 3-day lesson, students are thoroughly engaged in all elements of the language arts—reading, writing, listening, speaking, and thinking about literature. Because of the required oral presentation, individual written essays, and peer responses to both individual and group ideas, students are motivated to participate actively in the group discussions and to attend to the various presentations. As a result of such an engaging lesson, students find themselves becoming caught up in the process of trying to understand this intriguing character and realizing that cooperative thinking can be stimulating and enjoyable.

CONCLUSION:
THE WHOLE IS GREATER THAN THE SUM OF ITS PARTS

Teachers who employ cooperative learning methods promote thinking because these collaborative experiences engage students in an interactive approach to processing information. Research on cooperative learning substantiates its benefits: greater retention of subject matter, improved attitudes toward learning, increased opportunities for "higher order" processing of information, and enhanced interpersonal relations among group members.

Graphic organizers are practical tools that help students organize information and ideas. Research on the use of graphic organizers points out that these cognitive tools can help students to represent abstract information in more concrete form, depict relationships among facts and concepts, relate new information to prior knowledge, organize thoughts for writing, and assess understanding of new concepts. By combining these two instructional approaches, teachers can derive mutual benefits for enhancing the quality of student thinking and learning.

FOR FURTHER INFORMATION

Clarke, J. (1990). *Patterns of thinking: Integrating learning skills in content teaching.* Boston: Allyn and Bacon.
Dansereau, D. F. (1985). Learning strategy research. In J. W. Segal, S. F. Chipman, & R. Glaser (Eds.), *Thinking and learning skills, Vol. 1: Relating instruction to research* (pp. 209-239). Hillsdale, NJ: Erlbaum.
Fogarty, R., & Bellanca, J. (1989). *Patterns for thinking, patterns for transfer.* Palatine, IL: Illinois Renewal Institute.
Jones, B. F., Palinscar, A. S., Ogle, D. S., & Carr, E. G. (1987). Strategic teaching: A cognitive focus. In B. F. Jones, A. S. Palinscar, D. S. Ogle, & E. G. Carr,

Strategic teaching and learning: cognitive instruction in the content areas.
Alexandria, VA: Association for Supervision and Curriculum Development.

Lyman, F. T., Jr. (1989, September/October). Rechoreographing: The middle-
level minuet. *The Early Adolescent Magazine, 4*(1), 22-24.

McTighe, J., & Lyman, F. T., Jr. (1988). Cueing thinking in the classroom: The
promise of theory-embedded tools. *Educational Leadership, 45*(7), 18-24.

Novak, J. D., & Gowin, B. D. (1984). *Learning how to learn.* New York: Cambridge University Press.

Pehrsson, R., & Robinson, A. H. (1985). *The semantic organizer approach to
writing and reading instruction.* Rockville, MD: Aspen Systems Corporation.

Williams, P., & Reeves, B. (1987). *1987 Writing supplement* (pp. 13-41). Baltimore: Maryland State Department of Education.

13

Cooperative Questioning
and Critical Thinking

Charles Wiederhold and Spencer Kagan

How can critical thinking attitudes and skills be incorporated into cooperative learning groups? Through student-generated questions. This chapter describes the Q(question)-Approach, a method of ensuring student-generated questions at many levels of thinking. The approach is based on Bloom's *Taxonomy* (1956) and ensures teacher control of the levels of thought and an equal distribution of thought across all levels of the taxonomy. More importantly, it empowers students as question generators. The essence of the approach is best presented by the following example:

Four students in Room 19, a fifth-grade classroom, are seated with their desks facing each other. They are the Tigers, a cooperative learning team composed of Tim, José, Susan, and Maria. The class topic is endangered species. Each team is expected to generate research questions on that topic. José spins two brightly colored Q-Dials (see Figure 13.1). He gets *What Can?*, one of the 36 possible questions generated by six words on each dial. He writes the two words on his paper and passes the dials to Susan, whose spins give her *Where would?* As Susan passes the dials to Maria, José thinks for a few moments and writes his first question: "*What can* be done to stop the killing of dolphins?"

By the time the dials have gone to Tim, Susan has completed her first question, "*Where would* a whale hide?" In a few minutes the Q-Dials have gone around to each student twice. Each student checks for additional information in a science text, and in a few more minutes the Tigers have generated eight questions about endangered species. The cooperative learning structure being used by the Tigers is a variation of Roundtable, which asks students to create their own questions using specialized student-question generation materials.

The student question generation structures and materials discussed in this chapter are reprinted by permission of the authors and Resources for Teachers, Inc.

Figure 13.1. Q-Dials

Members of the Tigers read their questions, and they are discussed by the team. Fifteen minutes into the class period the teacher reminds the team that they have 5 more minutes to combine their questions into a research topic. After a brief discussion, Maria suggests that animals that live in water and animals that live on land should both be part of the research question. After checking additional source materials, the group agrees that there is plenty of material available to more completely research the topic and write a team report.

They struggle a bit with the question wording but finally settle on "Which animals are the most endangered in the United States?" and "Why are ocean mammals endangered?" The Tigers all raise their hands to let the teacher know they are ready with their question. The teacher writes the Tigers' question on the chart paper, adding it to the research questions generated by the other teams of students.

The bell rings and the period is over. The fifth-grade class files out the door with questions on their minds about animals, extinction, and life on the planet. The activities engaged in by the Tigers represent the fourth step in the complex group investigation model known as Co-op Co-op (Kagan, 1990).

The activities described differ from traditional whole-class teacher-directed instructional practice in two significant ways: (1) The questions are generated by the students rather than by the teacher, and (2) the questions are processed cooperatively by students within cooperative learning teams rather than by individual students in isolation.

The students in Room 19 are using questions in ways they have never used them before. They are using their own questions, based on their own knowledge, to explore and make connections about curriculum content.

Typically a teacher at the front of the classroom asks a series of questions directed to a whole class of 30 students (Goodlad, 1984). The students with correct answers quickly raise their hands. The teacher calls on a student; a verbal response is given. The teacher either acknowledges a correct answer, calls on another student, restates the question, calls on more students, answers the question himself or herself, or asks another question. Students who don't know "the answer" sit in dread fear of being called on or simply tune out. Students with "the answer" quickly raise their hands, and usually neglect to process several possible answers with the skills of a critical thinker. The questions themselves, according to a large body of research, tend to be at the recall or comprehension level in the majority of classrooms. Students who sit in strategic classroom locations are offered the most questions, and students who are perceived as bright with good verbal skills are offered the best questions (Good & Brophy, 1973).

The creation of questions in the form of quizzes, tests, and classroom dialogue, together with the production of student answers, constitute up to 80% of the learning time in most competitive classrooms. Unfortunately, about 70% of those questions are at the two lowest levels of intellectual processing. The cause-effect link between questions asked and thinking applied is well documented in the educational literature (Dean, 1986; Perez, 1986; Ciscell, 1987; McTighe & Lyman, 1988; Kloss, 1988; Wiederhold, 1989). If the questions are simple, so is the thinking.

FREEING STUDENTS TO QUESTION

If classrooms are to change from the whole-class question-answer structure to the Q-Structures practiced in Room 19, at least four factors must be considered: (1) teacher attitude, (2) cooperative learning, (3) critical thinking, and (4) student question generation. Each has the capacity to empower students as flexible, autonomous learners. Used together, they offer a powerful curriculum delivery system that is exciting, whole, and driven by student thinking as well as by prescribed content.

In working with teachers in critical-thinking classes, it is clear that the teachers most successful at implementing critical-thinking strategies are the same teachers who are successfully using cooperative learning. What seems to set them apart is that they are comfortable in a role of facilitating student-centered learning and shedding the old role of teacher as dispenser of knowledge.

Cooperative learning among students has been described and practiced in a variety of forms. The structural approach to cooperative learning (Kagan, 1990) serves as the basis for sample Q-Structures presented in this chapter. The Q-Structures provide for individual accountability, positive interdependence, and face to face interaction.

Critical thinking refers to a set of abilities and behaviors that allow students to look beyond the information presented, make connections, develop cognitive organizers, and create personal meaning. Critical thinking is concerned with problem finding as well as problem solving (Bergland, 1985). Critical thinking involves the application of multiple criteria in evaluating the possible benefits of a variety of solutions. It is introspective and reflective. Critical thinking involves persistence, toleration of ambiguity, careful analysis (Paul, in press), nuance judgment (Resnick, 1987), and interpretation. Above all, critical thinking is creative and involves risks as students work at the edges of their competence (Perkins, 1990). Critical thinking begins with curiosity and develops through the questions we ask.

Student question generation empowers students to ask their own questions about the content being studied. As an alternative to whole-class question-answer, we suggest that the most powerful use of questions is in cooperative learning teams with students empowered to ask questions of each other across all levels of Bloom's *Taxonomy*.

In field-testing the Q-Structures, it became clear that students were very capable of generating their own higher order questions, as long as they had a tool for framing the questions and sound cooperative structures for processing the responses. The teams with which we have worked have become communities of active inquiry, full of imagination and curiosity as students design their own questions and produce their own thoughtful responses.

USING THE Q-MATERIALS

The critical thinking intervention used in Room 19 is the result of the structural approach (Kagan, 1990) to cooperative learning incorporating planned student-generated questions—the Q-Approach. The intervention is designed to focus students' thinking on their own questions about content and process in the classroom. Through combining various elements such as team interviews or partners' paraphrasing with student-generated questions, cooperative learning structures take on an entirely new meaning and empower students to process information in a way that fosters critical thinking.

The Q-Matrix upon which the Q-Approach is based was originally developed by the first author in 1988 as a research tool. Observations by independent observers using the matrix to classify questions were found to be highly reliable (0.94). The Q-Approach was extensively field-tested in 23 classrooms that ranged in grade from K to Advanced Placement high school (see Wiederhold, 1991). Inspiration for this work is from John Dewey, whose discussion of the importance of student-generated questions has also inspired other educators such as Davidson (1990).

The questions created by the Tigers were based on the word pairs in a 6×6 cell matrix—the Question Matrix (see Figure 13.2). The word pairs are prompts or samples of how questions might begin. The word pairs are generic and are adaptable to any content. The cells in the Question Matrix are arranged simply, in a hierarchy that considers many levels of intellectual processing and eliminates exhaustive lists of sample questions. Moving in any direction from the *What is?* cell in the upper left hand corner, students are moving toward questions that require higher order thinking and creativity.

Using word pairs to have students generate their own questions at any level of thinking is straightforward and simple. Students choose any word pair from either the Question Matrix or from other Q-Materials that are constructed based on the matrix. Alternatively, the level of word pairs may be controlled by the teacher by either assigning a specific word pair or limiting student choice to groups of word pairs. Some groups of questions deal with categories of information such as events, situations, choices, reasons, and means. Other groups of questions deal with possibilities, probabilities, prediction, and imagination. Students use a word pair as the first part of their question, followed by appropriate content. With practice, students learn to embed each of the words from the word pair into more complex questions. For example, they move from "*Which might* be the best way?" to "Considering our alternatives, *which* of the top three do you think *might* work for our team?"

A simple example of a question beginning using the "What is? word pair is "What is the capital of Oregon?" The "Which Might?" word pair can work as a question beginning in "Which might be the best way to solve this problem?" Critical thinking enters cooperative learning if students generate questions at a range of levels of intellectual functioning. Through the use of several Q-Structures, cooperative learning structures that facilitate student question generation, students are encouraged to be aware of and choose the levels at which they will address thinking and content. Critical thinkers engage in metacognition: thinking about one's

Figure 13.2. Q-Matrix

1. What Is?	2. Where/ When Is?	3. Which Is?	4. Who Is?	5. Why Is?	6. How Is?
7. What Did?	8. Where/ When Did?	9. Which Did?	10. Who Did?	11. Why Did?	12. How Did?
13. What Can?	14. Where/ When Can?	15. Which Can?	16. Who Can?	17. Why Can?	18. How Can?
19. What Would?	20. Where/ When Would?	21. Which Would?	22. Who Would?	23. Why Would?	24. How Would?
25. What Will?	26. Where/ When Will?	27. Which Will?	28. Who Will?	29. Why Will?	30. How Will?
31. What Might?	32. Where/ When Might?	33. Which Might?	34. Who Might?	35. Why Might?	36. How Might?

own thinking, recognizing personal biases, and consciously developing broader worldviews (Costa, 1984).

Groups of four students, together with a structural approach to cooperative learning, form the basis for the classroom activities illustrated in this chapter. Two sets of partners work together and cooperatively switch roles and materials in the question-response interview structures. Cooperative learning in this context is presented as a set of elements, structures, materials, and lessons using sets of question generation materials or Q-Materials.

Some structures are designed to help students generate their own questions and other structures are designed to help students process questions with other students. The elements that are initially used to generate questions ensure individual accountability. Each student within the group is required to individually generate questions. Other elements combine to form structures, such as Two Way Q-Interview, which is used to process the questions. The use of structures ensures positive interdependence, individual accountability, face to face interaction, processing skills, and social skills. Each structure is made up of steps that show students what to do, how to do it, and when to do it.

In field testing of the student question generation materials, the structures first introduced to students were elements. As elements, they do not stand alone. Elements are individually modeled for students. For example, the element Individual-Question is only the first step of the complex structure Two-Way Q-Interview. Individual-Question provides a question prompt in the form of a word pair that focuses student thinking and produces a student-generated question, but without the complex Q-Structure two-way Q-Interview or another complex structure, the student has no way to process the question other than to continue thinking about it.

The elements can be configured in a variety of ways to form Q-Structures. Within each structure the choice of word pairs will dictate whether the structure will produce high consensus or low consensus questions. Complete lessons focus on a specific content area and are usually composed of several structures linked together.

WHAT A TWO-WAY Q-INTERVIEW SOUNDS LIKE

We can examine the cooperative-learning and critical-thinking elements of a complex Q-Structure—the Two Way Q-Interview—by stepping into Room A-9, a high school science classroom. The teachers are field-testing the question generation materials and structures.

The biology topic was one the students in Room A-9 had been working on with questionable interest. The topic was sponges. The students weren't the only ones finding sponges a bit dreary. In the past, both biology teachers found the study of sponges something that is done more for the test than the learning. Each year, when it was time to study Porifera, the teachers expected and got about the same reaction from their students.

Students are in teams of four. After an initial introduction to a study of sponges, a topic is assigned with the following directions: "Pretend that you will be talking to a team of scientists who are planning innovations for the year 2000. Some of the scientists are oceanographers. Decide what questions you might ask them about sponges and the role sponges might play in the year 2000." Students are given color-coded quadrant cards based on the Question Matrix along with 3×5 cards for recording their questions. Some of the questions students wrote about sponges were: "When did the first sponge get discovered?" "How might sponges change color?" "What will sponges be used for in the future?" Within 5 minutes the class has generated 90 questions about sponges.

Next, when partners finish writing their questions on 3 × 5 cards, they proceed to the element partners question. Partner 1 asks the first question and partner 2 responds, while partner 3 asks a question and partner 4 responds. As we walk around the room, we stop at one team and listen to two students, Brad and Jamie. Brad has just asked, "What might sponges eat?" Jamie responds, "I don't know. They live in the ocean and they don't move. Their food must come to them, probably microscopic stuff, you know, plankton. I wonder if they eat all the time."

After Jamie has finished responding to the question, Brad looks at Jamie, repeats her comments almost word for word, and asks her if his paraphrase was accurate. Jamie nods approval.

Brad then says to Jamie, "I thought your answer was good. I wasn't sure either, but your answer makes sense." Praise is a processing step or element that is used by the partner who asked the question. It is a strong self-esteem builder. In this step partners are creating an emotionally safe environment for each other. When an answer to a low consensus question is incorrect, praise may still be given for trying, but the answer should be corrected. After paraphrasing and praising, partners move on to the next element or step, augmentation.

Augmentation is a processing step. After praising, Brad augments the answer by adding, "I think we may want to send this on to the scientists or look it up. Is their food supply threatened?" After augmenting the response, partners reverse roles. Jamie asks Brad her first question and he responds. Simultaneously, partner 4 asks a question to which partner 3 responds. Partners repeat the steps of Two Way Q-Interview until all of the questions generated by each partner have been responded to by the other partner.

Notice that individual accountability is incorporated through individual questions generated and stated by each student in the room. Face to face interaction is incorporated in the interview process through listening, responding, paraphrasing, praising, and augmenting. Positive interdependence is provided in that one student's thinking increases the probability of engaging the other student's critical thinking.

Social skills are incorporated through the use of quiet voices and praising as well as during listening and paraphrasing. Paraphrasing is also a powerful self-esteem builder for the student whose idea is being listened to carefully enough to be accurately restated. No put-downs is the rule in any of the Q-Structures. Learning to frame clear questions is essential to the entire process of learning. Framing clear questions about a subject helps to focus and organize student thinking about that subject.

On the particular day students in Room A-9 were introduced to the Two Way Q-Interview structure, something changed. The students had been working in teams of four but they had not yet worked with any of the Q-Structures nor formally generated their questions. Teachers observing the sponges lesson were enthusiastic about several aspects of the use of student question generation. They gained many insights into what students really understood, what they didn't, what misconceptions they held, and the levels of thinking that went into their student-generated questions and responses. The lesson was a transformational experience for both the students and the observing teachers.

CONCLUSION

In the classroom scenario just presented, students were doing the thinking actively and cooperatively. Using a model such as the student question generation model can make student questions the focus of cooperative lessons, allowing students time to think critically: first in constructing questions, second in asking them, third in responding, and again in paraphrasing, praising, and augmenting them.

How much teaching/learning should be direct instruction, cooperative learning, or cooperative questioning? All three instructional methods are needed at different times. Students need direct instruction in steps and procedures, and often in knowledge acquisition. Students need structure and practice working cooperatively. Finally, students need opportunities to share their thinking and their questions. Students benefit from the shared thinking and social skills of their peers, and the power of the students themselves as sharers of a rich content base. The question materials and structures release a tremendous group curiosity and foster win-win participation in school.

Competitive whole-class instruction, if used as the major relationship structure between student and teacher, cannot be effective in producing citizens prepared to participate in a healthy democracy based on critical thinking and critical questions. Regardless of the small gains or losses on standardized achievement tests, in whole-class question-answer, some win, too many lose, and some are ignored. The social cost of such a system is great.

Historically, teachers have asked the questions and students were expected to provide the answers, often as narrowly focused factlets. In *Pedagogy of the Oppressed*, Paulo Freire (1988) describes a "banking concept" of education in which facts are deposited into containers called students for withdrawal at some future date. How much one can withdraw is measured primarily by multiple-choice and true-false tests. The real "withdrawal test," of course, comes from real life, beyond the class-room. This is the test we must not fail.

Much of the concern about the quality of education in the United States today has focused on poor student performance on standardized test instruments. We suggest that motivation and ability to generate and research questions at a range of levels of intellectual functioning also be a criteria for measuring educational success. The cooperative learning and critical-thinking skills sought by many teachers for their students are rarely addressed in the educational reform rhetoric. There are no national norms for a learner's self-esteem, spirit of cooperation, spirit of inquiry, creativity, helping and communication skills, or for a learner's apprecia-tion of differences. We recommend that educational reforms start where the educational product is delivered, in classrooms, in schools, between students and teachers. And we further suggest that the reforms address the issues of empowered learners cooperating in school in order to be able to cooperate in the home, the workplace, and in a pluralistic society.

Students will enter a fast-paced information driven world that is more diverse and less predictable than before. They cannot afford to enter that world as the passive recipients of factlets or as socially un-skilled or uncaring people. What will be needed in the future are individ-uals with practiced social skills, information retrieval skills, an openness about new problems, a good information base, a cooperative spirit that includes an appreciation of cultural and ethnic differences in a cultural democracy, and the ability to base one's thinking on well-constructed, imaginative questions. We hope that the student-generated question ap-proach presented in this chapter contributes in this direction.

REFERENCES

Bergland, R. (1985). *The fabric of mind*. New York: Viking Penguin.

Bloom, B. S. (Ed.). (1956). *Taxonomy of educational objectives*. New York: David McKay.

Ciscell, R. (1987, May). Increasing teacher–student interaction. *The Middle School Journal*, 17–19.

Costa, A. (1984, November). Mediating the metacognitive. *Educational Leader-ship, 42*, 57–62.

Davidson, N. (1990). *Cooperative learning in mathematics*. Reading, MA: Addi-son-Wesley.

Dean, D. (1986, Summer). Questioning techniques for teachers: A closer look at the process. *Contemporary Education, 57*(4), 184.

Freire, P. (1988). *Pedagogy of the oppressed*. New York: Continuum.

Good, T. L., & Brophy, J. E. (1973). *Looking in classrooms*. New York: Harper and Row.

Goodlad, J. (1984). *A place called school: Prospects for the future*. New York: McGraw-Hill.

Kagan, S. (1989, December). The structural approach to cooperative learning. *Educational Leadership*, 12–15.

Kagan, S. (1990). *Cooperative learning resources for teachers*. San Juan Capistrano: Resources for Teachers.

Kloss, R. J. (1988, February). Toward asking the right questions. *The Clearinghouse, 61*, 245–248.

McTighe, J., & Lyman, F. T., Jr. (1988, April). Cueing thinking in the classroom: The promise of theory-embedded tools. *Educational Leadership, 45*(7), 18–25.

Paul, R. (in press). *Dialogical reasoning*. Alexandria, VA: Association for Supervision and Curriculum Development.

Perez, S. A. (1986, October). Improving learning through student questioning. *The Clearinghouse, 60*, 63–64.

Perkins, D. (1990, February). On knowledge and cognitive skills. *Educational Leadership*, 50–53.

Resnick, L. B. (1987). *Education and learning to think*. Washington, DC: National Academy Press.

Wiederhold, C. (1989). *An examination of questions asked by teachers*. Ann Arbor: UMI Press.

Wiederhold, C. (1991). *Cooperative learning and critical thinking: The question matrix*. San Juan Capistrano, CA., Resources for Teachers.

Enhancing Writing Through Cooperative Peer Editing

Carla J. Beachy

For the middle school student, or almost any writer for that matter, putting intangible thoughts into a meaningful written product can often be a challenging process. This process includes deciphering and understanding the assignment, collecting and organizing details, and composing a draft. All that and we're *still* not finished! There is the editing to do and then, of course, the revising. In each of these phases of the writing process, cooperative thinking can provide students with valuable ideas and suggestions to improve their writing. The focus of this chapter will be specifically on the revision phase, because students who have gotten their thoughts into written form have a tendency to believe that the words have now become sacred, written in stone, and are not to be moved, changed, or deleted in any way, shape, or form. In other words, revision becomes little more than recopying the original text neatly in pen and on looseleaf.

One method that I have found to be successful during the revision stage is the cooperative learning strategy of peer editing: Fellow students help one another to improve their compositions through the editing process. In my experience as a middle school English teacher, I have found that the peer editing process organizes and guides students in editing, helps to clarify their thinking, motivates them during each phase of the process, improves the final product, and finally ensures success for all students.

KEY COMPONENTS OF THE PEER EDITING PROCESS

The Writing Prompt

In my classroom, all composition assignments are given in the form of a teacher-written three-paragraph prompt modeled after the *Maryland*

Writing Supplement (Williams & Reeves, 1987), an essay test used to measure competency in writing. The form, audience, topic, and purpose of the composition are always stated in both the first and third paragraphs of the prompt, while the second paragraph contains the instructions for the details that should be contained in the writing assignment. I create my own prompts, which usually reflect the theme of the literature unit or interdisciplinary unit that we are working on at the time. All composition assignments involve the five parts of the writing process as discussed in Donald M. Murray's *Write to Learn* (1987):

1. Collecting details
2. Focusing on or choosing specific details
3. Ordering those details into a meaningful pattern
4. Developing or drafting the composition itself
5. Clarifying or revising

The Grading Checklist

The grading checklist (also called the *editing checklist*) is another vital part of the composition assignment. This is created by the teacher and is distributed after the prompt is analyzed by the class. The grading checklist includes all of the major details of the second paragraph of the prompt, plus any additional skills requirements and mechanics. Each item on the grading checklist is given a point value, with content receiving a greater point value than mechanics or sentence structure. On the grading checklist, students are given space for both a self-evaluation and a peer or editor evaluation. Ordinarily, students are not asked to give a point value to their composition but rather to check off whether or not the requirement has been satisfactorily accomplished. If an item is left blank, the student author knows to go back and revise.

The grading checklist thus becomes another assignment sheet to be used in conjunction with the prompt. The checklist also helps to organize the writers and guide them through the sometimes complicated writing task in a step-by-step manner. I have found that the grading checklist serves to keep the students on task and increases accountability for each part of the writing assignment. Of course, the checklist is also valuable for use as an evaluation tool by student, editor, and teacher alike.

How Thinking Is Enhanced

Writing is difficult because it involves putting invisible thoughts into solid form; however, my students have found the task is much more approachable with the use of the prompt, the grading checklist, and an editing partner. Thinking begins with the unlocking, or the analysis, of the writing prompt. Included in this part of the assignment is always a webbing (McTighe & Lyman, 1988) or outlining of the second paragraph and then a brainstorming and focusing of details. Of course, the type of thinking that occurs during the actual writing of the composition depends on the assignment itself. A narrative would require use of sequencing, while an explanatory piece might require a main idea with supporting details or comparison/contrast. During the evaluation stage of the peer editing process, students are using many different levels of thinking: finding the main idea, sequencing, comparison, analysis, and evaluation.

The procedures for teaching and learning the composition process occur throughout the school year in every composition assignment. As students become more confident with the process, less teacher direction is required and more student independence is allowed and encouraged. The goal is for students to be able to write their own writing prompts and develop their own checklist, thus providing ownership and self-direction in future writing. In addition, it is hoped that students will acquire more confidence in their writing since the prompt, checklist, and editing are there to provide opportunities for success.

IMPLEMENTATION IN A SEVENTH-GRADE CLASSROOM

Group Size and Formation

Both research and past experience have proven to me that middle school students enjoy and need to work in groups; however, research and past experience have also proven to me that it is important for the teacher to establish classroom management during the first 3 weeks of school (Evertson & Emmer, 1982). Each of my English classes has students with the same level of ability; classes are categorized as gifted and talented, above average, average, or below average. Therefore, I begin the school year using whole group instruction, with student seating arranged in alphabetical order or arbitrarily. Sometime during the first week of school, however, I take a writing sample from each student, and I am soon able to assess individual progress in writing. I then pair the students: strong with weak, or average with weak or strong. No mention of individual writing abilities is ever made by me, and since pairs change monthly, students do not label each other as strong or weak in writing skills. As the year progresses, pairs grow to triads and then to small groups of four or five students. Pairs, triads, and groups change monthly with new seating arrangements, providing for variety in both physical and social environment.

Fostering Cooperation

I usually begin the school year with Kurt Vonnegut's short story "No-Talent Kid." Students enjoy this humorous account and learn to accept their own strengths and weaknesses as a result of class discussions about the story. It is also an opportunity for students to get to know each other by sharing their own talents and ultimately discussing their own strengths and weaknesses in writing. The composition assignment for this story requires an understanding of the main character, Plummer, and of his strengths and weaknesses. In this assignment, which is given in the form of the three-paragraph prompt (see Figure 14.1), the students are asked to pretend that they and one of the characters are on a school field trip and have become separated from their group. They are to explain to their

Figure 14.1. "No-Talent Kid" Prompt

Imagine that you and one of the characters from our story are on a school field trip. You and the character become separated from your group and get lost. Now, write a letter to your teacher telling what happened when you and the character were lost.

Before you start writing, think about how you and the character got separated from your group, what you and the character did while you were lost, and what you did in order to find your group. Think about how the character reacted in the situation, being certain that this is consistent with his personality.

Now, write a letter to your teacher telling what happened when you and the character were lost.

Form: _____

Audience: _____

Topic: _____

Purpose: _____

teacher how they got lost in the first place, what they did while they were separated from the group, how they found the group, and how the character reacted in the situation. His reactions, of course, should be consistent with his personality as developed in the story.

The students begin this assignment by first "unlocking" or analyzing the prompt for form (friendly letter), audience (the teacher), topic (getting lost on the school field trip), and purpose (to explain or inform). We call this the "FAT P" or "Fat Paper." Then as a total group we do an outline web of the middle paragraph of the prompt. The importance of this outline is emphasized throughout the writing process because it contains the basic requirements of the composition. Students are given various web or graphic organizer examples in displays in the classroom and in a handout of various web shapes (see Figure 14.2) that they are to keep in the composition section of their notebook. An entire class period is devoted to organizing different types of details on the various graphic organizer shapes. Usually, students are allowed to choose which graphic organizer to use in their compositions. In this particular writing assignment the students are using several different thinking skills. They are recalling events and characters from the "No-Talent Kid" story, and they are sequencing the events of their own story. In addition, they are predicting how a character will react in a new situation and employing the concept of cause and effect in their plot.

The Students' Roles as Authors and Editors

After this, students brainstorm details for each section of the web. I always encourage the writers to record all ideas, no matter how divergent. Then we focus or select the details that best reflect the main idea. After ordering or organizing these details, students write the first draft. The self-evaluation of the first draft is done after carefully reviewing the editing checklist (see Figure 14.3). I always make a big deal out of the students signing their name where it says "Author" on the checklist. Using a transparency, I have the students read over the checklist step by step, being certain they know the point value for each section of the checklist. (The *total* of all the sections is always 100). Students do the self-evaluation, then revise and write a second draft. After this, the students exchange papers with their partner, usually the person seated next to them. (If a student is absent or if there is an unequal number in the class, we sometimes have to make a three-way switch, but students never seem to have a problem with organizing themselves.)

Next, I distribute green pens so the students can see any editing marks on their second draft. Students enjoy using the green pens, which

Figure 14.2. Graphic Organizers

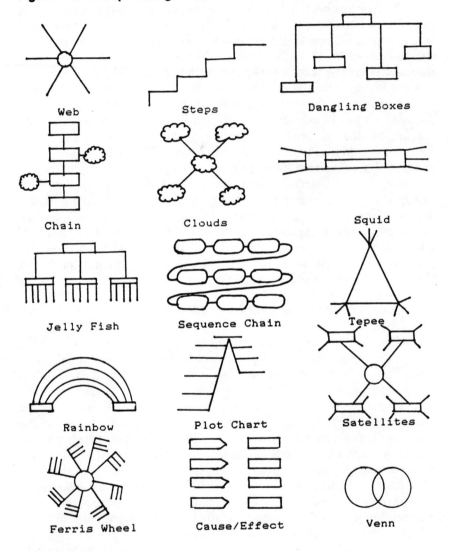

Figure 14.3. "No-Talent Kid" Editing Checklist

Author _____

Peer Editor_____

If the answer is "yes," place a check (✓) in the appropriate box. If the answer is "no," leave the block blank.

	self	peer	teacher
1. Does the writer use the correct FATP?			5
2. Does the opening paragraph capture the reader's interest and make a general statement about the theme of the narrative?			1 0
3. Does the body of the composition discuss the following topics in a clear and consistent manner and use specific details from the story? - A vivid sense of how the two characters spent their lost time			6 0
- An explanation of how the two characters found their group			
- A description of how the main character reacted to the situation which is consistent with his personality			
4. Does the concluding paragraph review the main points of the narrative in an intriguing manner?			1 0
5. Did the author proofread for mechanics: spelling, capitalization, and punctuation?			1 0
6. Did the writiner include all parts of the writing process: the prompt, the web, and all drafts?			5
			1 0 0

also serve to give them a sense of importance as the editor. Ample class time is allowed for this portion of the writing process. In fact, I encourage the editors to read the authors' papers several times before making any editing marks on the composition and the grading checklist. I also urge the editors to read the papers aloud to pick up sentence fragments, run-ons, or awkward sentences. Talking with the partner is permitted and encouraged during the editing process. Editors know that if they have a question about a detail in the composition they should discuss it with the author. I emphasize the importance of the peer editors signing their name to the space that says "Peer Editor."

I also emphasize the point that good friends help to make their partner's paper the *best* paper possible. In other words, it is the editor's job to point out errors or problems in the author's writing. One group that often experiences monumental difficulties in writing and revision is the below-average group. Before I started using the editing checklist, when we switched papers in class students comments tended to range from "You're stupid!" to "This composition is perfect! You don't have to change anything." The checklist definitely helps the below-average students to know what to look for when reading their partner's paper. It also helps the students to avoid inflammatory remarks.

After the author/partner's papers are edited, the compositions are returned and each author analyzes the editor's remarks, suggestions, and editing marks. Again consultation is encouraged between editor and author. Finally, the authors choose whether or not to make certain revisions. Authors then write the final draft, which is usually due in a day or two, depending on the length of the compostion.

The composition is turned in with the grading checklist stapled on top of the final draft, which is placed on top of all other drafts, the web, and the prompt. Compositions are not accepted without all steps of the writing process. If a student happens to be absent on the day we do the peer edit, then an older sibling or a parent is permitted to do the peer edit.

The Role of the Teacher

When it is my turn to evaluate the composition, I always begin by making sure that each step in the writing process has taken place. In fact, on compositions done in the first part of the school year, I might have a part on the grading checklist that gives 5 or 10 points for having all parts completed. Then I read the composition once for content and again for mechanics. The grading checklist is filled out and assists me in giving an objective, unbiased grade to a complicated and often subjective process.

Of course, the real thinking work begins for the teacher *before* the writing assignment is even given to the students. At the very beginning of the unit, the teacher has to determine what objectives and skills are to be introduced and, hopefully, mastered during the unit. Then the teacher needs to develop a prompt reflecting the theme of the unit and requiring the students to demonstrate competency in the major skills learned during the unit. In addition, the prompt must appeal to the needs, interests, and imagination of the students and challenge their abilities while providing opportunity for success. The peer editing, or grading, checklist must be developed and should fairly reflect the instructions on the prompt. It is wise to have ample copies prepared for the students, and a transparency should be made of all handouts for large group instruction.

During the unit, the teacher needs to provide opportunity for direct instruction of thinking skills. I have found thinking skills instruction easiest to accomplish through frequent use of graphic organizers throughout the unit. Students collect information on these organizers, which help to clarify their understanding of a particular concept, and students may even be able to use some of these details in the future composition. For example, during an interdisciplinary unit on Colonial America, the social studies teacher and I introduced the Venn diagram. We then took the students on a field trip to Mount Vernon, a wealthy colonial farm, and the Claude Moore Farm, a poor colonial farm. Students were asked to develop poster-size visual organizers that compared and contrasted the many aspects of the two farms. In English, we asked students to focus on one aspect of their choice—for example, clothing—and write a composition comparing and contrasting the two farms, using the details they had collected on their visual organizer.

The teacher also has to think about the author/editor pairs, triads, or small groups. It is important to provide a variety of partners throughout the school year. Of course, teachers learn very quickly that there are some students who just cannot work together, although on the middle school level this is usually a temporary situation. I have found a weak writer to improve immensely when paired with a strong writer. Strong writers rarely deteriorate when paired with a weak writer; on the contrary, their self-confidence seems to be greatly enhanced by the experience of helping a classmate.

During the writing process, the teacher's task is to monitor progress, answer questions, ask questions, give pep talks, guide uncertain students, and model appropriate behaviors. The teacher must be certain that the students understand, however, that it is their responsibility to do the actual writing, editing, and revising of the composition. On occasion, I will write along with the students, demonstrating my interest in the process. Sometimes experiencing the same frustrations that the students are having helps me as I review my instructional materials and revise them for future classes. It also helps me to be aware of possible difficulties so that I can provide strategies to overcome these problems. The students are impressed to see that even a teacher sometimes struggles in writing and needs to edit and revise frequently.

The Role of the Parents

When compositions are returned, I always give a grade distribution so that students know where they rank in the class. I never publish or announce individual grades, however. Next, the compositions go home for the parents to look over. At the beginning of the school year during Back-to-School Night and in a letter that goes home to each parent, I tell parents that their job in this process is to acknowledge their child's hard work and accomplishments and to encourage continued improvement on the next assignment. Most parents are more than happy and appreciate being able to participate, and the required parent signature emphasizes the importance of writing in the curriculum.

The Final Assessment

The final phase of the project is to place the written piece in each author's folder where all compositions are kept during the school year along with a writing progress sheet. On this progress sheet, we place the date of the composition, the type of assignment, the skills that were emphasized, and each individual student's strengths and weaknesses (+ and −) on the assignment. Also included are the percent and letter grades. At mid-year I have the students reevaluate their strengths and weaknesses on all writing assignments to date. I also encourage them to look for trends or patterns, especially in their weaknesses. Then I have the students formulate an action plan for improving their writing during the remainder of the school year. We return to these action plans before future compositions as a reminder of goals, and at the end of the year we assess whether or not we were able to make the planned improvements.

Grouping as the Year Progresses

As the school year progresses and classroom procedures are readily followed by students, group sizes shift from pairs to triads, and finally to small groups of four or five. I always try to create variety by including in each group students of different writing abilities, genders, races, person-

alities, and interests. For at least one composition during the school year, I allow students to choose their own groups and to establish their own roles and procedures in the editing process. Often, they enjoy naming their groups and creating a poster to display at their area.

When studying *The Light in the Forest*, my above-average students choose their own Native American name and create a nameplate for their desks. I even choose a Native American name for myself. Then during the unit we use only our Native American names and decorate the classroom in a Native American motif. Students create a sequel to the novel, working in their groups or "tribes" to write and edit it. Students are encouraged to use Native American language, and to use symbolism from the novel or even to create their own. This writing assignment provides ample opportunity for both critical and creative thinking. Students must demonstrate comprehension of the novel. They must also analyze the author's style of writing, write in that style, and create their own plot. Finally, they must use their interpretation of the novel in order to predict the protagonist's actions and thoughts in their own sequel.

The students are motivated to have the highest composition grade average for their tribe. During the editing and revision stages, students must use the thinking skills of comparing/contrasting, sequencing, and evaluating. After the compositions are returned, we enjoy sharing the compositions with the entire Native American nation in the celebration of our accomplishments.

Grouping at the End of the School Year

By the end of the school year, my students are able to evaluate each other's work in an expert manner. This is also the time when students enjoy doing group projects. For example, in my gifted and talented classes we often read Jack London's *The Call of the Wild*. This novel provides an excellent opportunity for research on topics from Alaska to wolves. As a total group we brainstorm a list of possible topics and then focus by limiting the list to five or six of our favorite topics. Students then choose groups by interest, giving a first and second choice to ensure equal group size. I then have the individual groups come up with their own expectations for the project; this would include a grading checklist, of course. By the end of the school year most students are very capable of creating their own assignment prompt and grading checklist. In the past, the different groups' grading checklists have been very similar in both general content and value despite the fact that the specific topic for research was different.

Although this particular novel unit was done with gifted and talented students, it is also possible to have average students create their own grading checklists by providing exemplary models of compositions or projects for them to analyze first. Students seem to enjoy this activity most if they are allowed to work in groups first to create their own evaluation checklist on large newsprint and then to compare these group checklists with those of the other groups in the class and finally with the original checklist. Again, this exercise allows students to analyze and evaluate another's work and provides ownership in future assignments.

SUMMARY

It's a wonderful feeling to "have written." Yet the writing process itself is a difficult, often lonely task, and the work of editing and revising can be downright tedious or even omitted. However, the assistance of a clear-thinking editor can make the revision stage of writing a little more pleasurable and certainly more successful. That is why I use peer editors and the editing checklist to enhance the writing process in my classroom. Writers benefit from the insight of others and grow in confidence as they assist fellow writers. They do this while enjoying the company of someone else involved in the same struggle with words. With practice, this cooperative struggle will lead to improved thinking, writing, social skills, and even self-esteem, as the writers succeed in the process of writing and can proudly announce that they "have written."

REFERENCES

Evertson, C., & Emmer, E. (1982). Effective management at the beginning of the school year in junior high mathematics and English classes. *Journal of Educational Psychology, 74,* 485–489.

McTighe, J., & Lyman, F. T., Jr. (1988). Cueing thinking in the classroom: The promise of theory-embedded tools. *Educational Leadership, 45*(7), 18–24.

Murray, D. M. (1987). *Write to learn.* New York: Holt, Rinehart and Winston.

Williams, P. M., & Reeves, B. M. (1987). *Maryland writing supplement: Project Basic instructional guide.* Baltimore: Maryland State Department of Education.

15

Designing Cooperatively Thoughtful Science Lessons

Anita Stockton

Science educators are trying to keep up with a world of rapidly advancing technology. Science knowledge, and the demands on teachers and students, are increasing exponentially.

Our colleagues in business and industry plead with us to send them graduates capable of working with a team to solve problems. The ability to think at higher levels is a prerequisite for many diverse positions. Skilled educators can orchestrate a mix of inquiring minds (reactants) working in cooperative settings to produce students (products) who meet these qualifications.

The science classroom is a natural place for the teaching of thinking skills in a cooperative learning setting; and, frequently, the limited supply of laboratory equipment has actually necessitated working in pairs or groups. However, science educators have not always grouped students to produce maximum learning.

SOME COOPERATIVELY THOUGHTFUL TECHNIQUES

The work of Johnson and Johnson (1987, 1989) and Kagan (1989) has yielded data that inform us that some groupings are more effective than others. Groups of four, with one high-achieving student, two average students, and one low-achieving student can maximize peer teaching and individual learning. Constructing the group task so that all members must become active participants in order to succeed facilitates group interaction. Some appropriate structures for science classrooms are discussed in the following sections.

Roundtable

The Roundtable structure is used effectively to review lessons or to brainstorm what is already known. For example, at the beginning of each school year, students are routinely introduced or reintroduced to laboratory equipment and safety rules. Traditionally this review of safety rules is accomplished by distributing a printed list or having the teacher, at the front of the room, call on volunteers to recite rules. This method casts students in the role of sponges or receptacles of knowledge. Calling on students one by one, while all others supposedly listen, limits student participation. Once a student is called upon, others relax, minds wander, and the identified student is the lone participant. A different approach might be to seat students in groups of four with one pencil and one piece of paper among them. One student writes a safety rule, says it out loud, and quickly passes the paper to the next student. The second student does the same thing. This continues around the table during the allotted time interval. Groups then share their lists. During the Round-robin all participants are thinking about the question or list so that they may contribute ideas when the paper and pencil are passed to them. This Roundtable technique makes *all* students active participants and thus active learners.

Labs with Roles

The cooperatively thoughtful science classroom assigns students roles for each laboratory activity. Recorders, time keepers, materials handlers, and communicators are actively engaged in collecting data, managing time and equipment, and analyzing data.

When the group is stuck on a procedure or question, students first put their heads together. If group members are unable to answer their own query, the communicator goes to at least two other groups to seek answers. Only then may help from the teacher be sought. This technique encourages students to become independent learners, places the responsibility for learning directly on students, and encourages peer teaching.

The teacher is freed of the tedium of answering the same question over and over again. Students who answer questions gain prestige and self-esteem because they are able to help classmates. Students are also motivated to read the directions more carefully when they discover that the teacher will not give out the answers!

The recorder is responsible for preparing the written portion of the activity. Sometimes this is the only paper collected. Requiring all members of the group to sign this report promotes ownership and en-

courages responsibility. Carefully constructed group tasks ensure that all participants are required to provide meaningful input in order for the group to succeed.

If differences of opinion emerge, each student is offered the option of submitting a minority report representing his or her work, to be graded individually. This option is not often exercised in a cooperatively thoughtful classroom. Students quickly learn that cooperation makes the task more manageable. Students strengths are highlighted. Peer teaching helps struggling students to improve their skills and understandings.

A Sample Lesson on Chemical Reactions

These techniques are often integrated in middle school science classrooms in Baltimore County, Maryland. Students sit in clusters of four. In preparation for a laboratory activity, they reflect on basic chemical reactions. They then list terms associated with these reactions in a Roundtable structure. Students write words such as *reactants, products, synthesis, decomposition, single* or *double replacement, precipitate, gases* on a piece of paper as it is quickly passed among the four group members.

The teacher then asks groups to share their lists, clarifies meanings, and discusses the upcoming experiment. Groups add words suggested by others. Most students are attentive and anxious to add to the collective knowledge base.

Using the jigsaw technique, a strategy that casts students in the roles of experts for the purpose of peer teaching, home groups of four students are asked to find out all they can about the four basic reaction types. Expert subgroups move to assigned areas of the lab to perform some experiments that demonstrate synthesis, decomposition, single replacement, and double replacement reactions.

When questions occur, communicators seek help from members of other groups. Peers are often able to answer questions. The teacher observes motivated students who want to become knowledgeable about their topic so that they can share this with the home group.

The synthesis expert group burns magnesium ribbon, turning away as instructed to avoid the bright light given off. They consult with one another before deciding on a word equation. Exchanged among the group members are questions such as,

What happens when something burns?
What is combined?
What is the product?

Since four heads are better than one, students often come up with correct concepts. The word equation "magnesium plus oxygen yields magnesium oxide" is written. A little research leads to the ability to write the equation:

$$Mg + O_2 \longrightarrow MgO$$

and subsequent balancing:

$$2Mg + O_2 \longrightarrow 2MgO$$

Other expert groups are simultaneously working on synthesis and single and double replacement reactions.

Experts then return to their home groups to discuss their findings. They do this proudly, eager to share their newly gained knowledge. The teacher, assuming a "guide on the side" posture, hears information freely exchanged and adds comments, corrections, and suggestions as needed. Recorders summarize findings and prepare the group report. All members of the group sign it, indicating agreement.

Often students are tested with an offer of bonus points if all students attain a specified grade. In this win-win situation, much peer teaching occurs. Slower students gain help and fresh ideas from classmates. Chests swell when criterion grades are made and bonus points earned. Tutors pat each other on the shoulder and grins abound. Those who do not get the bonus points vow to do better next time.

HIGH LEVEL QUESTIONS

Teaching students to ask and answer higher level questions provides a vehicle for deeper processing and greater understanding of content. Thinktrix, developed by Frank Lyman (1987), provides a method for doing this (see Chapter 11 in this text). As students read new material they construct questions. Visual cues remind them of questioning levels from recall through evaluation.

Symbols represent levels of questions. For example, an R represents recall level questions. These are related to who, what, where queries. Students quickly learn that recall questions are low level and easily answered.

Cause-and-effect, example-to-idea, idea-to-example, comparison, and contrast questions are related to analysis and synthesis levels of thinking. Students find them challenging and quickly learn to ask these types of questions.

Evaluation questions are perhaps the most challenging and fun. These questions introduce students to the real world and wean them from the "right answer" syndrome.

Often wheels depicting these symbols are placed in prominent positions in the classroom. Movable arrows are used to identify question types as students pose them. This technique helps students understand the nature of their questions and acts as a prompt to help them to formulate higher level questions.

A Classroom Application of Thinktrix

One effective method of teaching students to generate higher level questions is to use "weird facts" (see Chapter 11 in this text). After reading that all oysters start out as males and as they mature turn to females, one student exclaims, "That's really weird, why do they do this?"

Pointing to the visual clue for cause and effect, Mr. Sam, the teacher, notes, "That is a cause/effect question. Let's explore further."

Another student notes that some snails do likewise. Mr. Sam points to the example-to-idea symbol and asks if other examples exist. Students busily delve into reference books looking for animals that change sex as they mature.

Mary notes, "I don't think this is a good way to do things; suppose a disease infects only young oysters, all the males may die!"

Mr. Sam asks what kind of question Mary has asked. After some discussion, the symbol representing scales of justice is noted and the question is identified at the evaluation level. A lively discussion ensues; students are asked to support arguments with facts.

Discussions triggered by stimulating ideas (weird facts), such as scallops have blue eyes, squids have pens, and frogs have teeth in the roofs of their mouth, are often peppered with questions. Skillful use of visual cues lead student questions and discussions to higher levels and subsequent processing of information at the analysis, synthesis, and evaluation levels.

Once question types are identified and linked with visual cues, teachers may ask students to write a specific question type for homework. One biology teacher assigned a reading on evolution and asked students to write an idea-to-example (analysis level) and one example-to-idea (synthesis level) question for homework.

The next day, in lieu of a drill, students orally asked their questions, called on volunteers who identified the question type, and answered the question. The teacher became the guide on the side as students discussed answers among themselves. Disagreements over question type led to more cooperative small group discussion for deeper analysis and greater understanding of problematic questions. This discussion went on for about 15 minutes, with students discussing new materials at the analysis, synthesis, and evaluation levels.

During the whole-class discussion, Kim began by asking peers to compare the theories of Lamarck and Darwin. Clued by the word *compare*, John easily identified the question type but then proceeded to describe how the theories differed. A discussion of the terms "compare and contrast" led to consensus that comparison requires finding likenesses and contrast requires finding differences. The symbols were linked with the terms, and the class reached consensus on the definition of these terms that would serve them well throughout the year.

Danny asked how desirable traits were passed from one generation to another. As Pam pondered this question, she decided that she was dealing with cause-and-effect relationships. This understanding helped her ferret out stored knowledge about genetics and link this with the idea of survival of the fittest.

Student-to-student discussions of this type mix the reactants (inquiring minds, provocative material, and the Thinktrix organizer) to yield products, students capable of thoughtful processing of content. These students are more likely to succeed in college and the workforce.

Group Reading for Different Purposes

Another method of helping students ask and answer higher level questions is Group Reading for Different Purposes. All members of the class read the same material, but each group reads to accomplish a different task. Group 1 may be asked to identify two causes and two effects in the text. Group 2 may locate two facts and two opinions. Group 3 might suggest alternatives to those offered in the reading, and Group 4 might ask questions of the author.

Students begin by reading a selection from a newspaper article entitled "Peasants in Rural China Raise Babies in Bags of Sand." It tells how a rural community in China solves its child care problems by putting children in bags of silt up to their chests while adults tend the fields. Students are anxious to discuss this situation. A member of Group 1 reads the following statement but does not identify it as a cause or effect: "In these areas, the use of sand bags to rear children is extremely common."

Think time is given; then students pair to share ideas; then total group sharing occurs. Jim notes, "This is an effect because it is dry in the area." Robin adds, "It is also an effect of the extreme poverty in the area."

Sam adds, "But it could be a cause of slow physical development in these youngsters!" This comment triggers other responses. Soon class members are analyzing this practice from the standpoint of healthy development of children (both physically and mentally), the economics of the area, and social mores. Social issues and environmental science are blended in the Group Reading for Different Purposes technique, yielding similar results to the Thinktrix.

Group 1 shares another statement and another discussion ensues. Group 2 then shares a statement from the article but does not identify it as a fact or opinion: "The silt is soft, so it does not harm the babies' bottoms." Other members of the class examine this statement, discuss what evidence supports or refutes it, and come to consensus. Again a multilevel discussion from many viewpoints is triggered.

Jane shares an alternative plan generated by Group 3. "We propose that the elders in this community stay home from the fields to tend the children." A lively discussion addressing the economics and feasibility of this solution prompts Ron to note, "This discussion really has no right answer, we are making an evaluation!" Thus connections between the Group Reading for Different Purposes technique and Thinktrix are again illustrated.

Group 4 poses questions for the author and the total group attempts to reply as they think the author might reply. Barry asks, "Is it possible for the elders to stay home from the fields to watch the children?" Joyce answers as if she were the author, "No, the labor of the elders is necessary to harvest an adequate crop." This framework stretches the imagination, encourages creativity, and leads to the evaluation of ideas. Students gain insights into their own abilities and that of their peers to process complicated problems. Hopefully, they also gain confidence in their ability to deal with these problems.

SCIENCE, TECHNOLOGY, AND SOCIETY ISSUES

The primary goal of science education in our era is to produce scientifically literate citizens. While much is written about what being scientifically literate really means, most agree that students should become informed about scientific principles, the technology that our knowledge of these principles has spawned, and the social consequences of this technology. Scientifically literate third graders, therefore, know something about waste recycling and pollution and also know what they can do personally to help preserve the environment.

Value lines and talking chips (See Kagan, 1989) are especially effective techniques for helping students think critically about science, technology, and society (STS) related issues. Critical thinking involves taking a position on an issue and being able to logically defend that position. The value line represents a continuum from strongly agree to strongly disagree. Faces often are used to represent these positions.

An STS statement such as, "The power company should build another nuclear power plant in my state," "Surrogate motherhood should be outlawed," or "Eugenics will produce a super race," offers students the opportunity to take a position. Working in groups of four, students mark the line and initial their marks for their beginning opinions.

Using pens or pencils as chips, they then provide reasons for their positions and lay their "chips" down after they have spoken. No one may speak a second time until all four members of the group have spoken once. They may change their position on the value line after this first round, and in fact often do, because they have had the opportunity to hear what others are thinking. Speakers often think about their thinking (metacognition) while generating reasons for their positions. For example, when students learn about solar energy they often rethink the need for nuclear energy.

A second round provides the opportunity for group members to share their revised positions. This technique makes discussion very meaningful. Students are required to listen to each other, and speakers must produce logical ideas because they will be carefully scrutinized by peers. (For a more elaborate discussion of "constructive controversy," see Chapter 8 in this text.)

ADAPTING TRADITIONAL CURRICULUM

Traditional curriculum guides often give instructions to teachers such as: review the symbols for specific elements, discuss the four basic reaction types, perform a laboratory activity, and write a report. Teachers implement this plan with varying skill. At one extreme, individual students are called upon to name the symbols as the instructor writes them on the board. This one-on-one interaction frees the nonparticipating students from any responsibility. Often, over half the class members are off task during such a lesson. The speaking student is, at the least, attentive, and at the most, telling what is already known. Others may be listening, doodling, or reading.

As the teacher continues to write equations for reaction types, most copy this information dutifully, processing it with varying degrees of understanding. The instructor seldom checks for understanding because only a few students have the opportunity to share their thinking in this format.

Taking their laboratory manuals, students in pairs, trios, or quartets then move to the lab to perform reactions and observe results. In the least effective traditional classrooms, directions are read line by line with little comprehension of the total picture. More aggressive students monopolize the discussion and the equipment. Reports are written individually with less capable students frequently writing answers gleaned from others. One misconception is often repeated in report after report, reflecting a lack of general understanding.

In cooperatively thoughtful curriculum guides, such as Baltimore County's thinking skills appendices for ninth grade science, biology, chemistry, or environmental science (Baltimore County Public Schools, 1986, 1987, 1990a, 1990b), teachers find strategies that will address these pitfalls. Including these in the written curriculum will improve the chances of their becoming part of the delivered curriculum. Teachers are instructed to use the Roundtable technique to review chemical symbols. In this scenario, groups of four are allowed one piece of paper and a pencil. The Roundtable technique gives each student an opportunity to list the symbols he or she can recall. More importantly, it provides time to think about what is known and the opportunity to learn what others know. A few minutes for each group to share answers is required.

The curriculum guide gives explicit directions for strategies such as jigsaw, which may then be used to make the laboratory activity more meaningful. Home groups, consisting of four students, are divided into subgroups to become experts on synthesis, decomposition, and single and double replacement reaction types. Experts from each group meet in an assigned area of the laboratory and perform several reactions of a specific type.

Home groups then reassemble and learn about each of the four reaction types from other experts. The laboratory report is prepared cooperatively by the home group and signed by all members. Any member of the group is allowed the option of preparing an individual report.

In this classroom, students have been afforded the opportunity to think, speak, and listen. The jigsaw technique makes every student an expert on something. This can increase self-esteem if the expert is really able to explain ideas, peer teaching becomes the norm, and learning is increased. Students are generating knowledge, not merely absorbing it.

USING THE INCLUSION PROCESS

The understanding of science is based on the ability to reach logical conclusions. Teachers often complain that students do not think or are unable to think. What they often mean is that they are unable to synthesize information, make it meaningful, and reach logical conclusions.

These thinking skills must be taught explicitly. The Inclusion Process, developed by Toni Worsham (Worsham and Stockton, 1986), provides a mechanism for doing this. Using this framework, students metacognitively reflect on how to reach logical conclusions, cooperatively define the skill, and generate a list of the steps used to apply the skill. Think-Pair-Share and Think-Pair-Square-Share are used to do this (Lyman, 1989). This procedure in the Inclusion Process is called a focus lesson because it zeroes in on a specific thinking skill and provides students with an understanding of what the skill means and how it is applied (Chapter 5 in this text.)

Numerous application lessons provide opportunities for students to apply each thinking skill. Definitions and steps are referred to frequently. Applying the skill in other disciplines provides additional opportunity for reinforcement and practice. Graphing is a skill required not only in science but also in mathematics and social studies. Students often have problems reading graphs or constructing their own.

Using the Inclusion Process, Ms. Freeman asked her biology students to look at several graphs typically pictured in high school biology texts. These illustrated heart and respiration rates in relation to exercise. Students shared observations such as:

"They have titles."
"They have two variables."
"Respiration rate increases with exercise."
"So does heart rate!"

By using Think-Pair-Share and scaffolding questions such as, "What happens to the heart rate when exercise occurs?" "What happens to the heart rate after rest?" "How can we show this?" students generated a definition of the thinking skill of making a graph. This definition, "Making a picture that shows the relationship of one variable to another," was posted for all to see and to be modified as students gained more experience with this skill.

Ms. Freeman then had students generate some of their own data. They exercised for varying lengths of times and monitored their pulse rates. Pulse rates were also monitored during the postexercise rest period. When asked to present this data in a meaningful way, Keith noted that a graph was the way to go. Working in pairs and referring to the posted definition of making graphs, students developed graphs with varying degrees of success. Most attacked the task with confidence, however.

Midway through the lesson Ms. Freeman paused and asked students to reflect on what they were doing. Steps for making a graph were generated, discussed, modified, sequenced, and rearranged. These steps were posted for future reference. They included:

Gathering data
Organizing the data
Seeking meaningful relationships among the data
Displaying the data to show these relationships by using a pie graph,
      bar graph, or line graph
Titling the graph
Labeling the graph

Students then returned to the task of contructing their graphs, this time with success for all participants. The cycle of admonishing students to *think* was broken. This direct instructional process acted as a catalyst with which students interacted to emerge with the knowledge and skills to construct meaningful graphs. For more examples of cooperative learning experiences in science, see Hassard (1990).

ASSESSING THINKING

When students learn in a cooperatively thoughtful manner, testing should also occur in this manner. Allowing groups the opportunity to cooperatively solve problems becomes an appropriate assessment approach. Questions are designed to stimulate group thinking. "How do you determine what substance this is?" "How do you find out what it will react with?" "What can you do to determine its properties?" Students can devise methods of determining physical and chemical properties, record observations carefully, organize data, and reach logical conclusions as part of an assessment.

Thought processes and group interaction may be evaluated by a process observer. Students may be trained to do this, thus eliminating the expense of this labor intensive technique. Journals and data record books provide more information. Student-generated criteria may be used by the process observer to evaluate peers. Process observers look for behaviors that facilitate group attainment of a goal such as asking pertinent questions, seeking additional information, and building on the ideas of others. They also look for behaviors that are supportive to group members, such as praising or helping.

Assessment of thought processes using open-ended questions that require written responses may be administered to groups or individuals. Students may be given some data such as flame colors for metallic ions and asked, "What does this mean?" "What correlations can you infer?" "What cause and effect inferences can you make?" "What other data do you need?" Written responses to questions of this type yield much information about the thinking abilities of students.

THE NECESSITY OF STAFF DEVELOPMENT

In order to promote change in classrooms, teachers must be empowered with strategies that increase student learning. They must have a repertoire of skills and teaching strategies to make this happen.

School districts have long recognized the need for staff development and often hire consultants to drop in for a few days to deal with this. Such "quick fixes" have few long-term results. Each district needs its own team of experts. The formation of a nuclear staff development team is one key to change. It also gets the most for the district's money.

Training a cadre of people takes time. The Science Cadre Initiative in Baltimore County provided a year for members to attend workshops and conferences and to have the opportunity to try some of these techniques in their own classrooms. Two years would have probably been more realistic. The initiative was supported by federal funds earmarked to train and retrain science and mathematics teachers (Eisenhower Mathematics and Science Education Act, 1988). Six key science teachers were trained.

In addition to their regular teaching duties, these six fledgling staff developers took a graduate course and attended conferences addressing thinking skills offered by the Maryland Association of Science Teachers and the Maryland Association of Supervision and Curriculum Development. They heard lectures by noted experts in the field and attended sessions conducted by practitioners working in schools. They tried to sort out those strategies appropriate to science content, the maturity level of their students, their teaching styles, and the learning styles of their students. Their classrooms became laboratories for piloting and modifying appropriate strategies.

At the end of this training year, cadre members met to decide what they wanted to share with colleagues. A syllabus for an in-service course was written, with each teacher assuming responsibility for teaching a portion of the sessions. Trainers chose those techniques and strategies that they had successfully piloted in their classrooms.

The in-service course was offered in six 2½-hour sessions spaced about a month apart. It met after school, and a relaxing atmosphere was fostered through informal presentations, minds-on and hands-on activities that cast participants in the role of doers, and refreshments. Participants were encouraged to try some of the strategies in the month between sessions. Time was allotted at the beginning of each session for sharing successes and failures.

This course has attracted over 40 participants each year during the 3 years it has been offered. Teachers have become enthusiastic about strategies that have made teaching and learning fun again. Supervisors are observing student-centered lessons in which youngsters are assuming responsibility for their own learning. Baltimore County science classrooms are becoming cooperatively thoughtful as a result of this staff development program.

Other teachers have adapted these techniques, taken courses, and attended conferences. They are often asked to share ideas with colleagues during professional development activities. Thus, the corps of trainers is growing.

SUMMARY

The value of teaching thinking skills in a cooperative setting has yielded many positive results. The work of Johnson and Johnson (1987, 1989) and Kagan (1989) indicates that not only do students achieve better, but they also have enhanced self-esteem and more confidence in themselves as learners. The Baltimore County experience supports this. Science classrooms have become arenas for thoughtful processing of content and ideas.

The transition from traditional classrooms to classrooms that cast students in the role of active learners and generators of their own knowledge depends on many factors. These include integrating appropriate strategies in curriculum guides, staff development, parent training, and ongoing support and recognition for teachers. To use a chemical analogy, when the structure is sound, all reactants are put into place; if the activation energy is sufficient, the products will be exceptional.

REFERENCES

Baltimore County Public Schools. (1986). *High school biology*. Baltimore: Author.
Baltimore County Public Schools. (1987). *Physical science 9*. Baltimore: Author.

Baltimore County Public Schools. (1990a). *Environmental science*. Baltimore: Author.

Baltimore County Public Schools. (1990b). *High school chemistry*. Baltimore: Author.

Eisenhower Mathematics and Science Education Act. Elementary and Secondary School Improvement Amendment, January 25, 1988. (Public Law 1000-297).

Hassard, J. (1990). *Science experiences cooperative learning in science*. Reading, MA: Addison-Wesley.

Johnson, R. T., Johnson, D. W., & Holubec, E. J. (1987). *Structuring cooperative learning: Lesson plans for teachers*. Minnesota: Interaction Book Company.

Johnson, R. T., Johnson, D. W., & Holubec, E. J. (1989). *Cooperation and competition: Theory and research*. Edina, MN: Interaction Book Company.

Kagan, S. (1989). *Cooperative learning resources for teachers*. Riverside, CA: Resources for Teachers.

Lyman, F. T. (1981). The responsive classroom discussion. The inclusion of all students. In A. Anderson (Ed.), *Mainstreaming Digest* (pp. 109-114). College Park: University of Maryland Press.

Lyman, F. T. (1987). The thinktrix: A classroom tool for thinking in response to reading. *Reading: Issues and Practices*. Westminster, MD: Yearbook of the State of Maryland, International Reading Association, 4, 15-18.

Lyman, F. T. (1989, September/October). Rechoreographing: The middle-level minuet. *The Early Adolescence Magazine*, 4(1), 22-24.

Worsham, A. M., & Stockton, A. J., (1986). *A model for teaching thinking skills: The Inclusion Process*. Bloomington, IN: Phi Delta Kappa Educational Foundation.

16

The Use of Small Group Learning Situations in Mathematics Instruction as a Tool to Develop Thinking

Tom Bassarear and Neil Davidson

Several recent publications have called for a fundamental reformulation of mathematics education in the United States (Mathematical Sciences, 1990; National Council, 1989a, 1991; National Research Council, 1989). One of the themes that runs through all of these documents is the need for more situations in which students work together in small groups to discuss mathematical ideas and to solve problems.

A primary cause for so much attention to mathematics education is the growing awareness of the lack of thinking skills among our students. Consider an example taken from a recent National Assessment of Educational Progress (1983, p. 14). This examination, administered every 4 years, is taken by tens of thousands of American schoolchildren. One set of 13-year-olds was given the following problem: 3.04×5.3. Approximately 72% circled the correct answer. Another set of 13-year-olds was given the same numbers but asked to estimate the answer. The choices were 1.6, 16, 160, 1600, and "I don't know." Less than 21% chose 16; in fact almost 28% chose 1.6! Unfortunately, this is not an isolated example. Many more examples indicate that our students' procedural knowledge (that is, their ability to do computational problems) is "reasonable." However, when we assess their ability to apply these procedures, their ability to solve nonroutine problems, their ability to generalize their knowledge, the results are almost universally distressing.

One of our biggest concerns about the growing use of cooperative learning is that it will simply be seen as another technique used to teach students mathematical procedures but not to help students develop higher order thinking. Therefore, some time is needed to examine the kind of mathematical knowledge we are suggesting our students should possess and to examine some of the processes by which learners construct their understanding of mathematics. The ensuing discussion on cooperative learning in mathematics classrooms can then be seen in a larger context.

THE NCTM *CURRICULUM AND EVALUATION STANDARDS*

The *Curriculum and Evaluation Standards for School Mathematics* (National Council, 1989a) articulates characteristics of mathematically literate students. The first four standards for all three levels (grades K-4, grades 5-8, and grades 9-12) bear the same titles: Mathematics as Problem Solving, Mathematics as Communication, Mathematical Reasoning, and Mathematical Connections. This comes from the belief that these four aspects ought to permeate all mathematics instruction. Below are several items from the standards document that provide a sense of the reformulated goals of classroom instruction. The authors state that the students should be able to

> Use problem-solving approaches to investigate and understand mathematical content (grades K-4, p. 23)
> Discuss mathematical ideas and make conjectures and convincing arguments, and evaluate those conjectures and arguments (grades 5-8, p. 78)
> Develop, analyze, and explain procedures for computation and techniques for estimation (grades 5-8, p. 94)
> Apply integrated mathematical problem-solving strategies to solve problems from within and outside mathematics (grades 9-12, p. 137)

Clearly the National Council of Teachers of Mathematics (NCTM) is insisting that the development of higher order thinking must be seen as a primary goal of mathematics instruction in the United States. It is not hard to see how cooperative small-group learning would be a part of the new mathematics curriculum. Such an ambitious curriculum cannot be accomplished by having the students work by themselves, with most interaction in the classroom occurring between student and teacher. There is simply too much for the teachers to "teach." We might argue about how much to use small groups and appropriate situations for using groups, but that time is needed for mathematical discussion with other students is clear.

A FRAMEWORK FOR INSTRUCTION IN MATHEMATICS

The NCTM *Standards* essentially examines what our students ought to know and points to some instructional practices that teachers might use to help their students construct that knowledge. However, it does not embrace a specific pedagogical perspective, leaving that decision to the teacher. It is important, however, for teachers not only to have a coherent sense of what they want their students to learn but also a framework for organizing the classroom, in other words a curriculum:

> An operational plan for instruction that details what mathematics students need to know, how students are to achieve the identified curricular goals, what teachers are to do to help the students develop their mathematical knowledge, and the context in which learning and teaching occur. (National Council, 1989a, p. 1)

Jerome Bruner (1966) has articulated five major aspects of a theory for instruction, aspects for a teacher to consider when planning the learning environment. The following discussion focuses on three of those principles:

1. The need for exploration
2. The need to present new mathematical ideas in a concrete fashion
3. The need to separate failure from punishment

When encountering new mathematical ideas—for example, long division in elementary school and factoring trinomials in high school—students benefit from exploring at the concrete (or manipulative) level. If the mathematical procedures associated with these ideas are prematurely introduced, students' manipulation of the procedure is often rote. One example of this is the widespread mechanical use of the FOIL method (first, outer, inner, last) in algebra to enable students to multiply binomials such as $(x + 10)(x + 3)$. However, if problems are posed and manipulatives used, the students can explore mathematical situations. For example, students can use the "guess and test" problem-solving strategy with tables and algebra tiles to determine how to factor the trinomial $x^2 + 13x + 30$. Elementary students doing long division can use base 10 blocks to determine how to distribute 72 desks equally among three rooms.

By encouraging exploration at the concrete level, we want the students to solve problems using the knowledge they presently possess; we want them to make and test their hypotheses. However, most students are not accustomed to stating tentative hypotheses as opposed to giving answers to questions clearly stated by the teacher. Therefore, the teacher must create a learning environment that minimizes the risk involved in making tentative hypotheses and maximizes the informativeness of error. One of our college students articulated this point powerfully. She stated that during the early part of the semester she had become discouraged whenever she made a mistake. However, over the course of the semester, she realized that she had learned more from her wrong answers than from her right answers, and she now viewed every mistake as an opportunity to learn!

Giving a wrong answer is one of the most dreaded things that can happen to a student. However, the college student had come to realize that failure is a natural and inherent aspect of most learning. Just as a child "fails" many times before mastering a physical skill or the English language, so too does a student often "fail" before mastering a concept and its connection to other concepts and procedures. In this chapter, we are trying to encourage the kind of knowledge that develops through a cyclical process in which the student hypothesizes and obtains feedback on his or her growing understanding. This process is in contrast to a more binary perspective on learning in which one either does or does not know something.

CLASSROOM EXAMPLES

Learning Multiplication

Most people reading this chapter will remember learning or memorizing the multiplication tables, probably in the third grade. Some learned them easily, some learned them with difficulty, and some never learned all of them. Most will remember the quizzes, usually timed, whose goal was to force students to internalize the products. If the goal of such instruction is to get the multiplication facts "in," such a teaching procedure makes some sense, but if we refer to the NCTM *Standards*, the goal for instruction is far greater today.

Consider this dialogue between two students who had learned the tables up to 5×5 and now were asked how much is 10×4.

John: It's five more sets of 4. Look. Five more sets than 20.
Andy: Oh! 20 plus 20 is 40. So it's gotta be 40. No.
John: Yeah!

Andy: No. 4, 8, 12, 16, 20, 24, 28, . . . [*keeping track on his fingers*].
John: 40.
Andy: 40.
John: Yeah, I know . . . 'cause ten 4s make 40.
Andy: Like five 4s make 20.
John: Four sets of 10 makes 40. Just turn it around.
Andy: Five sets of 4s make 20 and so five more than that.
John: Yeah, just turn it around. Just turn it around.
Andy: 5 times 4 is 20, so 20 more than that makes 40.
John: Just switch them around (Cobb, Yackel, & Wood, 1989, p. 139).

From a Brunerian perspective, the students are exploring and checking their hypotheses. In this brief example, their answer is correct. However, in cases where their conjectures are wrong, the wrong answers are interpreted by the students as feedback that they need to examine their thinking. Hence, failure at this early stage is simply a sign to reexamine their thinking. Such exploration at this early age lays the foundation for the development of number sense and estimation and allows the students to have a better connected sense of mathematics. For example, an older student might need to estimate the product of 71 and 28. Students with Andy's and John's background are more likely to be able to reason that since this means seventy-one 28s, the product will be close to 70×30, that thirty 70s is equivalent to ten 70s added three times, and thus an estimate is $700 + 700 + 700 = 2100$. In this sense, they have anticipated the distributive principle, a concept that eludes most high school students who do not understand its use in the FOIL method mentioned earlier. Other small-group activities that fit nicely with the learning of multiplication include looking for patterns and relationships in the multiplication table and using geometric array models of multiplication.

Prime Numbers Lesson

One of the most attractive aspects of cooperative learning is that it can be integrated so nicely with other teaching practices that are receiving increasing attention, such as writing in the content areas and critical thinking. Following is a sketch of a lesson on prime numbers that could be given at the middle school level or, with some modifications, with preservice elementary teachers. The objective of the lesson is to introduce prime numbers. In this setting, the class has been divided into groups of four.

The teacher begins, "Today, we are going to learn about prime and composite numbers. Rather than me tell you what they are, let's play a game and see if you can figure out what "prime" and "composite" mean. I will start with the number 2 and place each number under "prime" or "composite." When you think you can predict where the next number will go, just jump in. And it's O.K. if your hypothesis doesn't work. As we have found, wrong guesses often contain seeds of truth." Slowly the teacher says and writes, "Two is a prime number, so is three, four is composite, five is prime, six is a composite." The teacher then asks students to think individually about the number seven and whether it is a prime or composite. Students then discuss this question in pairs. Then they share responses with the whole class.

> *Student 1*: Seven will go under prime.
> *Teacher*: Why?
> *Student 1*: 'Cause it doesn't have any factors.
> *Teacher* [*Looking at the rest of the class*]: Agree or disagree?

This is an intentional question with two purposes: by turning the question back to the students, the teacher provides more opportunity for thinking, and the teacher is weaning the students from their reliance upon the teacher as the authority.

> *Student 2*: Sort of. She should have said it doesn't have any factors other than itself or one. [*Student 1 accepts the qualifying statement.*]
> *Teacher*: Other opinions?
> *Student 3*: I look at it a bit differently. A number is prime if you can't divide it by anything other than one and itself.
> *Teacher*: This sounds convincing too. You know, there are many different ways to express the idea of prime numbers. We're going to do another Think-Pair-Share for a few minutes. Here is what I want you to do: First, write a definition of prime numbers, in your own words. Next, share your definition with another person in your group and either come up with one definition or agree that both definitions are valid. If you have time, discuss your definitions with your whole group.

The students now work, first silently, then in pairs, then in groups. The teacher walks around the room to gain a sense of the students' understanding and to provide direction and help if needed.

Teacher: Let's see what we have.

Student 1: A prime number is a number that has just one and itself as factors.

Teacher: Agree or disagree?

Student 2: Basically I agree, except he should have said whole number. [*Student 1 agrees.*]

Teacher: Another definition?

Student 3: A number that can be divided only by itself or one.

Teacher: Agree or disagree?

Student 4: That's not quite enough. You really need to say "can be divided without remainder" because that's what you really mean. [*Nods from students indicate agreement. The teacher adds "without remainder" to the previous definition.*]

Student 5: But that's what *divisible* means!

Teacher: So we can use that word to make our definition more succinct. Can someone state a definition of prime number that uses the word *divisible*?

Student 6: A prime number is a whole number that is divisible only by itself and one.

At this point, there would be some time to develop a formulation of the meaning of composite number as one that is not prime. A next step might involve having the students determine which of the numbers between 50 and 75 are prime. In this case, the teacher can accommodate different learning styles by allowing the students to choose to work in pairs or in groups of four. Since some groups will invariably finish before others, the teacher can also provide a follow-up question for such groups, such as determining whether 611 is a prime number. Now that the students are working in small groups, the teacher has some time to walk around the room and to have mathematical discussions with students, to provide hints where needed, to diagnose misconceptions, and to do some direct instruction if needed. The ensuing discussion would focus on how students determined which of those numbers are prime.

By having each student share a tentative formulation of prime numbers with another person, the teacher is encouraging every student to explore, to do some thinking. In the whole-class discussion method, it is often the case that only a few students are actively thinking. By beginning with pairs instead of the whole group, the teacher reduces the likelihood of a dominant student making an articulation that others could just copy. Also, by stressing that there are different valid ways to represent the concept, the teacher is further encouraging the students in small groups to construct and write formulations of prime numbers in their own words.

Problem Solving

Although there has been an increasing emphasis on problem solving in mathematics classes, the term *word problems* still evokes strong negative reactions from many students and teachers alike. The introduction to the *Professional Standards for Teaching Mathematics* (National Council, 1991) acknowledges difficulty in convincing teachers to modify old teaching strategies, and the National Assessments of Educational Progress continue to document the lack of problem-solving abilities in most students (National Council, 1989b).

Before discussing how cooperative learning can support the development of students' problem-solving abilities, let us consider the purpose of problem solving in mathematics classes. Traditionally, textbooks have shown students techniques to solve different kinds of problems such as rate problems, mixture problems, and coin problems. Students then do many problems until they have "mastered" one kind of problem. However, in the context of the new NCTM *Standards* (1989a), problem solving has two related functions:

1. Posing and solving problems can facilitate the learning of mathematical content. The problems can elicit misconceptions, nuances of the concepts, and various models for representing the concept.
2. Solving problems and discussing students' strategies for solving problems develops "mathematical power." For example, students have an increased ability to solve problems not isomorphic to ones they have done in class, to solve problems where they do not use all the given information, and to solve problems where more than one solution is valid.

In this context, it is helpful to consider some characteristics of problems that serve this larger purpose (Clarke, 1988):

1. The problems require more than recall of a fact or reproduction of a skill.
2. They have an educative component; that is, the student can learn from attempting them, and the teacher will learn about the student(s) from the attempts.

3. They are, to some extent, open; that is, there may be several different ways to go about solving the problems, and/or there may be several acceptable answers.

With respect to problems for use in small-group learning, Crabill (1990) has suggested that we select problems that are easy to visualize physically and are clearly defined—even though they may not be easy to solve.

Let us now consider more provocative mathematical problems, how they serve the larger function of problem solving, and how small-group learning fits nicely with this purpose. Consider the following question:

Janet wants to make a garden in her backyard, and a friend has given her 100 feet of fencing to surround the garden. What is the biggest garden she can enclose with the 100 feet of fencing?

In working through this problem, the students come to understand that one can make rectangles that have the same perimeter but different area. Students in upper grades can also discover that a circular fence will enclose even more area than a square fence. A cooperative learning structure that works well for this type of problem is called think-pair-share, mentioned earlier. Students are given a minute or two to work on the problem alone and then asked to work together with a partner (with perhaps one pencil and paper) to solve the problem. Afterward, the teacher facilitates a discussion of the problem—different ways students went about solving the problem and strategies they found helpful.

Other problems that work well in the think-pair-share mode include: "Construct a rectangle that has a perimeter of 36 units and an area larger than 75 square units" and "What happens to the perimeter of a rectangle if its length is doubled and the width remains the same?"

A cooperative learning strategy also well suited to enhancing thinking is group discussion. Consider the following problem:

A farmer looks out the window and sees a number of chickens and lambs in the farmyard. The farmer counts 32 heads and 80 feet. How many chickens and how many lambs are in the farmyard?

Each group works to solve the problem but also makes sure that each person in the group is able to understand the solution. There are a variety of strategies for having the groups share their solutions and the different ways they went about solving the problem (see Kagan, 1990). Groups can share their solutions and strategies with the group next to them. Another strategy for sharing diverse solutions is called "stand up and share." After all groups have successfully solved the problem, the teacher requests all class members to stand up. The teacher then asks someone to explain his or her solution. Other students who solved the problem that way then sit down. The teacher then asks a student still standing to explain another way of solving the problem, and then all students who solved the problem that way sit down. This procedure continues until all the different ways of solving the problem have been articulated.

Group discussion is also well suited to larger problems. Consider the following two questions:

> What year was it 1 million seconds ago? (Problem contributed by Ruth Parker.)
> How many squares can you find on a checkerboard?

The first problem is a striking, intrinsically interesting word problem and involves reasoning through a process of multiple conversations with seconds, minutes, hours, days, and years. The second problem makes connections between geometry, arithmetic, and algebra. It involves locating hidden figures (spatial visualization task) and counting them in a systematic way. The use of concrete materials (e.g., tiles) is helpful; recall the earlier discussion of Bruner. For more problems and guidelines for group problem solving, see Davidson (1990a, 1990b).

A cooperative learning structure called "jigsaw" provides a stimulating alternative for seatwork when a concept has been introduced and time is needed to practice more problems. In a traditional class, the teacher might do several problems in succession with the whole class. Consider the following variation of the jigsaw structure in a class with 16 students that has been divided into groups of four. Each group counts off by four so that each student is assigned a number: 1, 2, 3, or 4. The students then regroup into "expert" groups with all 1s sitting together, all 2s together, and so on. The teacher then gives each group a different problem. Each group is given time to solve and discuss the problem so that each student is able to explain a solution procedure. Then the students return to their original groups, and each student is given time to explain his or her problem solution to the other members of the group.

In summary, there are varied ways to structure group problem-solving discussions in mathematics. Students working together can often solve problems that are beyond the abilities of individuals at that developmental stage.

ASPECTS OF COOPERATIVE LEARNING
THAT ENHANCE THINKING

Developing Thinking Versus Producing Answers

It is important to note that, like many other teaching practices, the successful use of small-group instruction is not automatic. Without carefully worded instructions to the contrary, students will often focus on procedural aspects (i.e., getting the answer) at the expense of developing related thinking abilities such as examining how they arrived at the answer, how they verified their answer, how they monitored their progress, and how they decided which problem-solving strategy to use. Even when teachers emphasize the value of such thinking, students often fail to pay much attention to such processes, especially if their grade is based only on the correctness of their solution. Therefore, alternative forms of assessment (see Clarke, 1988; Kulm, 1990; Stenmark, 1989) are needed that encourage thinking and discourage blind guessing.

When teachers consider more nonroutine problems that require thinking, it is easy for much class time to be spent addressing question after question by confused students. If a student asks a question and only a few other students have that same question, the other students will likely not attend to the ensuing explanation. However, when a portion of class time is spent in small-group discussion, several positive things can occur. First, the students can often address other students' questions more effectively than can the teacher because they have just learned the concept and their explanations are often more understandable to each other. Second, in the effort to communicate one's understanding of a concept, that understanding is generally strengthened. Third, the discussions can often capture various misconceptions or point to the need for connections to be made. Fourth, in walking around the room, the teacher can have more effective mathematical discussions with small groups than he or she can have with large classes. Hence, mathematical communication that fosters thinking is enhanced in several ways by small-group interaction.

Developing Multiple Representations of Mathematical Concepts

Small group instruction can be used to facilitate discussions of mathematical models, an essential aspect of learning mathematics. For example, consider the definition of intersection of sets as it appears in most texts:

$$A \cap B = \{x \mid x \in A \text{ and } x \in B\}$$

Both the text and teachers will often offer models (or representations) of this concept to help the students. However, there are many available models. One student may prefer the model of intersection of two highways, while another likes the model of "what the two sets have in common," while yet another better understands the Venn diagram representation. Any model communicates some aspects of the concept but either distorts or fails to communicate other aspects of the concept. When the goal of instruction is for the students to construct their own models of the mathematical concepts, which they then test through discussion and doing problems, then the teacher cannot possibly demonstrate all of the models and the tacit aspects that underlie the related concepts. However, when students solve problems in groups, share their solution strategies, and discuss the utility of various models, then the tacit and subtle aspects of the models and their representations emerge and can be discussed in the groups and with the whole class. Bruner (1966) discussed the value of having more than one way of representing concepts and mathematical ideas, and this idea has been incorporated by the NCTM *Standards*, with their emphasis on students' needing to develop "mathematical power." Other mathematical concepts benefiting from discussion of models include adding and multiplying negative numbers, solving proportions, and fractions. Also enhanced are proofs in geometry (Chakerian, Crabill, & Stein, 1986; Serra, 1989), computer modeling of real-world situations (Sheets and Heid, 1990), and discussion of paradoxes, logic puzzles, and classical riddles.

Facilitating Changing Beliefs About Teaching Mathematics

Another advantage of cooperative learning deals with in-service programs for teachers. The *Professional Standards for Teaching Mathematics* (National Council, 1991) proposes a very different kind of mathematics classroom than is found in most schools today. However, an axiom in teacher education is that "teachers tend to teach the way they were taught." Many teachers report that their initial response to the new NCTM standards is often one of being overwhelmed, that now they have to "fit in" even more things into an already crowded curriculum. In our workshops with teachers, we use cooperative-learning structures to discuss the math *Standards*, and we have the teachers try some cooperative-learning structures in their own classrooms. We have seen striking changes in classrooms as a result of using cooperative learning when it has been framed in the context of the *Standards* and higher order thinking. When teachers pose questions that require thinking, ask students to discuss those questions in small groups, and the teachers then circulate around the room, some fundamental changes begin to occur. Students engage in animated discussions about the validity of each other's definitions and formulations, teachers begin to have mathematical discussions with students, and students ask questions back. Students and teachers begin to see that the answer itself is not the whole story, and that sometimes a student can get the right answer and be lucky, while another student or group can have the wrong answer (because of a minor error) but yet have developed a much more powerful solution procedure that extends to other problems. Students and teachers begin to see that while one solution may be more "elegant," other solutions (for example, using diagrams or inductive reasoning) are just as "mathematical." In other words, they begin to see that "mathematical" thinking is not completely synonymous with symbolic manipulation to get right answers.

Accommodating Different Learning Styles

More and more attention is being given to the variety of learning styles learners bring to any classroom. With respect to mathematics education, we speak of impulsive vs. reflective learners, field dependence vs. field independence, concrete vs. abstract learners, those who like to work alone and those who like to work together, and gender differences. These differences are real and need to be addressed. Teachers utilizing cooperative learning need to be aware of students' different learning styles.

A recent workshop with teachers illustrates this point nicely. A task was presented to the teachers, and they were allowed to choose among three cooperative learning structures: think-pair-share, pair-share, and group discussion. Those persons choosing think-pair-share were to find a partner, do the task silently by themselves, then discuss their solutions with the partner. Those persons choosing pair-share were to find a partner and then do the task together. Those persons choosing group discussion were to form groups of four or so and do the task in a way agreed upon by all members. Afterward, the teachers explained their choice of cooperative-learning structure as follows:

- *Think-pair-share.* "I needed to familiarize myself with the problem first." "I need to work at my own pace. If I am paired with someone faster, I will just let them do it and explain it to me." "I learn more quickly and efficiently on my own." "I could read and reread as many times as I needed to. If I feel under pressure, I bail out."
- Pair-share. "I didn't want to work alone but a group was too many people, too many distractions." "I tend to panic when I'm working

alone; having a partner is reassuring." "Working with a partner is multisensory—talk, hear, write, listen, bounce ideas."
• Group discussion. "If one person can't explain, someone else can." "More people, more brains." "More fun." "You can divvy up the work."

One cannot always accommodate every different learning style, and there is merit to having learners develop competence in different situations. However, by acknowledging the validity of different learning styles and by accommodating those differences when possible, we can make the mathematical learning environment more favorable for all learners.

Reducing Student Anxiety

Another important rationale for the use of cooperative learning in mathematics is that there is a large, well-established literature on mathematics anxiety (Beery, 1975; Hembree, 1990; Reyes, 1984). There are many intelligent persons who abhor mathematics and freeze not only on mathematics tests, but feel anxious and incompetent in the classroom. Our experience is that many such anxious students, who would never talk in the regular class, are able to talk and ask questions in a small group. We often teach courses in mathematics for elementary teachers. Every year, either in the anonymous course evaluation form or in person, several students will tell us that the use of small groups was a powerful catalyst, that they had not asked a question in a mathematics class ever in high school for fear of looking stupid, but they were able to ask questions in a small group. And they were able to find, to their amazement and relief, that they were often not alone!

CONCLUSION

We are in the beginning of an exciting period in mathematics education. The recent NCTM *Standards* books (National Council, 1989a, 1991) strongly resonate with an emphasis on higher order thinking. The focus on problem solving, communication, reasoning, and making connections cannot be attained without teachers possessing the ability to use cooperative small-group instruction strategies at appropriate times. It is important to emphasize that cooperative learning is one of the tools that teachers need to help their students become more powerful thinkers.

Frequent use of cooperative learning methods in mathematics can foster the following benefits for students:

- Opportunities to discuss and clarify concepts, freely exchange ideas, ask questions, give and receive help, explore situations, look for patterns and relationships in sets of data, and formulate and test conjectures
- Learning varied approaches for solving the same problem
- Support for problem solving, logical reasoning, and making mathematical connections
- Learning to communicate in the language of mathematics
- The chance to learn from "mistakes" in a nonthreatening environment
- Decreasing math anxiety and increasing math confidence
- Accommodation of diverse learning styles
- Making friends with group members across boundaries of race, class, and gender
- Increased ability to cooperate with others and develop social skills
- A lively, engaging, and enjoyable mathematics class

REFERENCES

Beery, R. (1975). Fear of failure in the student experience. *Personnel and Guidance Journal, 54*, 190–201.

Bruner, J. S. (1966). *Toward a theory of instruction.* New York: Norton.

Chakerian, G. D., Crabill, C. D., & Stein, S. K. (1986). *Geometry: A guided inquiry.* Pleasantville, NY: Sunburst Communications.

Clarke, D. (Ed.). (1988). *Blackline masters to support the Mathematics Curriculum and Teaching Program.* Carlton, Australia: Curriculum Corporation.

Cobb, P., Yackel, E., & Wood, T. (1989). Young children's emotional acts while engaged in mathematical problem solving. In D. B. McLeod & V. M. Adams (Eds.), *Affect and mathematical problem solving: A new perspective* (pp. 117–148). New York: Springer-Verlag.

Crabill, C. D. (1990). Small-group learning in the secondary mathematics classroom. In N. Davidson (Ed.), *Cooperative learning in mathematics: A handbook for teachers* (pp. 201–227). Menlo Park, CA: Addison-Wesley.

Davidson, N. (Ed.). (1990a). *Cooperative learning in mathematics: A handbook for teachers.* Menlo Park, CA: Addison-Wesley.

Davidson, N. (1990b). Small-group cooperative learning in mathematics. In T. Cooney (Ed.), *Teaching and learning mathematics in the 1990's* (pp. 52–61). Reston, VA: National Council of Teachers of Mathematics.

Hembree, R. (1990). The nature, effects, and relief of mathematics anxiety. *Journal for Research in Mathematics Education, 21*(1), 33–46.

Kagan, S. (1990). *Cooperative learning: Resources for teachers.* San Juan Capistrano, CA: Resources for Teachers.

Kulm, G. (Ed.). (1990). *Assessing higher order thinking in mathematics.* Washington, DC: American Association for the Advancement of Science.

Mathematical Sciences Education Board and the National Research Council. (1990). *Reshaping school mathematics: A philosophy and framework for curriculum.* Washington, DC: National Academy Press.

National Assessment of Educational Progress. (1983). *The third national mathematics assessment: Results, trends, and issues.* Denver: Education Commission of the States.

National Council of Teachers of Mathematics. (1989a). *Curriculum and evaluation standards for school mathematics.* Reston, VA: Author.

National Council of Teachers of Mathematics. (1989b). *Results from the fourth mathematics assessment of the National Assessment of Educational Progress.* Reston, VA: Author.

National Council of Teachers of Mathematics. (1991). *Professional standards for teaching mathematics.* Reston, VA: Author.

National Research Council. (1989). *Everybody counts: A report to the nation on the future of mathematics education.* Washington, DC: National Academy Press.

Reyes, L. H. (1984). Affective variables and mathematics education. *The Elementary School Journal, 84*(5), 558–581.

Serra, M. (1989). *Discovering geometry.* Berkeley: Key Curriculum Press.

Sheets, C., & Heid, M. K. (1990). Integrating computers as tools in mathematics curricula (grades 9–13): Portraits of group interactions. In N. Davidson (Ed.), *Cooperative learning in mathematics: A handbook for teachers* (pp. 265–284). Menlo Park, CA: Addison-Wesley.

Stenmark, J. K. (1989). *Assessment alternatives in mathematics: An overview of assessment techniques that promote learning.* Berkeley: Lawrence Hall of Science.

17

The World-of-Work Connection
Thinking Cooperatively
for Career Success

Paul Hilt

American employers are sending employees to training courses in record numbers. The American Society of Training and Development, as reported in the *Philadelphia Inquirer* ("Training in Problems," 1990), surveyed 200 of the nation's biggest companies and found that 41% offer training in writing, 31% in computation, and 22% in reading. However, there were topics that received even more attention: 58% of the nation's biggest companies offer training in problem solving, while 43% offer classes in teamwork, interpersonal skills, oral communications, and listening. Business now recognizes the importance of an expanded set of basic skills to America's success. As a result, the role of educators is taking on a new dimension.

Teachers are becoming "business partners"; as business organizations have come to realize that they alone cannot upgrade American workers' skills, they turn to the educational system to help meet the challenges facing America. "If I've learned one thing," states Robert Kirkpatrick, the chairman of CIGNA Corporation, "It's that the answer to virtually all of our national problems—from international competitiveness to improving our standard of living to the very security of our nation—ultimately rests on one word . . . education" ("Work in America," 1990, p. 2). This new visibility of education as a priority presents a major opportunity for educators to be heard and recognized for their influence on America's world position. The ways in which educators respond will significantly impact our society's future health. Today's teachers must understand *and* teach the practical concepts of teamwork and innovation. This is where industries are placing their greatest emphasis and hope.

"Go Team! The Payoff from Worker Participation" exclaims the cover of *Business Week* (1989, July 7). In a *Fortune* cover article on self-managed teams, Texas Instruments chairman Jerry Junkings says, "No matter what your business, these [self-managed] teams are the wave of the future" (Dumaine, 1990, p. 52). Teams look different from one company to another. However, they typically consist of 5 to 12 multiskilled workers who rotate jobs and produce a complete product or service under minimal supervision.

Innovation is the ability not only to create a solution but also to implement it. Innovation is essential for the United States' ability to compete in the global marketplace and to survive within an ever-changing world economy. In fact, many industries have found that the only means to deal effectively with change is innovation. But despite their importance in America's future, teamwork and innovation are not always partners.

Teams are not automatically innovative and innovation does not rely solely upon teams. It is the combination of these two trends that offers American business a potent mechanism for achieving the high levels of productivity needed to maintain global competitiveness.

The most productive teams work well cooperatively: in order to achieve common goals, they devise flexible strategies as they conduct their day-to-day activities. They also innovate continuously. The result? An ability to create new and improved work procedures, a crucial component of continued productivity.

Without this ability, America's workforce will risk not meeting the requirements of the shifting environment within which it exists. Unstable economic conditions, mergers and acquisitions, environmental trauma, changing consumer needs, and increased competition—all require workers to be effective group problem solvers.

An increasing emphasis on teamwork and innovation has direct implications for the classroom—specifically for the teaching of thinking through cooperative learning. In order for the growing trends of increased teamwork and innovation to fully transform the American workplace, new workers must acquire an array of skills beyond what have traditionally been referred to as the "basics"—reading, writing, and computation. According to a report sponsored by the U.S. Department of Labor (Carnevale, Gainer, and Meltzer, 1988), tomorrow's workforce will need skills of a more sophisticated nature. These "new basics" include an array of workplace abilities such as interpersonal communications, problem solving, self-initiated learning strategies, and group effectiveness.

Today's students will enter a world of work where teams of workers with well-developed interpersonal skills continuously innovate in order to meet organizational goals. Teaching thinking through team learning can be the cornerstone of an educational effort that focuses on the new basics and answers society's cry for skilled workers. This approach can help students achieve future success as responsible citizens and productive workers.

In this chapter, the ways in which teaching thinking through cooperative learning can help students succeed in the workplace will be explored.

INNOVATION

Innovation in the workplace involves combining invention *and* action to create a new product or service or to implement a new method of working. Invention is a process that uses higher order thinking skills with an emphasis on creative thinking, critical thinking, and problem solving. This process might be called "action-oriented problem solving." Many steps are involved in the process of inventing new solutions:

1. Intuitively sensing the existence of a problem or opportunity
2. Critically evaluating the problem
3. Gathering pertinent information about its causes
4. Sorting through a volume of information and selecting the pieces essential to the problem
5. Creating alternative solutions
6. Choosing alternatives consistent with goals despite uncertainties and ambiguities (VanGundy, 1984)

All of these thinking abilities are drawn upon when one invents.

Action, the other aspect of innovation, involves planning with an emphasis on decision making and metacognition. Like invention, many steps are involved:

1. Thinking about options
2. Discussing strategies with others
3. Remembering that mistakes are only failures if something is not learned from them
4. Implementing action steps
5. Monitoring results
6. Analyzing why some strategies work and others do not
7. Making adjustments so that plans can match reality (VanGundy, 1984)

How can students learn to invent solutions to problems and also to take action in order to make their solutions a reality? One way is by working on projects that challenge their problem-solving and idea-implementation abilities. Several guidelines may help to develop fully students' skills in this area.

Real Issues

First, a teacher should select issues that exist in the real world. An issue could be one that exists in an individual person's life (e.g., getting a part-time job or coping with drugs in school), or it could involve a broader issue involving the local community (e.g., municipal laws affecting teen behavior in malls and other public places). Sometimes, a concern of a more global nature (e.g., pollution of the oceans and its impact on recreation) is appropriate. Real issues send a message that students are using their time in a meaningful manner. If the real-world issue relates to the lives of students and also takes advantage of their prior knowledge, then there is a higher likelihood that students will take an interest in the learning experience. William Herrold, Jr. (1989) underscores this point: "Student efforts will increase as learning for a reason takes the place of covering the subject" (p. 41).

In a keynote speech at the 1990 annual meeting of the Association for Supervision and Curriculum Development, Eliot Eisner urged the audience to "let kids formulate their own problems. Let them practice related to their own purposes. Don't always give them the problem. Most students have little practice doing problem selection." If we follow Eisner's advice, students must have a chance to become more involved in the learning process.

Engaging student interest by focusing on relevant problems is critical. Students will begin to realize that what is taught in the classroom has value in the world outside the classroom and ultimately in the world of work. If their motivation is stimulated, they will begin to appreciate that learning is pertinent and beneficial to their lives, and that creating solutions can be exciting and fun. This kind of awareness is critical if a student is to develop an orientation toward lifelong learning—an attitude that employers increasingly suggest is vital to success in the workplace (Carnegie Forum on Education and the Economy, 1986). If workers cannot learn as a result of their own initiatives, they will be less adaptive to change.

As students learn to solve real issues, they are confronted with the "gray areas" that typically surround most real-world problems. They realize that life is not certain and that right and wrong can be hard to determine when the answer is not dependent on multiplication tables or phonetics. "Educators must introduce ambiguity," says Eisner (1990).

"Students must learn to deal with ambiguity and make trade-offs. Schools can't just provide clarity."

Active Involvement

Second, teachers should provide activities that actively involve students. Frank Newman (1990), president of the Education Commission of the States, believes that "schools must be radically changed to include more hands-on learning" (section 4, p. 13). Action is a means to engage students, to generate challenges, and to gain involvement and commitment to learning. Action projects can often be done in groups. This allows group members to establish a shared context, or common experience, from which to build new knowledge. Many sources of opportunities for active student involvement exist. A good source is the local community, with its unending need for fresh ideas and energetic action applied to such issues as homelessness, vandalism, recycling, and drug abuse.

Action projects provide students with direct feedback from the environment itself, rather than from traditional sources, such as a test or quiz. The uncertainty of outcomes from action projects enables students to experience the ambiguity of problem solving referred to by Eisner and also enables them to understand that there is rarely a single "right" answer to real-world problems.

In *Developing Minds*, Art Costa (1985) emphasizes active student involvement in learning. "According to Piaget's constructivist theory, all knowledge arises—or is constructed—from interactions between learners and their environment" (p. 129). The teacher can help facilitate this interaction. Through a thorough understanding of both the curriculum content and the background of students, a teacher can construct a bridge between the two. This will help the content become more accessible to students. "Much research," states Costa, "has also shown that *active* learning has a positive effect on students' development of decision-making and problem-solving skills, and their attitude toward school, teachers, the content to be learned, and learning itself" (p. 129).

The first two guidelines—real issues and active involvement—can best be illustrated by briefly examining examples combining both. In Southern California, eighth graders in a social studies program called "We Care" ("Innovative social," 1989) solve real-life problems using information they learn in the classroom. The program has achieved dramatic test score increases on statewide exams. More importantly, students have seen that their efforts have impact. In one case, students uncovered a problem while visiting a balloting site during local elections. They found "unnecessary complexity" in the existing voting ballots. As a result of student efforts, the County of Los Angeles changed its voting procedures. An interesting aspect of the program is that students aren't allowed to complain. If they see a problem in the course of their studies, they are required to figure out how to act on it.

In another example (Hilt, 1989), students in Maryland became concerned about the pollution of a local river. Water samples were gathered by students over time and these samples showed that pollution in the river was increasing. On their own time, students observed a construction site dumping pollutants in the river. Because students acted promptly on their discovery, the construction site was actually closed until the situation was corrected.

Why are learning approaches like these effective? One reason is that the more accurately the learning experience mirrors how problems are actually solved by competent adults, the greater the likelihood students will learn to behave like competent adults. Research in cognitive science (Brown, Collins, & Duguid, 1989; Raizen, 1989) emphasizes the importance of "situated" learning. Situated learning takes place through active involvement within a physical and social context, and not as a result—as in the traditional classroom—of being taught a series of discrete, decontextualized facts. Sue Berryman (1989), director of the Institute of Education and the Economy, points out some of the "critical mistakes" made in education:

> At present, knowledge and skills are taught in a setting—the formal classroom—very unlike settings at work or in real life. This teaching out of context impedes the transfer of school learning to settings outside the classroom. . . . Often a skill is decomposed into subskills, and each subskill is practiced separately. But it is seldom true that learning each of the subskills separately produces competence in the skill itself. (p. 3)

Reflecting Upon Thinking

A final guideline to keep in mind when developing action-oriented projects is to supplement action steps with metacognitive activities, such as a teacher's use of open-ended and probing questions: "What happened?"; "Why did it happen?"; "What else could have happened?" Encouraging students to "think about their thinking" will expand the learning that students receive from their experiences and will help them achieve higher level results. Students will more consciously begin to discuss strategies and develop plans. This kind of thoughtful activity is a characteristic of successful enterprises in the world of work.

In a *Harvard Business Review* article entitled "Team as Hero," social and political commentator Richard Reich (1987) dispels the cultural myth of the lone entrepreneur as the sole source of America's innovation. Innovation—and with it, America's global economic position—is less dependent on the isolated entrepreneurial genius inventing the big breakthrough idea than it is on the team as a collective agent continually improving upon its own efforts. Reich states:

> In collective entrepreneurship, individual skills are integrated into a group; this collective capacity to innovate becomes something greater than the sum of its parts. Over time, as group members work through various problems and approaches, they learn about each others' abilities. They learn how they can help one another perform better, what each can contribute to a particular project, how they can best take advantage of one another's experience. Each participant is constantly on the lookout for small adjustments that will speed and smooth the evolution of the whole. The net result of many such small-scale adaptations, effected throughout the organization, is to propel the enterprise forward. (p. 81)

Increasingly, workplace innovation depends on the individual's ability to problem-solve as part of a team. *Business Week* has published special issues devoted entirely to innovation (1989, June 16; 1990, June 15). One of the most compelling points made in these issues is that a team approach is now considered to be one of the most effective ways to encourage innovation in the workplace.

TEAMWORK

In order to become more competitive in the world marketplace, America's businesses have been redesigning their workplaces. A significant element in this redesign effort has been the importance of teams to higher productivity. "The team concept is spreading rapidly in industries such as autos, aerospace, electrical equipment, electronics, food processing, paper, steel, and even financial services" (Hoerr, 1989, p. 57).

A productive organization cross-trains its team members. As a result, productivity is less dependent on the individual, and the team becomes stronger and more capable. The organization then achieves the high degree of flexibility necessary to deal with rapid change. In addition, team members become multiskilled—expanding their personal inventory of abilities and becoming more valuable workers in the process.

This team-oriented focus in the workplace has direct implications for the classroom. If we want workers to display cooperative team behavior in the workplace, students must first have opportunities to develop this behavior in school. Cognitive science research (Raizen, 1989) supports this view:

> Competent individuals are not dependent solely on the knowledge inside their own heads. They use the environment (made up of both physical and human resources) to reformulate and accomplish their tasks. Working in groups, they often construct knowledge together that advances the communal task and makes the group and the individual within it more proficient. (p. 54)

The value of group efforts are also well recognized by business. "Society functions best when all parties are brought together in collaborative and cooperative relationships," says Walter Shipley, chairman of Chemical Banking Corporation (Doyle, 1989, p. E18). Teaching thinking through cooperative learning can help students to begin developing the group effectiveness skills that they will need when they enter the world of work. Several of these important skills are: oral communications, listening, self-knowledge, interpersonal skills, valuing diversity, and working toward common goals. A discussion of each of these skills follows.

Oral Communication

A report on the new workplace basics (Carnevale et al., 1988) emphasizes that "success on the job is linked to good communication skills. In fact, recent studies have indicated that only job knowledge ranks above communication skills as a factor for workplace success" (p. 11). Classroom activities that encourage verbal interaction, minimize teacher dominance, and provide opportunities for oral presentations can help students hone their oral communication skills. A good example is a lesson on sequencing that involves practice of both written and oral communications.

> Students select a skill to demonstrate, write out step-by-step instructions, have another student observe them following the directions in proper sequence, recite the directions (checking for grammatical errors), and then give oral directions to a different student to see if the person can perform the skill desired. (Owens & McClure, 1989, p. 14)

Cooperative group learning draws students into the learning process and, thus, reduces the teacher's role as sole provider of information.

Student group work inherently provides many opportunities for the practice of oral skills. Another example involves oral communication as both the content and the means of the classroom activity.

> A language arts teacher wants students to understand roadblocks to communication. She explains different types of roadblocks such as ordering, threatening, preaching, blaming, psychoanalyzing, and name calling. Each roadblock is put on a note card and students are given one to roleplay, using their personal or work experiences. (Owens & McClure, 1989, p. 14)

An example (Shanker, 1990) that illustrates the importance of developing oral communication skills can be seen in a new educational assessment model being used in Victoria, Australia. A portfolio reflecting a student's educational accomplishments is created. Among the key components of the portfolio are two student oral presentations—one to a group within the school and another to an audience outside the school. The student is evaluated based on the presentation and the question-and-answer period that follows. Having to explain a subject to an audience is an effective way to demonstrate how well an individual grasps a subject. This method is considered to be a more accurate demonstration of student mastery than traditional methods. In addition, evaluating performance based on accomplishment is how job performance is assessed in the world of work.

Listening

Building listening skills is considered by some to be even more important than oral communication skills. "The average person spends 8.4 percent of time writing, 13.3 percent reading, 23 percent speaking, and 55 percent listening" (Carnevale et al., 1988, p. 11). The best workplace training programs develop a *variety* of listening skills—listening for content, listening to conversations, listening for long-term contexts, listening for emotional meaning, and listening to follow directions (Carnevale et al.).

Group learning methods provide many opportunities for students to listen to one another. Since the different types of listening skills involve various elements of effective thinking—in particular, critical thinking—classroom activities can be designed to take advantage of the natural interactions that occur when students learn cooperatively. Student conversations can be a means to both apply critical thinking and to improve student listening abilities (Johnson, Johnson, Holubec, & Roy, 1984).

Helping students to examine metacognitively their listening behaviors builds listening skills and also provides an appropriate activity for students to become more aware of their own thinking. As students become comfortable reflecting upon and talking about their thinking, they will see the value of making thinking visible—their own as well as the thinking of others. In the world of work, making thinking more visible helps workplace teams to clarify areas that can be problematic: conflicting information, unstated assumptions, unclear goals, and opposing strategies. Exposing such issues can be of considerable value for overall workplace team effectiveness.

Self-Knowledge

An important aspect of metacognitive awareness is an ability to expand one's self-knowledge. The theory of multiple intelligences, proposed by Harvard psychologist Howard Gardner (1983), suggests that beyond the two intelligences traditionally recognized by Western culture—linguistic and logical-mathematical—there are several other intelligences as well: visual-spatial, musical, kinesthetic, interpersonal, and intrapersonal.

Of these, a vitally important one, intrapersonal intelligence, is the least recognized. Intrapersonal intelligence is the ability to understand one's self. Ultimately, such knowledge is the basis for self-change.

What does understanding oneself have to do with teamwork? One of the most effective means to understand the behavior of others is to first understand one's own behavior. In order to create a truly productive workplace, group skills *and* self-knowledge are important (Weisbord, 1987).

One way students can learn about their own thinking is for teachers to introduce a learning style model—such as those developed by McCarthy (1980), Dunn and Dunn (1978), Meyers-Briggs (Golay, 1982)— in the classroom. This will aid students by providing an organizing principle for human behavior and a way to increase their intrapersonal intelligence. A learning style model can help students understand more about themselves—and about others. When students become more aware of and gain a better understanding of the different learning styles in the classroom, this adds a new, complementary dimension to the teaching of thinking. An awareness and appreciation by students of others' learning styles will help to strengthen their ability to interact with others. This will be of considerable value to them when they encounter different styles in the world of work.

Interpersonal Skills

Successful cooperative learning rests on the development of students' interpersonal skills. As teachers help students become more experienced in group-learning processes, students develop group skills such as learning to give and take direction, assisting others, dealing with stress, being flexible, judging appropriate behaviors, and developing empathy. All these skills will be valuable to them when they make the transition from school to work. "There are very few work situations," states Senta Raizen (1989) in a paper summarizing the implications of the latest cognitive science research on education, "that do not involve people learning and working in conjunction with others; hence, becoming proficient in the requisite social skills is as important as becoming expert in the practical and theoretical knowledge skills" (p. 50).

Diversity

"Why did you choose that strategy to deal with the problem?" "What other alternatives could exist?" "What do you think would happen if you didn't know this particular piece of information?" A teacher's use of reflective or metacognitive questions such as these enables the thinking strategies of the individual to be shared with a group of students. Each student benefits because his or her perspective is broadened by others' viewpoints. In addition, a student's personal inventory of alternatives is expanded. This helps individual students recognize an important workplace concept—the value of diversity.

Students learn how people see things differently, and how those differences can be a strength. A rich mixture of diverse views broadens one's perspective and is a vital ingredient for innovation. Students learn that an open and exploring mind helps to transform "difference as a potential source of conflict" into "difference as a desired resource to be sought and cultivated. In order to avoid stagnant or lockstep thinking, difference stimulates fresh approaches to problems and thus becomes a valuable group asset. (For an additional perspective, see Chapter 8.)

Additionally, students learn that working effectively with others often depends on one's own attitudes and dispositions. Exposure to the positive benefits of diversity in the classroom can foster an appreciation that benefits students when they enter the world of work. Using the diversity of team members can be a challenging skill to develop, yet one that is highly valued by employers (Carnevale et al., 1988).

What classroom activities can foster a greater sensitivity to and appreciation of diversity? One innovative program (Champagne & Sofo, 1990) in Pennsylvania asked students to conduct video interviews of their peers from a variety of ethnic backgrounds. The students brought in objects most representative of family origins and were interviewed on camera. This activity generated a high degree of student interest and fostered an appreciation of cultural differences. In another version of this model, students conducted video interviews of several of the most prominent subcultures within the student body—such as preppies, heavy-metal types, and jocks. Each subculture had a different dress style, language, and different social norms. The video helped break down subculture stereotypes and enabled students to observe their peers as individuals with unique thoughts, feelings, talents, and dreams.

Common Goals

Working in groups exposes students to common goals and increases their comfort in working with others toward that end. This is critical to success in the workplace, for it is the common goal (being the best national medical products company, for example) that spurs workplace teams to high levels of productivity. By learning to acknowledge a goal outside of themselves (for instance, improving the quality of life for the aged through quality medical products), workers recognize the personal benefits (inner satisfaction; bonuses from profit-sharing plans) that can be gained from achieving that goal.

Teachers can help students increase their appreciation of the value of common goals by articulating the benefits of group thinking efforts—for both the class and the individual—while the learning activity progresses. One recommended approach encourages teachers to periodically ask students to identify the benefits resulting from a particular activity. "How is it useful for you to have experienced this activity?" "How can you see this benefiting you in the future?" "How did this activity benefit the class as a whole?" The more meaningful and engaging classroom activities become, the more students will personally experience the benefits of the learning effort.

Successful teams develop in industry due in part to common goals and shared experiences. Team members are deeply involved in an activity that they can talk about in the workplace. Perhaps more importantly, they talk about it informally during nonwork time: lunch, breaks, and after-hour social situations. In the classroom, when students' minds are sufficiently engaged, they will more likely discuss activities outside the classroom—thus enriching the learning experience.

CONCLUSION

In order to survive, the American workplace is compelled to rethink its very makeup and structure, making it a setting for better thinking through teamwork and innovation. Not coincidentally, the same situation faces American education.

What is presently called "work redesign" in business and industry is called "restructuring" in education. The essence of these two concepts is the same: in order to produce results of the highest quality, it is necessary to reorder fundamentally the values, goals, and relationships that guide day-to-day activities. There is no single prescription for implementing the ideas suggested in this chapter. Each school and each learning environment is unique. Much will rest, however, on the attitudes and efforts of individuals within the system.

At the heart of teaching innovation and team skills is practicing it oneself. Teachers know that students hone in on them as individuals, exclusive of the subject being taught. Students observe and remember all sorts of personal things about teachers. Teachers must model teamwork and innovation behaviors, or students will surely recognize the conflict between "do" and "say." Thus, adopting a focus of teaching thinking through team learning requires a commitment by the school staff to group problem solving and self-development at the very same time it encourages these activities for students. It's a mutual journey.

Some schools and teachers already understand this concept: restructuring at a schoolwide level parallels restructuring at the classroom level. In the school, teachers and administrators develop skills in shared decision making, collaborative problem solving, team building, and interpersonal communications. In the classroom, as teachers implement innovative practices involved in teaching thinking through group learning, students gain skills in critical thinking, decision making, creative thinking, problem solving, and group learning and interaction.

As teachers invest time and effort to develop further their own collaborative skills, they will enhance their ability to teach thinking through cooperative learning. What teachers do outside the classroom will benefit them in the classroom and vice versa.

Some ways for teachers to develop these skills within the school environment are to

- Participate in school restructuring programs
- Become actively involved in interdepartmental committees addressing school environment issues

- Instigate initiatives that cross grade levels
- Reach out to involve colleagues in common projects
- Encourage themes across the curriculum
- Personally develop problem-solving skills
- Visibly use problem-solving techniques with colleagues
- Create support groups to further encourage personal development

In the current educational environment, both students and teachers are increasingly exposed to new collaborative ways of interacting and thinking. The timing of these parallel efforts at restructuring the educational system offers a unique and exciting opportunity for development—not only for students, but for teachers as well.

REFERENCES

Berryman, S. E. (1989). *Portents of revolution: The cognitive sciences and workplace literacy* (Occasional Paper No. 8, p. 3). New York: Teachers College, Columbia University, Institute on Education and the Economy.

Brown, J. S., Collins, A., & Duguid, P. (1989). Situated cognition and the culture of learning. *Educational Researcher, 18*(1), 32–42.

Carnegie Forum on Education and the Economy. (1986). *A nation prepared: Teaching for the 21st century*. New York: Author.

Carnevale, A. P., Gainer, L. J., & Meltzer, A. S. (1988). *Workplace basics: The skills employers want*. Alexandria, VA: American Society of Training & Development.

Champagne, D., & Sofo, R. (1990, March). *Stallone, Schwarzenegger, Roger Moore, Sydney Poitier, and Molly Ringwald as teachers*. Workshop presentation at the annual conference of the Association for Supervision and Curriculum Development, San Antonio.

Costa, A. L. (1985). Teacher behaviors that enable student thinking. In A. L. Costa (Ed.), *Developing minds: A resource book for teaching thinking* (p. 129). Alexandria, VA: Association for Supervision and Curriculum Development.

Doyle, D. P. (1989, October 20). The problem. *Business Week* [Special advertising section: Endangered species: Children of promise], p. E18.

Dumaine, B. (1990, May 7). Who needs a boss? *Fortune*, p. 52.

Dunn, R., & Dunn, K. (1978). *Teaching students through their individual learning styles: A practical approach*. Reston, VA: Reston.

Eisner, E. W. (1990, March 4). *What's worth teaching?* Keynote speech at the annual conference of the Association for Supervision and Curriculum Development, San Antonio.

Gardner, H. (1983). *Frames of mind: The theory of multiple intelligences*. New York: Basic.

Golay, K. (1982). *Learning patterns and temperament styles.* Newport Beach, CA: Manas-Systems.

Herrold, W. G., Jr. (1989). Brain research: Brain-compatible learning. *Educational Horizons, 68*(1), 41.

Hilt, P. (1989, November 4). *Thinking trends in the world-of-work.* Workshop presentation at the Maryland Center for Thinking Studies, Baltimore.

Hoerr, J. (1989, July 7). The payoff from teamwork. *Business Week,* p. 57.

Innovative social studies program stresses action. (1989, April). *Brain/Mind Bulletin,* p. 3.

Johnson, D. W., Johnson, R. T., Holubec, E. J., & Roy, P. (1984). *Circles of learning: Cooperation in the classroom.* Alexandria, VA: Association for Supervision and Curriculum Development.

McCarthy, B. (1980). *The 4mat system: Teaching to learning styles and right/left mode techniques.* Barrington, IL: Excel.

Newman, F. (1990, April 15). Four quick fixes for our schools. *New York Times,* section 4, p. 13.

Owens, T., & McClure, L. (1989). *New developments in improving the integration of academic and vocational education* (p. 14). Portland, OR: Northwest Regional Educational Laboratory.

Raizen, S. A. (1989). *Reforming education for work: A cognitive science perspective.* Berkeley, CA: University of California, Berkeley, National Center for Research in Vocational Education.

Reich, R. B. (1987). Entrepreneurship reconsidered: The team as hero. *Harvard Business Review, 65* (3), 81.

Shanker, A. (1990, March 5). *The case for restructuring schools.* Keynote speech at the annual conference of the Association for Supervision and Curriculum Development, San Antonio.

Training in problems. (1990, February 26). *Philadelphia Inquirer,* section D, p. 1.

VanGundy, A. B. (1984). *Managing group creativity: A modular approach to problem solving.* New York: American Management Association.

Weisbord, M. (1987). *Productive workplaces* (p. 87). San Francisco: Jossey-Bass.

Work in America honors Sigler, Williams, Kerr. (1990, January). *Work in America,* p. 2.

Index

About the Editors and Contributors

Neil Davidson is a professor in the Department of Curriculum and Instruction at the University of Maryland, College Park, specializing in mathematics education, teacher education, and staff development. His doctoral dissertation at the University of Wisconsin, completed in 1970, dealt with the development of the "small-group discovery method" of mathematics instruction. His books include *Abstract Algebra: An Active Learning Approach* and the edited volume *Cooperative Learning in Mathematics: A Handbook for Teachers.* He has published articles on cooperative learning in a variety of journals. He served for 3 years as president of the Mid-Atlantic Association for Cooperation in Education, and is the current president of the International Association for the Study of Cooperation in Education. He is an internationally known consultant and workshop leader in cooperative learning. He currently serves as director of a doctoral program in staff development at the University of Maryland.

Toni Worsham is currently the Director of the Maryland Center for Thinking Studies (MCTS), and has been a leading practitioner in the field of thinking improvement for the past 11 years. She has been an educator for 25 years, teaching at all levels, elementary through graduate school, in both public and private schools. Toni has held both administrative and supervisory educational positions. She earned her Ph.D. at the University of Maryland. Her doctoral research led her to develop the "Inclusion Process," a procedural framework for thinking improvement used in schools (K–12) and school systems in at least 14 states. Toni consults on thinking improvement research across the country and has published in leading educational magazines. Her Inclusion Process has been published by Phi Delta Kappa as part of its fastback series.

Tom Bassarear is an associate professor of mathematics education at Keene State College in Keene, New Hampshire. He obtained his doctorate from the University of Massachusetts and has taught mathematics from grades 4 through 12 in public and private schools in the United States and Nepal. He regularly conducts workshops for teachers (K–12) on cooperative learning and the new mathematics standards. His primary research interest concerns how students' attitudes and beliefs about mathematics can help and hinder their ability to learn, and he has published on this topic.

Carla J. Beachy is an English teacher at Glenwood Middle School in Howard County, Maryland. She has been a presenter on the local and state levels on the topics of thinking skills and classroom management. She was graduated cum laude in English Education from Towson State University in 1971 and has received her M.Ed. from the University of Maryland.

James Bellanca is president of IRI Group, Inc., an educational consulting company. He attended the University of Illinois, Champagne-Urbana, and spent the first 16 years of his professional career as a high school English teacher and staff developer. In 1975, he founded IRI Group. His interest in the real impact of staff development in the classroom setting propels his work with the adult learner. Jim has authored *Cooperative Think Tank* and *Team Stars* and coauthored *Patterns for Thinking-Patterns for Transfer, Blueprints for Thinking in the Cooperative Classroom, Catch Them Thinking, Teach Them Thinking,* and *Keep Them Thinking III*.

Lenore Judd Cohen coordinates the Montgomery County Teacher Education Center, a collaborative endeavor between the University of Maryland and the Montgomery County Public School System. She has been involved in staff development and preservice education since 1972. Lenore received her doctoral degree from Temple University in 1983. Lenore's main research interest is in the theory-practice connection and how to assist beginning teachers in that transfer.

Geoffrey Comber is cofounder of the Touchstones Discussion Project. He is co-editor of the Touchstones series of volumes of texts for discussion. For the past 26 years he has been on the faculty of St. John's College, where discussions are used extensively for teaching all subjects. In 1954 he became an associate of the Royal College of Music. He completed his graduate work in music (M.A.) and philosophy (Ph.D.) at Ohio State University in 1962. He has served as consulting editor for *College Teacher*.

Arthur L. Costa is a recently retired professor of education at California State University, Sacramento. He taught graduate courses to teachers and administrators in curriculum, supervision, and the improvement of instruction. He edited the book *Developing Minds: A Resource Book for Teaching Thinking,* is the author of *The Enabling Behaviors, Teaching for Intelligent Behaviors and Supervision for Intelligent Teaching,* and is coauthor of *Cognitive Coaching, Techniques for Teaching*

Thinking. He has also written numerous other articles and publications on supervision, teaching strategies, and thinking skills. Dr. Costa has made presentations and conducted workshops for educators throughout the United States and in Canada, Mexico, Europe, Africa, the Middle East, Asia, and the South Pacific. Active in many professional organizations, Dr. Costa has served as president of the California Association for Supervision and Curriculum Development and as a president of the national ASCD from 1988 to 1989.

Robin Fogarty is the director of training and development for Illinois Renewal Institute, Inc., as well as editor-in-chief of Skylight Publishing, Inc. Robin has taught every level from kindergarten to college. She received her Ph.D. in Curriculum and Human Resource Development from Loyola University of Chicago. Her research focus is in cognitive instruction, especially in the areas of thinking skills, cooperative interactions, metacognition, and transfer of learning. Publications include numerous articles, coauthored works—*Patterns for Thinking, Patterns for Transfer; Start Them Thinking; Teach Them Thinking*—and authored works: *Design for Cooperative Interactions* and *How To Integrate the Curricula.* Robin currently acts as editor of the newsletter *Cogitare* for the ASCD Network for Teaching Thinking.

Paul Hilt is president of Hilt & Associates, a Philadelphia management consulting firm serving business and education, and specializing in group facilitation and innovation and creativity. Paul also works with Research for Better Schools, a nonprofit educational organization, where he designs and delivers seminars reflecting the latest developments in educational practice and facilitates school improvement efforts. Paul is on the faculty of St. Joseph's University, where he teaches "Creative Thinking and Problem Solving," a graduate course designed for training and developing professionals, and "Motivation," as part of the executive MBA program. He received his MBA from St. John's University in New York City.

David W. Johnson is a professor of educational psychology with an emphasis in social psychology at the University of Minnesota. He has a master's and doctoral degree from Columbia University. He is the author or co-author of over 25 books on interpersonal relationships, including: *Human Relations and Your Career; Productive Conflict Management: Perspectives for Organizations; Reaching Out: Interpersonal Effectiveness and Self-Actualization; Educational Psychology; Joining Together: Group Theory and Group Skills;* and *Circles of Learning: Cooperation in the Classroom.* He has published over 250 research articles in leading psychological journals, and he is a recent past editor of the *American Educational Research Journal.* For the past 25 years he has served as an organizational consultant to businesses and schools, focusing on management training, team building, conflict resolution, interpersonal and group skills training, and drug abuse prevention.

Roger T. Johnson is a professor of curriculum and instruction with an emphasis in Science Education at the University of Minnesota. He has an Ed.D. from the University of California at Berkeley. His public school teaching experience includes teaching in kindergarten through eighth grade in self-contained classrooms, open schools, nongraded situations, cottage schools, and departmentalized (science) schools. He has taught in the Harvard-Newton Intern Program as a Master Teacher and was curriculum developer with the Elementary Science Study in the Educational Development Center. He is an authority on inquiry teaching, author of numerous articles, and coauthor of *Learning Together and Alone*.

Spencer Kagan who received his Ph.D. in psychology from the University of California, Los Angeles, in 1972 is author of *Cooperative Learning Resources for Teachers* and numerous books, book chapters, and scientific journal articles on the development of cooperation. He is a former professor of psychology and cooperating faculty, school of education at the University of California, Riverside. His early research documents the development of cooperative and competitive motives and behaviors among children of various cultures; more recent work focuses on the academic and social impact of cooperative and competitive classroom structures, developing cooperative learning methods, and training teachers in the methods. Dr. Kagan developed the structural approach to cooperative learning, and Co-op Cards, Co-op Co-op, Partners, 3-Step Interview, Roundtable, and New Pieces Jigsaw. Presently with Resources for Teachers, Dr. Kagan is a founding member and member of the board of directors of the International Association for the Study of Cooperation in Education.

Frank T. Lyman, Jr. is a teacher education coordinator for the University of Maryland, College Park, and the Howard County, Maryland, School System and director of the Saturday School at the Maryland Center for Thinking Studies. He works with preservice teacher candidates and experienced teachers in this university/public school collaborative arrangement. Prior to 1970, he taught 11 years of elementary school. In 1965 he was perhaps the first classroom teacher to use cognitive mapping (Thinklinks) with children (in Lexington, Massachusetts), and has invented and co-developed several other techniques and strategies since. Among these are Think-Pair-Share and Thinktrix. He has degrees from Haverford, Harvard, and the University of Maryland.

Nicholas Maistrellis is one of the creators of the Touchstones Project. He has worked extensively with teachers on how to use discussions in

social studies, mathematics, and science classes. He co-edited the series
of Touchstones volumes and has taught at St. John's College since 1968.
His graduate degree was taken at the University of Wisconsin in the
philosophy of science.

Robert J. Marzano received his Ph.D. in curriculum and instruction
from the University of Washington. He has been a classroom teacher in
New York City and Seattle and a professor of education at the University
of Colorado. Currently he is deputy director of training and development
at the Mid-continent Regional Education Laboratory in Aurora, Colorado. His primary responsibility is to develop research- and theory-based
programs and practices that can be used in K–12 classrooms. His areas of
interest include the teaching of thinking, literacy development, authentic
assessment, and instructional design. He has authored and coauthored a
number of books and articles on these and other topics including:
Dimensions of Thinking, published by the Association for Supervision
and Curriculum Development, *A Cluster Approach to Elementary Vocabulary Instruction*, published by the International Reading Association,
and *Reinforcing Thinking in the English Language Arts*, published by the
National Council of Teachers of English.

Linda Hanrahan Mauro is a faculty member in the School of Education and Human Development at George Washington University, where
she coordinates the graduate teacher preparation programs in secondary
education. In addition to making numerous national conference presentations on cooperative learning, concept attainment, and concept formation, Linda emphasizes these instructional models in the preservice and
in-service courses she teaches. Linda received a doctoral degree in English education from Rutgers University. She worked in public schools, at
Rutgers University, and the University of Maryland, and with Teacher
Corps prior to moving to GW. Linda has coauthored several articles on
teacher education and was named Promising Researcher by the National
Council of Teachers of English for her work on response to literature.

Jay McTighe currently works with the Maryland State Department of
Education coordinating a statewide school improvement program for
thinking skills development. He received his undergraduate degree from
the College of William and Mary, earned a master's degree from University of Maryland, and has done postgraduate studies at Johns Hopkins
University. He has published articles on thinking in a number of leading
journals and books, including *Educational Leadership* (ASCD), *Developing
Minds* (ASCD), and *Thinking Skills: Concepts and Techniques* (NEA), and
has consulted extensively throughout the country on this topic.

Pat Wilson O'Leary is a consultant in the area of cooperative learning. She earned her M.A. at Western Michigan University. She is coauthor

of *A Guidebook for Cooperative Learning: A Technique for Creating More Effective Schools* (Learning Publications Incorporated, Holmes Beach, FL, 1984) and is a featured columnist in *Cooperative Learning* (the quarterly magazine for the International Association for the Study of Cooperation in Education, Santa Cruz, CA). Currently Pat is gathering classroom ideas for work in primary, as well as administrative K–12 support for cooperative learning. She is also the editor of Cooperation Unlimited Inc.

Barbara Z. Presseisen is director of national networking at Research for Better Schools, the Mid-Atlantic Educational Laboratory in Philadelphia. A specialist in cognitive research and implications for curriculum, instruction, and evaluation, Dr. Presseisen chairs the Cross-Laboratory Committee on Higher Order Thinking Skills. A graduate of Brandeis, Harvard, and Temple, Barbara Presseisen has authored several works on school reform and educational improvement. Among her more recent publications are *Unlearned Lessons: Current and Past Reforms for School Improvement* (1985), *At-Risk Students and Thinking: Perspectives from Research* (1988), and *Learning and Thinking Styles: Classroom Interaction* (1990). Dr. Presseisen serves on the advisory editorial boards of *Educational Horizons*, *Remedial and Special Education*, and *Teaching Thinking and Problem Solving*.

Robert Samples is an independent scholar whose initial training was in the sciences of geology, geophysics, and astronomy. Since 1961, the major emphasis of his work has focused on the origins of creative thought. He has authored or coauthored seven published books and more than 200 articles. He has also authored and consulted on more than 200 award-winning films. Samples' current research focuses on brain-mind function, a redefinition of the affective domain, and the conceptual base for planetary consciousness. He is the international director of the Solstice Seminars and is listed in *American Men of Science* and *International Men of Science*. For the past 10 years the results of Samples' earlier studies have been applied in industry, public and private schools, colleges, universities, seminaries, and federal governments.

Richard D. Solomon and Elaine C. L. Solomon are the chief executive officers of their consulting and publishing company, the National Institute for Relationship Training, Inc. They conduct workshops and training events in cooperative learning, the relationship skills, team building, self-esteem strategies, conflict resolution and organizational change. They have coauthored several books including the *Handbook for the Fourth R: Relationship Skills*, volumes one and two. Richard Solomon and Neil Davidson coordinate the University of Maryland–Prince George's County Secondary Professional Development Center, a staff development program designed to induct teacher candidates into the profession. Richard is an adjunct professor at the graduate school of Loyola College, Baltimore, Maryland. Elaine is a psychology teacher in the Anne Arundel County, Maryland, Public Schools. She also teams with Richard in teaching several graduate courses at Loyola College.

Anita Stockton is a graduate of the University of Connecticut with a bachelor of science degree. Anita has taught high school biology and chemistry in several states. She received her masters of science education from the University of Georgia and Ed.D. in curriculum and supervision from the University of Maryland. Anita is currently the coordinator of science for the Baltimore County Public Schools and director of curriculum at the Maryland Center for Thinking Studies. She has coauthored *A Teacher's Guide to the Johns Hopkins Model of Human Musculature*, *Surface Anatomy: A Teacher's Guide to the Johns Hopkins Functional Model of the Human Skeleton*, and *The Inclusion Process—A Direct Instructional Model for Teaching Thinking Skills*.

Charles Wiederhold currently serves as coordinator of staff development for the Placer County Office of Education in northern California. During a 33-year career in education he has served as a classroom teacher, building administrator, and director of several regional programs in northern California. He is past president of the Rio Linda Teacher Association and the Central California Science Council. He has done graduate work at CSU Sacramento, CSU San Diego, and completed his doctoral dissertation at Pacific Western University. Publications include contributions to *Developing Minds: A Resource Book for Teaching Thinking* (ASCD, 1985) and *An Examination of Questions Asked by Teachers* (UMI Press, 1989). He is also the author of *Cooperative Learning and Critical Thinking: The Question Matrix* (Resources for Teachers, 1990).

Howard Zeiderman is one of the creators of the Touchstones Discussion Project and has designed and piloted interdisciplinary approaches to mathematics and science. He did his graduate work in mathematics, history of science, and philosophy at Cambridge University, England, and at Princeton University. Since 1973 he has been on the faculty of St. John's College, first in Santa Fe and currently in Annapolis, Maryland. He co-edited the series of Touchstones volumes and authored the *Guide to Teaching Discussions*.